TOUCHING THE WILD

LIVING WITH THE MULE DEER OF DEADMAN GULCH

Joe Hutto

Skyhorse Publishing

Skyhorse Publishing books may be purchased in bulk at special discounts for
sales promotion, corporate gifts, fund-raising, or educational purposes.
Special editions can also be created to specifications. For details,
contact the Special Sales Department, Skyhorse Publishing,
307 West 36th Street, 11th Floor, New York, NY 10018 or
info@skyhorsepublishing.com

www.skyhorsepublishing.com

ISBN: 978-1-62636-213-0

10 9 8 7 6 5 4 3 2 1

Library of Congress Cataloging-in-Publication Data is available on file.

Photos on pages 21, 22, 34, 56, 58, 66, 74, 76, 78, 82, 95, 97, 98, 104,
151, 155, 165, 167, 214, 232, 252, 268, 290, 292, and 295
by Leslye Hutto. All other photos by Joe Hutto, unless otherwise credited.

Printed in China

Acknowledgments/References

This book represents, not only a lifetime of work, but a perpetual collaboration involving many disciplines, influential educators, mentors, and those inspirational personalities, both academic and personal, who have contributed to my vision of the natural world. Regretfully, they are too numerous to mention all and I could surely write volumes on every one.

A few of my early personal influences include: Ornithologist Herb Stoddard, botanist Robert K. Godfrey, wildlife biologist Lovett Williams, and paleontologist Stanley J. Olsen, all of whom taught me that the most rigorous science was perhaps the most fun a human being can have, when the wonder and curiosity of a child can be sustained throughout a lifetime.

Among so many scholarly and philosophical contributors I must mention the works of Aldo Leopold, Olas Murie, Loren Eiseley, Nikolaas Tinbergen, George B. Schaller, Jane Goodall, Edward O. Wilson, Derek Bickerton, Arthur Zajonc, Konrad Lorenz, and Henry Thoreau. Their collective genius and influence cause me to wonder if I have ever had an original thought in my life.

Contributors to our understanding of the mule deer of the American West are many and I must name but a few that have had more direct bearing on this study. It is impossible to consider the mule deer without some mention of the standard reference: *Mule and Black-tailed Deer of North America*—a research anthology involving many important contributors, compiled and edited by Olof C. Wallmo. In addition, there are many more recent studies that have been referenced directly in this book that include the stellar work of: Werner T. Flueck, Susan Lingle, Hall Sawyer, Fred Lindzey, and Doug McWhirter.

Further, it is difficult to say anything of significance about the North American mule deer without mentioning evolutionary biologist and professor Emeritus of the University of Calgary, Valerius Geist. It was his influential advice and encouragement that once suggested that there was valuable work to be done and it was he who in large part inspired me to make a commitment to this extraordinary animal.

I will always be indebted to a team of supporters who have become more like family members than employers and colleagues. PBS Nature series Executive Producer Fred Kaufman along with Bill Murphy, Janet Hess, Janice Young, Laura Metzger Lynch, and Jayne Jun—WNET, New York, all shared a vision for the potential of this project. This vision was realized and brought to light in the truest sense by Passion Pictures based in London England. Producer David Allen and assistant Gaby Bastyra, along with a team of technical people that must be one of the most gifted assemblages of profoundly inspired human beings to have ever come together with a common purpose. The celebrated cinematographer Mark Smith along with filmmakers Dawson Dunning and Sammy Tedder, made living and working in the wilderness, often under the most difficult circumstances, an honor, a privilege, and a pleasure of the highest order.

I am indebted to State wildlife agencies all over the West including: Colorado, Nevada, South Dakota, Idaho, Montana, and, of course, Wyoming. Their research and management data has been crucial and their kindness and encouragement has been humbling. I wish there was a better means to convey to the general public how fortunate we are to have so many enlightened, gifted and dedicated people, so tirelessly intent on making a difference and doing the right thing. It is truly inspirational.

Thanks to Skyhorse Publishing and especially to my most talented and visionary editor, Lilly Golden, for whom, after so many years and so many projects, my respect, affection, and gratitude has become complete.

No small attribution is owed to my friend, partner, and wife Leslye. My love and gratitude is immeasurable, as this journey has also been hers—every step of the way.

Table of Contents

Preface

I have lived with a large herd of mule deer in the mountains of the Wind River Range in Wyoming every day for the past seven years. How, you may ask, can a person do such a thing, and why would he choose to do it? My response would be, how could you not? Given the opportunity, how could a person resist such a life? You can call it biology or, better yet, ethology, or, perhaps more generally, natural science. But a more accurate description of this particular study would be the expression of some irresistible necessity to find sanctuary in the proximity of wild things. *Necessity* would be the key word in this case. I am compelled to seek out and explore the lives of other creatures—not to know simply *what* these animals are biologically but, more interestingly, to know *who* they are and how their biological affiliation, as a member of a species, instructs them as individuals. Ironically, it is through understanding individuals that knowledge of a species can truly be revealed. Although there can be strictly quantitative approaches, *ethology*—the study of animal behavior in a natural setting—is by definition a rather subjective undertaking. But divining the "who" of an animal can be an unapologetic departure from hard science and an adventure into a qualitative behavioral realm. One of my hopes is to maintain that balance along a challenging narrow divide between science and sentiment. My other objective is to be the voice for this extraordinary animal, which at this time is in need of a powerful and persuasive ally—an advocate—and that advocacy will come only from the various people that by way of different but convergent paths come to know and love the mule deer. Ultimately, the North American mule deer is in trouble on a bewildering array of fronts. And if we do not take any action, we may watch this species fade into oblivion.

We need not fear the emotional ties that will inevitably develop as we draw near to some thoughtful creature that is, without question, returning our gaze—an undeniable participant in an inquiry that clearly has become mutual. Sentiment born of the simple and logical empathic recognition that as living things we all share certain distinct similarities can be a lucid window into the life of an animal, providing the means to keenly observe some subtle elegance and beauty that may otherwise be overlooked. Empathy provides us with the vision to gain understanding, not through some superior anthropomorphism, but through our objective biological membership as analogous living things.

The practice of ethology may be better suited for the obsessive personality. Studying animals in their natural environments can involve slogging through aquatic habitat, trudging up mountains, scaling tall trees, suffering in steaming heat with ravaging insects, or enduring bitter cold. You are hungry, you are cold, you have not slept, and you don't care. Not because your obsession is pathological or you have an inherent fondness for suffering, but because the level of entertainment is so high—the intensity of discovery so rewarding and undeniably fun—that your discomfort becomes irrelevant. You wouldn't trade the privilege of your exploration for anything on Earth. And then, perhaps—just perhaps, at last—you may become aware that your subject matter and the flood of knowledge being revealed could actually be important.

Since I was a child, I've been drawn to studying animals. When I was ten, I captured and raised every newborn creature I could get my hands on, from crows to coyotes. Eventually, in college, I had the opportunity to work with bears, big cats, and even baboons and mandrels. It was also during these years that I worked with many species of cervids—deer and elk—and immediately became intrigued with the many interesting aspects of their social behavior. The more complex animal societies such as those of crows, baboons, and various herd animals including bison and deer captured my imagination and seemed to offer the greatest chal-lenges—and opportunities. Even though I had been involved in land and wildlife manage-ment for decades with an emphasis on game animals, I later became drawn to many of these same popular species, not because they were important game animals, and certainly not because I was being handsomely paid, but because these animals were in fact prey species that are characterized by larger, more dynamic populations, and thus often display elaborate social organization. Growing up in a waterfowl hunting culture in the rich and diverse wetlands of northern Florida, I had always had a bit of an obsession with ducks and geese.

One of my first attempts to finally conduct a fully rigorous ethology using the phenomenon of imprinting involved a newly hatched nest of orphaned wood ducks. *Imprinting* is simply the means by which a newborn animal comes to identify its parent and, perhaps, to some extent, its affiliation as a member of a species. I lived with these birds in the water of a bay swamp as their parent every day from the moment they hatched until the survivors were adults at about six months of age. The experience was a life-altering revelation, as I gained entry into the life of the wood duck, revealing a world with nuances and complexities that were previously beyond my comprehension. These creatures proved to be infinitely—outrageously—more intelligent and interesting than I could have imagined. I was not only struck by the complete and fully articulated instruction inherent in their genome, but also amazed to understand the depth of their ability to reason through the labyrinth of their universe with true problem-solving intelligence. That was the intimate experience that made me realize the untapped potential for discovery among many wild species, and that this was a largely unexplored realm—wide open with possibilities that seemed to shake up my world. The wood duck project demonstrated that there was abundant and fertile new ground to be broken, and that this not only was serious business, but could even be considered important work.

Years later, after in-depth involvements with gray foxes, crows, and several birds of prey, I repeated a similar but even more intense imprinting study involving wild turkeys: I incubated, hatched, and lived with a large family of twenty-four individuals for more than two years in a remote "wilderness" setting, largely isolated from human contact. The project resulted in the book *Illumination in the Flatwoods,* which, to my great surprise, was well received, by many casual students of natural history and scientists alike. Astonishingly, an Emmy award–winning documentary film, *My Life as a Turkey,* based on the book followed and proved beyond a doubt that not only are people interested in the seemingly obscure lives of wild creatures—they are hungry to know how other creatures envision the world. And it has become clear that some people find emotional or possibly even spiritual consolation in

« Author with young wood duck, 1978.

⌃ The author with Stretch, one of the turkeys from his 1995 experiment involving
imprinting wild turkeys.

the notion that humans are fully capable of establishing complex and meaningful relationships with other independent living things in ways that do not involve dominion or control.

Then, a few years later, I found myself living under rather strange circumstances, among another society of obscure animals, as a field biologist on the Wyoming Whiskey Mountain bighorn sheep study, beginning in 2001. This time I found myself living on a remote mountain in the Wind River Range, at twelve thousand feet, far above timberline, embedded with a summering herd of Rocky Mountain bighorn sheep. I lived alone in the company of these rare animals for months at a time without seeing another human in an effort to uncover what mysterious circumstances were limiting lamb survival. As in previous studies, a society of wild creatures seemed to become my own social environment—and, to some extent, my own family. My involvement with some of these individuals lasted for years, and included successive generations of young with individual faces and personalities that also came to identify me as a safe and persistent feature in their unique landscape. My affection for all bighorn sheep—and of course for certain individuals—became a powerful and very personal force in my life.

Almost immediately following my involvement with the bighorn sheep study, I found myself once again living among another society of creatures that has captivated my time, attention, admiration, and affection, to the exclusion of most everything else. And so, after spending another seven years of my life within the society and ecology of another animal, it could be said that my human perspective has been altered in some way, and that my identification with my own species has been clouded.

My goal with the mule deer study was to observe behavior in a light that is brighter than that offered by our own narrow human experience, using a little common sense, and perhaps even some informed intuition, with the intention of obtaining insight by the most honest means in my possession. Each day I am reminded of Friedrich Nietzsche's words, which should precede every scientific inquiry and should be included in the intellectual gospel of every honest human: "Convictions are more dangerous enemies of truth than lies." When observing the natural world, our mission should be to approach any ecology or any organism without preconceptions and, more important, abandon that imperial sense of human superiority, which always suggests that we know something even when we clearly

⌃ Author in summer on 12,200-foot Middle Mountain. Photo by Dawson Dunning.

do not. A position of superiority always provides the worst possible perspective and is anathema to any clean and honest observation—whether scientific or not. The objective should be to metaphorically approach any phenomenon of the natural world with your hat in your hand. I find humility to be increasingly easy to come by after so many years immersed in the lives of other creatures. Like a great enigmatic onion, complexity increases as we peel away successive layers of the underlying mysteries that always characterize the natural world. Get down, get your nose on the ground merely following your common senses, get out of your own way, and simply pay attention.

With this approach, it is possible to ask the fundamental questions—*who* are the personalities and *what* are those extraordinary characteristics and capabilities that define the species? I have always not merely observed but developed relationships with other creatures, and,

⌃ Big Horn Sheep on Middle Mountain. Photo by Dawson Dunning.

occasionally, through our common bonds of trust, tolerance, perhaps mutual interest, or—even on occasion—shared affection, we have come to know one another. I am convinced that only through the possibilities provided by this level of interaction may an animal gradually begin to fully reveal itself.

Ethology is simply an effort to observe any wild creature under the most natural circumstances possible—preferably with no captivity, no cages, no restraints, and, presumably, little interference or disruption created by the observer. One option may involve observing at a distance with a good pair of binoculars, a camera, and a notebook, as some extraordinary organism goes about its life in its otherwise ordinary way. Or, as I prefer, the observer may choose to gain a more personal and rigorous perspective of the individual or group of individuals being studied. Obviously this approach dictates a necessity of encountering more logistic difficulties and investing more time on a more persistent basis to create a level of comfort in a creature ordinarily unaccustomed to the company of a nosy human. This is often referred to as the process of *habituation*—you become such a common feature within another animal's landscape that you are eventually proven to be at least reasonably safe.

Then, when the subjects of your relentless investigation become so bored with your presence, you may be ignored entirely.

In time you may find yourself immersed in the fascinating life of another animal, and, perhaps more remarkable, you find that another animal has permeated your life with the richness of its own. The animal has generously contributed to your life in ways you could never have foreseen. And do not fear or flatter yourself with the suggestion that your presence is likely to alter a wild creature's fundamental nature, for most animals in their natural setting are far more willful and headstrong in the way they express their innate behavior than you or I tend to be. If you find yourself embedded in the society of another creature, in all probability, the only behavioral changes that are going to occur will be your own. Predictably, you will be the one whose fundamental nature has been altered in surprising ways.

Eventually, however, you may discover that you have in some way been acculturated into the society of another species, and you are then afforded a most privileged access to the animals' vision of the world. You begin to see the ecology from their perspective—from their point of view. Your human presumption of imperial authority over the landscape may be lost—you become just another rightful constituent, and, by example, you begin to tread lightly. This is an account of such a relationship.

PART I

Some Interesting Mule Deer I Have Known

CHAPTER ONE

In the Beginning

⌃ Slingshot Ranch, early spring.

Leslye and I live on an old Wyoming homestead ranch that lies on the eastern foothills of the southern Wind River Mountains, several miles south of Lander. The ranch was first established in the 1880s and is often referred to as the old Corbett place, and in more recent years it has been known as the Slingshot Ranch. Ellamae Corbett, the first schoolteacher in the pioneer community of Lander, is known to have lived here, and her old ramshackle log house remains in disrepair, partially dug into the hillside above the cliff face.

Homesteads were established during this period in 120-acre increments and expanded by the gradual acquisition of surrounding lands, as people chose to sell or abandon their places. Located on the lower slopes of a rather prominent feature known as Table Mountain lying southwest of Lander, the ranch house, corrals, and buildings rest just above a cliff face that overlooks a small canyon and the creek that flows through the drainage known as Deadman Gulch.

Deadman Gulch inherited its name from an unfortunate incident that occurred just down the draw, in which three white men on a freight wagon traveling from South Pass to Lander in 1870 were apparently attacked by a war party of Sioux. The three mutilated bodies were discovered by later travelers, along with a broken wagon and a team of missing horses. According to the report issued from Fort Brown, which lay within the boundaries of present-day downtown Lander, the three men climbed into a wolf den on the edge of the draw at the approximate confluence of Deadman Gulch and Anesi Draw, engaging the Indians in a vicious battle. Judging by the hundreds of expended rifle cartridges, the men must have put up a good fight until they eventually ran out of ammunition. The three mangled bodies were retrieved and, with little ceremony, immediately interred close to the fort. While workers were making improvements on Lander's Main Street in the early 1900s, they stumbled on the grave containing the remains of the three men. One of the skeletons had a steel wagon hammer driven handle-first all the way through the head. The skull was retrieved with hammer still embedded and now rests permanently in the Lander Pioneer Museum.

We moved onto the Slingshot Ranch about seven years ago in the spring of 2006. The Slingshot was so named by Nan Slingerland, who bought the place as a "satellite ranch" to provide supplemental autumn grazing for her herd of cattle. Nan and her late husband

Henry owned the famous historic Red Canyon Ranch, which was eventually sold to the Nature Conservancy in the late 1990s. The conservancy now operates the ranch as an ideal, environmentally sustainable cattle operation. Nan retains enough land from the original fifty-thousand-acre ranch to continue running a viable herd of red Angus cattle. Her operation lies at the mouth of a spectacular glacial canyon where the Little Popo Agie River spills out of the southern Wind River Mountains. From our place we can see the high northern rim of the canyon, and Nan considered that our place was about a "rifle shot" away—hence the name "Slingshot." I met Nan and Henry many years ago, and I was employed as a working cowboy and managed their Red Canyon Ranch during the early 1980s; after I moved on, we maintained a friendship for many years.

After my years of involvement with the Wyoming bighorn sheep study in the northern Wind River Mountains from 2000 to 2007, I decided to again make Wyoming my permanent home. I immediately called Nan from northern Florida, where I have lived for most of my life. I inquired whether one of her old bunkhouses might be available until I could find more permanent accommodations—there was a dead silence on the phone. Then she cautiously asked, "Who have you been talking to?" I innocently said, "No one," but, as it turned out, the old homestead and house on the Slingshot Ranch had been vacated just the day before! After discussions about some form of eerie fate being at work, she said it was not only available but, apparently, "meant to be." Leslye and I moved in immediately, and the ranch became home to us and Leslye's two horses, Lilly and Gum Drop. Eventually realizing that we "belonged" to the Slingshot, Nan graciously agreed to sell us the operation a couple of years later.

The Slingshot is located a mile and a half from the highway at the dead end of a county road, and we are the last place up on the lower slopes of the mountain. Here the "Gulch" is contained by sandstone canyon walls, and our old house is perched a couple hundred feet back from the rim of a roughly vertical cliff face that rises sixty feet above the creek below.

When choosing a place to live, I find that it is always best to base my decision on the quality of my most immediate neighbors—not necessarily the folks living more than a half-mile away on nearby ranches (all great people, by the way)—but the neighbors who will be living outside my door. We immediately recognized that the Slingshot was richly endowed

⌃ Leslye at the corrals with Gum Drop.

with fine neighbors of all varieties. True, we had good irrigation rights, a deep well with potable water, and great hay meadows with gentle inclines that will roll a tractor over only once in a while. But it could be said that we fell in love with this old ramshackle ranch because of its rare ecology and teeming wildlife—definitely not because of the economic prospects of the ranching industry, God knows. The diverse ecology of the draw, the creek below, the surrounding sandstone cliffs, and the sage brush slopes that rise into the timbered mountains above all provide a rich diversity of habitat types, with a huge variety of vegetation for browsing and cover and, predictably, a corresponding abundance of animal life. Furthermore, old ranches and the irrigation they provide often create an island effect, as they establish a relatively lush refuge. After more than one hundred years, the house and compound are now surrounded by a small but well-established stand of ancient cottonwood, box elder, elm, and willow trees. Much of the space in and around the yard, as well as the understory between the larger trees, is filled with tangled thickets of fruiting trees and shrubs. Wyoming's first commercial apple operation was introduced on the present-day Slingerland Ranch, and I would suspect that some of the old trees on the Slingshot may have originated from original varieties planted in the 1870s. The rows of large willows and cottonwoods that encircle the yard are surrounded by dense shrubs and volunteer fruit trees that produce crabapples and several varieties of plums, while two species of wild currant and gooseberry grow by the thousands. Dozens of hundred-year-old lilac trees and shrubs provide dense green cover in warmer months, and for weeks in spring their lavender and pink blooms fill the air with their intoxicating fragrance. This old place has, in fact, become a sanctuary for a diverse variety of plants and creatures large and small, four-footed and two.

Having always maintained feeding stations for birds and animals, I immediately installed bird feeders in the yard and was soon dumbfounded by the variety of species that lived in the immediate area or were seasonal migrants. Wyoming experiences a real winter, with temperatures falling to far below zero for several months of the year, so most summer bird residents are migrants. The fabulous orange, black, and white Bullock's orioles tend their hanging basket nests in summer, until the young are well fledged, and then begin their long migration to South America a full month before cold weather begins to grip the Wyoming countryside.

Three hundred cliff swallows arrive at the Slingshot, like clockwork, toward the end of June, immediately driving the freeloading English sparrows from the cliff-hanging, mud-pot swallow nests, and then begin repairs by collecting new mud from the creek. Egg laying begins within days. As soon as the members of the new generation are fledged and become strong flyers, they fill the air in a great swarm every afternoon, receiving a crash course on collecting insects in flight. After a few brief weeks in late summer, and by some mysterious means, the signal is given, and all head south in one large migratory event—a full month before even a suggestion of cold weather arrives. Their departure is abrupt, leaving the late afternoon sky lonely and power lines barren, with only the company of nighthawks and winnowing snipe for consolation. We have nesting mallards on the creek and sandhill cranes on the wet meadow below the house, and, in early spring, Canada geese stand on the rim of the cliff in mated pairs and make a phenomenal racket every morning for an hour in some

⌃ Cliff swallow nests on cliffs just below the house.

strange annual ritual that I have never fully understood, for their actual nesting sites are miles away. Pheasants, chukar quail, Hungarian partridge, and the threatened sage grouse all nest nearby and bring their broods to browse around the yard with regularity. Tree sparrows and white crowned sparrows pass through spring and fall, but blue grosbeaks and black-headed grosbeaks all nest nearby with two species of towhees. Cassin's finches and their beautiful songs are common throughout summer, but the similar red house finches are year-round residents, as are the pine siskins. Dozens of red-winged blackbirds congregate in the yard throughout the day and tend their nests in the cattails down by the creek. Both ravens and magpies are year-round residents, with magpies nesting in the apple trees and in the scrubby willows along the creek. When an animal has been killed in the area, the ravens and magpies, along with one or two scavenging eagles, will always alert me. Few creatures die within a two-mile radius that I don't know about within hours. There are multiple species of warblers that wander along the creek and venture into the yard with the golden-crowned kinglets. The area is graced with a relative abundance of lazuli buntings, with ten resident pairs of successful nesters last summer. Buntings and gold finches are with us throughout spring into early winter. Western and mountain bluebirds as well as barn swallows return each spring, and many are enticed to select our nesting boxes that dot the fences along the hay meadows.

Upon the arrival of the first heavy blanketing snowstorm of winter, when most other birds have moved far to the south, we fill our feeders and stand back, prepared for the onslaught. Black rosy finches, one of the rarest birds in North America, with one of the smallest home ranges, literally descend on the Slingshot by the hundreds. Fearless rosy finches are peculiar to the northern Rocky Mountains and are further distinguished by a year-round occupation of the remote timberline and alpine areas above ten thousand feet, preferring to nest on the alpine tundra with the pipets. Rosy finches are a blackish (or sooty), medium-sized, stocky bird with a contrasting pinkish, wine-colored iridescence that is unlike any color I have observed on any other species.

⌃ Rosy finch visiting with the author. Photo by Dawson Dunning.

After hundreds of attempts to photograph these brilliant birds that will eat seeds out of your hand, I have yet to get that definitive shot that captures the outrageous color on their wings and flanks. A blanketing winter storm will send them down from the high country in tight flying flocks of one hundred or more. Along with a few chickadees and redpolls, they feed ravenously for two or three days, until high winds liberate the snow that has enshrouded subalpine trees, and then, instantly, everyone is gone—back to the high country until the next big snow.

Great horned owls are year-round residents that, along with the red-tailed hawks, successfully nest in the cliffs each summer just below the house. Sharp-shinned and Cooper's hawks streak though the yard with predictability, often leaving only a telltale puff of feathers floating slowly to the ground. Northern shrikes are always nearby in cooler times, and appear to be more aggressive, persistent, and successful predators than the sharpies are. Harriers may be seen floating over the hay meadows, occasionally dropping into the grass to collect voles and deer mice, but suddenly disappear in the dead of winter. When many sensible raptors have migrated south during the coldest months, the Arctic tundra-nesting rough-legged hawks begin occupying the area—as these beautiful and exotic birds must find the balmy winter climate of Wyoming a haven from the true rigors of the far north. Although relatively large buteo hawks, they are considered to be inflexible "mouse obligates" and mysteriously manage to hover, dive, and then pull voles from the deep snow all winter. I also observe rough-legged hawks scavenging carrion throughout winter when opportunities arise. We also have golden and bald eagles nesting in the area, both year-round residents.

Unlike other people who encourage and have a strong affection for these eagles, Leslye occasionally goes shrieking out into the yard during the day to scare them from the trees, crying, "Leave my bunnies alone!"—thereby proclaiming to all that we do not operate an eagle-feeding station on the Slingshot. On one occasion, we counted forty cottontail rabbits in the yard silhouetted on the moonlit snow, and we do what little we can to encourage their well-being. However, cottontails are the ultimate prey species, and the pendulum of their population swings widely. Like chipmunks, many of the bunnies have names and readily take horse cookies from Leslye's hand down around the barn. Leslye has also cultivated a relationship with the remarkable rodent known as the pack rat, which often lives in accommodating rock shelters, but also loves old barns or derelict buildings. Large and beautiful rats with un-rat-like bushy tails, they are extremely intelligent and display a complex social life. Leslye can call a name, and a pack rat will emerge from a hole in a log wall of the barn, walk out onto Leslye's lap, and casually take a horse cookie.

Finally, in the dead of winter, the mighty goshawks descend from the high country to feed on quail, pheasants, and the Eurasian collared doves that frequent the ranch by the hundreds. Kestrels build their nest in a cavity within in a dead snag of a cottonwood outside the back door every year. However, until we began relocating the resident bull snakes, the little hawks never managed to fledge even one young bird.

Bull snakes are important predators but are voracious feeders on nesting birds as well as their eggs and hatchlings. They are bold and aggressive, attacking large prey such as young

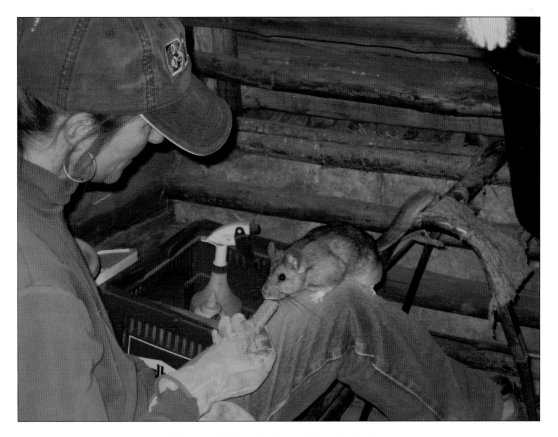

⌃ Leslye with Apple, the pack rat in the barn.

magpies and kestrels with impunity. I once watched a large bull snake consume an entire nest of mallard eggs in a single meal. I relocated that snake over a half-mile away, and he was back cleaning up the remaining duck eggs in less than an hour! On another occasion, Leslye caught by hand a marauding bull snake with a distinctive tail scar at the entrance of a cotton-tailed bunny burrow by the barn. She then deposited the five-foot snake a half-mile away by our cattle guard out near the county road. Again, in one hour, the snake was back and trying to dine on the same nest of baby bunnies. We have found that these snakes must be taken miles away to confound their remarkable homing skills. Bull snakes are strikingly beautiful and even-tempered, occasionally approaching a shocking length of seven feet in this area.

The cliff face below the house and barn runs for half a mile up the draw and provides an almost infinite variety of cracks, fissures, and overhangs, as well as multiple small crevasses and caves. The higher overhangs provide protected vertical walls for hundreds of mud-pot cliff swallow nests. The many cracks, fissures, and small caves often provide a little moisture, shade, and anchorage for vegetation, making all manner of homes and nesting sites for a wide assortment of other animals. We have an abundance of "least" chipmunks that truly appear too small to exist, let alone propagate in such great numbers. They are industrious and fearless little creatures that spend much time around the house, where we provide a ready source of sunflower seeds on the porch. We commonly sit on the front porch in the evening watching all the activity in the area, with chipmunks scampering across our laps as they fill their cheek pouches and then diligently head to some secure location to deposit their stash— then back they come for another load. Naturally, many of our chipmunks have names, and some will let me scratch them on their tiny heads while they shell sunflower seeds on the coffee table. Large, lumbering yellow-bellied marmots—"rock chucks"—live in and around the draw, and once a delightful and friendly female that we named Molly lived with us for a summer, making her home in the foundation of an old log shed outside our back door.

We have identified at least three hibernacula (snake dens) along the cliff wall. As spring begins warming the south-facing cliffs, various reptiles begin to emerge, sunning themselves by day and returning to their dens at night. The smaller-bodied snakes appear first, with the emergence of garter snakes, along with the gray-green racers and the scaly swift lizards that belong to a rather large genus of Iguanids. We have horned "toads"—lizards—living a

⌃ Leslye catching a bull snake.

 ⌃ Least chipmunk.

half-mile up the mountain in the sage brush and rock outcrops, but, curiously, none live in or around the cliffs. A week after the small snakes surface, on the warmest mornings, the heavier-bodied snakes begin to appear, as the bull snakes may be seen moving about but not yet wandering far from their sanctuaries. At last, the prairie rattlesnakes emerge, and for a week or two they may be seen coiled in lazy individual heaps, often by the dozen. They are sluggish as they try to restart a torpid metabolism that has been resting for several frigid months. It was not long after moving onto the Slingshot that we discovered that the prairie rattler was perhaps the single most abundant living thing in an ecology that was teeming with life.

At one time in my life I collected venomous reptiles to sell to universities, zoos, and research facilities, and, while earning my way through college, I also worked with dangerous

⌃ Prairie rattler near the house.

snakes as a professional reptile handler, giving twice-daily demonstrations at a zoo. All snake handlers get bitten—all of them—and I almost got what was coming to me on several occasions. After somehow surviving the immortal years of my late teens and early twenties, I realized that another line of work would be advisable and timely, so upon graduation I started working with somewhat less deadly species of animals. But I retain a deep affection for all reptiles and still have a high regard for rattlesnakes in particular. The prairie rattler is one of the more disagreeable rattlesnakes—an ill-tempered creature that is mercifully inclined to rattle at any small provocation, making them easier to avoid. It was our intention to attempt to live in harmony with all the rattlesnakes on the Slingshot, observing that they were here before us, and of course it was our consideration that they had every reason and right to be here. However, the prairie rattler has some of the most potent venom of any North American rattlesnake, and after three years of close encounters—every day—which included a miraculous "dry bite" to my hand while I was attempting to repair an irrigation head gate, at last, our favorable view of rattlesnakes dimmed. And in those three years, Leslye and I both experienced several other close calls. Then, one of Leslye's mares, Gum Drop, was bitten, not once but twice on the nose. I happened to see the bites occur in the meadow in front of the house as the horse squealed and took off at a run two hundred yards to the top of the hill. There she immediately collapsed in a heap like she had been shot with a high-powered rifle. Clearly in agony, she then pulled herself up and again ran straight to me as I stood by the fence another one hundred yards away. Sliding to a halt, she whinnied as if pleading for help and then ran down the hill and stormed into the open corral. Again her legs buckled under, and she collapsed like the life had suddenly been sucked out of her. I reminded myself that this was a one-thousand-pound animal and wondered what that same amount of venom would have done to me. Horses often recover from snake bites, but it was a horrendous ordeal that left Gum Drop standing with her head down, swollen like a basketball, unable to eat, struggling for every breath, with bloody serum draining from her nostrils for days. All we could do was administer an antibiotic to prevent secondary infection and have plastic tubes ready to insert in the nostrils should they swell shut. Leslye spent two long nights in the barn with the pack rats as the mare slowly recovered, and it was a full year before Gum Drop's head looked completely normal again. It became clear that our relationship with these snakes was not going to end well. The population had to be reduced. In the first year of our reduction program, we relocated or dispatched twenty-four individuals and optimistically hoped that we might see a reduced population the following summer. Beginning the following spring into summer, we were disappointed to remove another twenty-two snakes. Last summer our efforts began to pay off, and we removed merely five, but only after I had been bitten one more time on my irrigation boot by a hefty three-and-a-half-foot female with a bad attitude. Now we do not disturb the newborn rattlesnakes we occasionally encounter, but we continue to remove the larger adults that manage to come near the corrals or house. While out irrigating the hay meadows, visiting our prairie dog colony, or just roaming around, I still enjoy my occasional run-ins with the rattlesnakes, and I never disturb one that is not an immediate threat around the house or barn. Leslye, however, entertains a strong disapproval of rattlesnakes, and during warmer months, she packs "heat"—a "hog-leg"—on her belt in the form of an old Colt 38 Special loaded with "snake shot." When the UPS man drives up, Leslye always greets him in the driveway with a friendly smile, but he always raises his arms and says, "Yes ma'am!"

We also live in an area where many species of large mammals are seen in abundance. Antelope or "pronghorn" inhabit the sage brush slope of the mountain in large numbers. While bucks remain in sociable fraternal herds, the solitary does begin fawning in the hay meadows in late spring and may be seen throughout the summer. The does and fawns gradually reunite in herds that continue to swell into fall. The bucks join the does as the rut begins throughout

⌃ Leslye holding a prairie rattler by the tail.

late summer and fall, eventually becoming polite members of the greater herd by December. Great congregations of up to two hundred may be seen around the ranch in winter as they alternately browse the sage brush and occasionally spill out onto the snow-covered hay meadows.

When winter snows arrive, bears slip into their dens, while mule deer, elk, and moose must all migrate down out of high mountain basins and the timbered slopes that may be seen several miles up the mountain. We have observed only one bear on the Slingshot as he apparently fed on a dead fawn. Elk may be observed from our kitchen window on any winter day, often by the hundreds, as they pepper the steep open mountainside below the timber.

⌃ Pronghorn moving past mule deer in the gulch.

⌃ Higher on the mountain, the elk gather below the tree line.

They rarely visit the Slingshot, but I see the occasional track of a cow elk that has passed through in the night. Neighboring rancher Ed King mentioned counting 175 elk in a meadow that borders us one half-mile to the north. For years I have combed the slopes above the Slingerland Ranch in spring looking for shed elk antlers near a dramatic feature of the Little Popo Agie Canyon named Wolf Point. Wanting to see some beautiful country, Leslye and I recently backpacked up from Nan's house, spending three nights above Wolf Point, and we eventually hauled down six pairs of fresh shed antlers tied to our packs. From a ridge just above our camp in the timber, we could look down on the Slingshot—more than five miles and four thousand feet in elevation below.

The Shiras moose has been in a steady decline in Wyoming for many years, but the magnificent animals may still be seen here and there, although not in the great numbers of

⩘ Our Wolf Point antler camp.

twenty or thirty years ago. Because wintering moose prefer riparian habitat, Red Canyon and the three Popo Agie River drainages have always been a destination for these creatures.

Of course, with this many large animals surrounding us, their predators, too, are abundant. We live in the midst of mountain lions that in winter and spring are around the house day and night and leave their blood-stained scats below the cliff face for us to examine each morning. Unlike domestic cats, cougars prefer to leave their impressive scats uncovered, as if they should be admired by one and all. Coyotes are everywhere and band together in efficient killing packs in winter, effectively attacking mule deer and antelope.

Wolves have populated the Wind River Mountains in recent years, and we see at least a few every winter in this area. Now the mountain basins above the Slingerland Ranch have a predictable summer wolf population, and both the Slingerland and the Nature Conservancy

⌃ Wolf track above the ranch.

cattle suffer increased, but not yet unacceptable, losses as wolf numbers rise. As expected, elk numbers are beginning to decline in response to the wolf presence, but it is said that mule deer may be essentially defenseless when confronted by packs of this aggressive predator. Where wolves have dispersed or been introduced to islands off the northwest coast, black-tailed deer, close relatives to mule deer, were quickly reduced to extinction. It will be interesting to see how the Wyoming wolf reintroduction plays out, and only time will tell, as both wolf advocates and detractors have no real research data on which to base their opinions. For now the outcome is a crapshoot, but one thing is certain: the many species that were already in a state of decline now have to deal with the added stress of this powerful force on the landscape.

Other common predators that frequent the Slingshot Ranch include a healthy population of red foxes and bobcats, badgers, skunks, raccoons, and weasels.

⌃ Bobcat in the yard, striking at a passing bird.

I arrived at the Slingshot in May 2006, two weeks before Leslye, and began placing furniture and making some minor repairs and adjustments to the house. The first evening I looked outside the kitchen window, and standing by my pickup was a handsome young four-point buck, casually passing by. I thought to myself, "Great! We have a few mule deer around the place." I had no idea that we had just occupied a house that was located directly in the center of a home winter range of deer that had probably been enjoying the rich diversity of this little canyon for at least hundreds, if not thousands, of years. Judging by the sparse scatters of flint chips up and down the rims of the draw, humans have been at least marginally aware of these deer for millennia.

In spite of the diversity of our local ecology that supports an extraordinary abundance of species, it could be declared that this is, first and foremost, mule deer country. There are certain ecologies and particular habitats that seem to be characterized by a particular emblematic creature—the gilded thread that brings definition and clearly embodies the most essential spirit of the landscape. And the mule deer is that iconic creature. When walking across a plunging sage brush mountainside with small, steep-sided rocky canyons, awash in the color of spring flowers and lined with quaking aspens that enshroud sparkling, clear, rushing streams, it is the ever-present mule deer, quietly watching from some high promontory, that reminds us that we are walking on rare earth and that our presence is being noted.

⌃ Bohemian waxwing.

⌃ Leslye wearing a bohemian waxwing.

⌄ Quail on a cold day.

CHAPTER TWO

And Along Came Rayme

Throughout our first summer on the Slingshot Ranch, we were peripherally aware of our resident mule deer, which we would see occasionally in the draw or browsing the sage brush, but as with wild deer everywhere, they maintained a distance appropriate for any creature considered a big game animal. The summer resident population appeared evenly distributed throughout the area, and by midsummer we began to see the occasional doe with fawns grazing the meadows in late afternoon. However, by October, all things begin to change in the Wyoming high country. Nights become cool, blanketing the highest peaks in snow, while aspen and wild currents begin to wash the landscape in blazing reds, oranges, and luminescent yellows.

One cool afternoon in September, Leslye looked out the kitchen window, and standing in the front yard was a fine-looking mule deer doe. Leslye called me to join her at the window, and we stood enjoying the opportunity to admire this handsome animal, all the while assuming that she would soon become aware of our interest and move away. This deer seemed healthy and robust, with a new installment of winter hair well established. As we gazed from the darker interior of the house, the deer finally made eye contact. With ears canted forward and with large wet, black eyes, she stared back with great intensity and concern. We stood silent and motionless, certain that she would soon become fearful and the moment would be lost. However, to our amazement, she continued her obvious inquiry, which even included a quick halting step in our direction. But, then, she looked away, and without apparent fear or a backward glance, she slowly walked toward the back of the house and out of sight. Leslye and I finally made eye contact, and one of us quietly said, "Wow."

This doe became an immediate celebrity around the Slingshot, as she began to arrive each afternoon expressing some fascination with us that we, of course, always returned in kind. Soon we realized that she was a member of a family group, and when this particular deer entered the area around the house, we would also see her companions standing or browsing in the vicinity. One afternoon Leslye said, "The doe is in the yard," and I replied, "Which doe?" Leslye said casually, "What about Doe-Ray-Me?—Rayme!" So, without realizing it, we had assigned not just a name to a wild deer but rather an identity, and we began a tradition that would eventually involve more than seven years and well over two hundred individuals

⌃ Rayme, the deer who started it all.

with names, faces, and distinct personalities. In a matter of days we could walk out of the house, and Rayme would remain nearby—perhaps moving a few yards away, but showing little of the fear one would expect from a wild deer. I began to suspect that this particular deer must have had some unusual experience with humans that would account for her peculiar behavior. I even called the previous occupants of the Slingshot to ask if they had known or developed some sort of friendly relationship with a deer. The answer was no—they had seen many deer over the years, but there was no deer that seemed particularly tame or especially familiar with people. After a few months, I also had opportunities to check with all the adjoining ranchers and landowners, and none seemed to be aware of such a deer. Having horses, we customarily kept a fifty-pound bag of horse cookies, sold as "outfitter's wafers," that we used for treats or inducements while training or riding. We would toss one to Rayme on occasion as we left the house, and in a short time she became quite fond of the treat.

Soon, Rayme became a familiar resident around the house, and we discovered that all we needed to do was walk outside and say, "Rayme!" and she would mysteriously appear within seconds. And Rayme had this peculiar habit of staring at us through the window at night. We have thermal blankets that roll down over the cabin windows for really cold nights, but with the nearest neighbor half a mile away, in one hundred years, there had never been a curtain hanging on a window at the Slingshot. As a result, we live in something that must resemble a fishbowl as we walk around the well-lit house at night. Although a little disconcerting, we eventually realized that Rayme would literally follow us as we moved through the house, going from window to window, fascinated with our activities. At 10:00 p.m. you would look into the otherwise black square of a window and suddenly make out the face of a deer, almost pressed against the glass—there was Rayme—wide-eyed and watching our every move.

Rayme was a relatively large doe—a big, healthy-looking animal with a beautiful coat. Her facial mask was dark overall, with contrasting light markings around her eyes. Her crown was almost black, and her throat patch was pale. She also had large ears—even for a "mule" deer—and they were arranged relatively low on the sides of her head, a bit droopy, giving her an appearance that brought some element of the needy and the pitiful to mind. But, in all, Rayme was a handsome doe, and her rather painted-lady face was filled with expression. Ungulates or artiodactyls such as goats, cattle, sheep, and deer tend to lack the muscles that make facial expressions so obvious in creatures such as dogs, monkeys, and people. However, with enormous dark brown eyes, accented with those famously large, flirtatious eyelashes, plus the large and defining ears that were like semaphore flags, speaking mule deer volumes, this deer had a way of making her intentions known. Rayme somehow managed to make it perfectly clear not only that she was consumed with interest regarding our activities but also that she clearly wanted attention from us. There was something about our mere proximity that Rayme desired. For reasons that will always remain a mystery, Rayme found us—Rayme sought us out.

After daily ranch chores were completed, and weather permitting, we took to sitting on the front porch in the afternoons, and after tossing a few horse cookies to Rayme and engaging in polite conversation, she would eventually lie down, twenty feet away next to the lilacs, and with heavy, sagging eyelids, comfortably chew her cud.

Rayme's family group soon observed that the ranch and the occupants were safe, and that there might even be treats involved. In a matter of weeks the entire clan of fifteen other individuals was entering the yard, and immediately our focus and interaction became dispersed, in a very personal way, throughout this little herd. By observing various personalities and physical traits, Leslye soon assigned clever and relevant names to each individual, as each seemed to look and behave in ways that made it easy to distinguish that particular deer, even at a distance. Of course we could not tell what the affiliations were between the adults in the group, but the does with fawns had provided us with evidence regarding the family lineages that would eventually be so revealing in studying the significance and dynamics of the family unit in mule deer society.

We began calling one member of Rayme's group Raggedy Anne. Anne was an older doe, judging by the disheveled look of her pelage, or coat, that had tuffs of hair standing up in irregular patches. She was indeed raggedy. Her eyes appeared tired, but also there was a look in her eyes—not merely one of age or even sadness—but tragedy. She was a shorter, stockier deer with a top-line that sagged a bit, suggesting that she had been a mother many times. Anne had big, soft, dark brown eyes with unusual flecks of gray that appeared when the sunlight shone across her iris. Although extremely wary of us at first, Anne eventually came to trust us to an extent that was remarkable and unexpected. Anne was with twins that first year, and we named her doe fawn Rag Tag because both ears had been ripped down to the base by coyotes when she must have been a very small fawn. When we met her at about four months of age, both ears were completely healed. Her brother, Frosty, was pale overall, and his light gray-brown coat was entirely tipped in snow-white, giving him the appearance of being covered in a uniform winter frosting. Both fawns were frightened and confused when in our presence and would only stand nervously on the periphery of the group when they were all near.

We finally came to recognize a yearling doe in the group as being Anne's doe fawn from the previous year, as she rejoined her mother in the fall. This beautiful yearling doe became Charm, in reference to black scars that girdled both her lower front legs, like bracelets, just above the hooves. Her entire body was covered in large, dark patches and lines from obvious scarring. She must have been horribly mauled by coyotes or a mountain lion when she was a fawn but miraculously survived. She also had big, soft, dark eyes with heavy eyelids tipped in long lashes, and they seemed to reflect some deep sadness like her mother's did.

Another doe in the group that immediately captivated our attention was Notcha—a profoundly beautiful and elegant deer without a surviving fawn that year, but with a distinct notch taken out of her left ear. She seemed captivated by our attentions and had a particular affinity for Leslye. Another deer with a large, crescent-moon-shaped scar on her shoulder we came to know as Crescent. She had fawns that year whom we named New Moon and Luna; however, Luna eventually became Luno when his gender was finally revealed.

In late November, we began to observe our first rut at the Slingshot. At this time, mule deer bucks, like male animals everywhere, become distracted and obsessed to the exclusion of either food or rest. A large, beautiful buck we called Daddy Buck, joined our herd of twenty-five does and fawns, and although the occasional contender would wander by, this dominant buck's authority was rarely challenged. He was easy to recognize, not only because of unusually large antlers supported by a massive, swollen neck, but also because the antlers were "nontypical," with a rather gnarly configuration that lacked symmetry and with a smattering of extra small tines here and there.

⌃ Notcha.

Rutting mule deer bucks, although profoundly wary most of the year, can become almost oblivious to humans when preoccupied with prospective mates. If you are standing twenty feet from twenty does and fawns in the first week of December, the biggest buck may pass by close enough to touch you, offering only a nervous glance and a canted ear that dismisses your odd and inconvenient presence.

Daddy Buck immediately identified us as safe neighbors and in a few days became entirely comfortable with our presence. Dominant bucks normally lack the nervous insecurity that the younger two- and three-year-old bucks display around the herd. These older mule deer bucks, by comparison, seem to remain composed and rather dignified, having earned a secure standing among other deer. They can be surprisingly polite, merely making themselves available to a flirtatious doe while remaining highly conspicuous to other opti-mistic bucks, whereas younger bucks can be terribly annoying to does nearing estrus. Domi-nant bucks are also gentle and indulgent with the fawns and will even allow the little ones to share food, eating nose to nose. Buck fawns display a cautious but almost obsessive curiosity with the great bucks; they are allowed to sniff around the head and antlers as if they may be anticipating the possibility of one day also becoming such an imposing presence. In contrast, these behaviors would be considered horribly rude by most does, and would invite a brisk hoof laid squarely between the thoughtless fawn's ears.

A doe in heat may be attended by the dominant buck for twenty-four hours or until she has completed her cycle. During this season, bucks eventually become starved and exhausted,

⌃ Moses, a gentle giant.

⋒ Notcha with Moses.

so Daddy Buck would lie and sleep for hours during midday—and was obviously grateful for some high-protein supplemental food that we would offer him on occasion.

Daddy Buck was in attendance for two years before he was displaced, but he was with us only during the rut—then he would mysteriously disappear for the duration of the year. We saw him pass by the third year, but he politely surrendered the area to a more dominant and imposing buck we named Moses. When three-hundred-pound Moses swaggered into the yard with head lowered and ears canted back, we were reminded of the Red Sea parting, as thirty-five deer respectfully moved far to either side.

The first year was our introduction to this herd of deer that would eventually capture my attention and curiosity in ways that I had never imagined. Each year has been an exercise in uncovering successive layers of complexity that define the life of the mule deer and their extraordinary relationship to this diverse landscape. However, this was the beginning that would later offer possibilities that any scientist or ardent observer would find irresistible. Socrates said, "The unexamined life is not worth living." I would agree but further amend that by saying that, for some, it is the examination of other living things that makes life worth living.

CHAPTER THREE

An Inflorescence of Mule Deer

Even on a small ranch like ours, life can be consumed by the constant attention required of horses, fencing repairs, irrigating, growing and harvesting hay, and keeping noxious weeds at bay. Each summer our dear friends Jack and Robin Malmberg, with daughter Ingre, bring three teams of great draft horses, along with the appropriate one-hundred-year-old, steel-wheeled McCormick mowers, and spend a week cutting and baling our hay. It's a hard-working but delightful time, tending the land in a traditional way with the gentle giants that quietly and steadily pull us all along. The deer had migrated in May to their summer range, and we had no communication with them until summer came to an end, when we were delighted to see familiar deer faces returning. Last year's fawns were almost grown and independent but still entirely recognizable. And of course the familiar does from the previous years were returning and introducing us to their new fawns. These deer that we had known from the previous year, although somewhat nervous from being out of human company for six months, quickly recognized us and within hours were again familiar and comfortable to be within a few meters of us. Clearly, the new fawns judged from their mother's demeanor that even though we were a strange curiosity, we must be a relatively safe curiosity. Their behavior was distinctly different from the fawns we had met the previous year. In fact, the new, wide-eyed fawns were so accepting of us that it was hard to avoid the improbable suspicion that they had received some prior instruction on what to expect. Even the yearling fawns from the previous year were decidedly more

comfortable with our proximity than they had been when last we saw them—as though they had forgotten the exact previous spatial boundaries that we may have shared in those months last winter, and now these new boundaries were less rigidly defined.

After many weeks, we sadly concluded that Rayme had not survived the summer or perhaps the migratory gauntlet back to her home winter range. I still regret not getting to know her better, for clearly she was extraordinary. She had bridged the divide between her family and ours, and all that has transpired is her lasting legacy. Rayme was something of an oracle who voluntarily brought a message that merged one universe with another— she was the one who so generously and unexpectedly chose to share her unique vision of the world. Rayme opened a door I never knew existed.

As the season progressed, the deer began returning in waves that would include four or five at a time. One cool October morning after a light snowfall,

« Jack, Robin, and Ingre Malmberg cutting hay with 100-year old horse-drawn mowers pulled by their Belgians.

I was standing in the yard scattering some alfalfa hay, surrounded by a few deer, when I saw several other deer coming down through the sage brush from the mountain behind the house. Leslye had been particularly anxious, waiting for Notcha's return, but so far there had been no sign of her favorite deer. That morning, as Leslye stood in the window, I pointed to the arriving deer and suggested in some sort of sign language that one of the deer coming might be Notcha because of a left ear with a visible notch. I pointed, and Leslye nodded with a big grin. The gorgeous and distinctive deer entering the yard could only have been Notcha. But the new arrivals saw me and immediately stopped and became noticeably nervous. All five deer suddenly turned in fear and began trotting back out of the yard toward the mountain. Leslye exclaimed through the glass, "Say her name! Quick!" I called in a loud voice, "Notcha!" Then I repeated, "Notcha!" To our absolute astonishment, Notcha stopped and turned, staring momentarily, and, then, leaving the other deer, ran—yes, ran—at a gallop directly to me. We were stunned at the revelation that she not only recognized my voice and knew exactly who I was after six months without doubt, but, even more amazing, recognized her name! Following Notcha's example, the other deer soon joined us for a few minutes of casual greetings that included a few horse cookies. I returned to the house astonished. Why on earth would a wild deer have the capacity to so readily recognize and retain the oral association of some name that had been arbitrarily assigned to her in a previous year? I began to wonder how that particular kind of identification could be included in the deer's repertoire of social possibilities—and why. It was at that moment that I began asking a question that still haunts me: "Who am I am actually dealing with here, and what *are* the possibilities?"

⌃ Frosty, who had been a bit of a runt as a fawn, shown here well developed at three and a half years old.

With the exception of Rayme, all the deer seemed to have eventually returned, including Raggedy Anne with her new fawn, Mandy, plus the older twins, Rag Tag and Frosty, and Anne's oldest daughter, Charm. Anne's maternal herd seemed to be complete. Charm had arrived with an adorable waif of a fawn at her side, who had small, delicate features that brought the name Possum to mind. With a little, pointed, gray face and penetrating, jet-black eyes, the cute baby possum reference was almost unavoidable. Little Possum was immediately engaging and seemed to have a particular enthusiastic fascination with us. Within a week of our introduction, we found that Possum could not stay out of our pockets. While we did not think to reach out and touch the deer in our first winter with them, Possum invited us to breech the divide of physical contact. We found other deer, including Notcha, who seemed to enjoy the contact and sought it out.

The mule deer coat, or "pelage," is composed of uncommonly dense, heavy, coarse, hollow guard hair with a soft, almost downy, undercoat. On below-zero Fahrenheit days following relatively high humidity, these deer occasionally become completely enshrouded in hoar frost, a feathery, white covering of ice crystals. On cold, gray days without the advantage of direct sunlight, this frosting may remain with no inclination to melt, but the deer, having impeccable insulation, remains warm. On extremely rare occasions in spring, a cold, freezing rain can saturate the deer's coat, and a deer may shiver. A little direct sunlight, however, is an immediate remedy. People who study solar energy should take careful heed of the mule deer's remarkable hair. The moment the pale rising sunlight hits the mule deer's coat, even on the most brutally cold mornings, the hair suddenly spikes in temperature, feeling impossibly warm to the touch. Their coat has a remarkable ability to absorb and capture the sun's radiant heat with extraordinary efficiency. Many winter mornings while out browsing at daylight with the deer, my gloves will fail me as my hands begin to ache with cold. Quickly, I find an accommodating deer, remove my gloves, and bury my hands in its warm coat as it continues browsing along. In a minute, my hands are recovered enough to reenter my gloves, which have been warming inside my coat.

Another deer had returned from the previous year whom we had known and thoughtlessly assigned the unfortunate name Rodenta, because she and her apparent sister Dauby were both a bit—well—rat-faced. Now we saw Rodenta as a strangely beautiful doe with a

⌃ Charm at the gate.

distinctive Roman nose and exotic, almond-shaped eyes. Dauby, on the other hand, was always pitifully shy, with droopy, sad-sack ears, and invariably brought to mind Dobby the house elf from the *Harry Potter* stories. Several new faces arrived that fall but were undoubtedly members of the same local winter herd that had finally been convinced to enter the yard of our house. Crescent was again with us and in the company of a new fawn whom we named Retta, in reference to fawn spots that were retained in a reticulated pattern down both sides of her back. All of Crescent's subsequent fawns have displayed this peculiarity.

A young, insecure buck, whom we had known only as a shy and reclusive fawn from the previous year, also arrived that fall with his first set of antlers. And, as young, insecure bucks are prone to do, he could be a bit of a bully around the does and fawns. He had an unrefined head and a somewhat coarse facial appearance, and because of his rather bad attitude, we named him Stinky.

❧◦❧

We quickly recognized that there was something special about Raggedy Anne. In the midst of constant minor mule deer bickering and rancor concerning issues of status and hierarchy achieved through expressions of dominance or submission, we noticed that Anne was never the focus of these disputes, nor was she ever inclined to express any superiority toward any other deer. Gradually, as we came to recognize some of the more subtle communication that was unfolding around us, we observed, for example, that when Anne's space was being

⌃ Raggedy Anne—the face of a veteran.

violated, she would simply look and raise her chin, and, without fail, the offending deer would acquiesce, moving away with barely a glance. It was clear that Anne was the dominant doe, the mild-mannered matriarch, a most humble queen, and for our first season with the deer, we had never known this to be the case. Anne was treated with deference by all the other deer. With no need to reinforce her position of authority, she seemed almost passive and disconnected from the busy social activities around her. All does defer to all antlered bucks, but, still, throughout the winter months, the related bucks are inclined to follow the maternal herds. However, we always noticed that when the deer were on the move, it was usually Anne who would first begin walking away from the group with her immediate family in tow, and, then, the other deer—bucks included—would tag along soon after.

When we first met Anne, she was a fully wild deer who was obviously unfamiliar with humans and was slow to be fully trusting, but in her third winter with us, she suddenly had a change of heart. Many deer who are initially uncomfortable and suspicious may eventually lay their apprehensions aside with an expression that looks and feels more like a surrender than a mere compromise involving possible conditions. Suddenly, one day, a deer who was previously fearful may in a single moment walk forward in an ordinary manner and take a cookie from your hand. It sometimes feels as if the deer has shrugged off its apprehensions in one single, conscious declaration of faith. In one gesture, you see a historically wide, fearful eye soften, and with no further trepidation, a deer will walk up and stand by your side. I witnessed this transition over and over again. It is as if these deer have a rigid, biologi-cally defined flight distance of about ten or fifteen feet that, when maintained, allows a possible escape from an attack. But, surprisingly, once the deer allow themselves inside that zone, rather than becoming overwhelmed with anxiety, they instead seem relieved of the instinctive obligation to maintain the flight option. It seems as though the flight switch is suddenly flipped into the "trust" position. I have at last proven to the deer, and they are at last satisfied, that I can be trusted. There are, of course, some deer that even after many years will approach for contact but are always wary and uncomfortable.

One day in early fall, in this way, Anne declared that she could trust me with her life: her eyes went completely soft, her ears dropped slightly, and with a brisk, momentary flick of the tail, all fear seemed to vanish as she approached with no apprehension. This was clearly not the result of gradual habituation but a sudden and conscious revelation based on my persistence in never doing her harm. If there was habituation involved, it was entirely my own. Thereafter she never hesitated to approach for a treat or even to be stroked, and she enjoyed a light scratching along the sides of her neck. And as if exercising some sort of discrete etiquette, she would ever-so-gently grasp a cookie with her warm, soft mouth and wait for my release. Then, while chewing, in a gesture of complete trust, she would look away into the distance, canting her ears and her attention toward the far side of the canyon—still maintaining her eternal vigil for any possible danger—but a vigil that no longer included me in her universe of possible threats. Winning Raggedy Anne's trust and confidence—winning her heart—was one of the great rewards of my life and hinted at the many possibilities that still waited to be revealed.

⌃ Rag Tag.

Late one afternoon, following time spent in close proximity involving a few treats and grooming with Raggedy Anne and her family, Leslye and I eventually walked into the house and made eye contact; Leslye slowly shook her head and said with a tone of near disbelief and wonder, "What a gift."

Within days of Anne's acceptance, her fawns made similar concessions. Frosty would cautiously approach to take a treat, but Rag Tag essentially shrugged one day and came marching up to retrieve multiple cookies, as if she had been doing this all her life. Rag Tag was also a "breakthrough" deer in that she was not only one of the first to enjoy being scratched and groomed but the first to begin returning the favor. As I scratched her neck, she would bend around, alternately licking and nibbling on my coat or occasionally grooming my hair and face. Mutual grooming is an important aspect of mule deer social interaction and bonding within the herd. A mule deer will not engage in mutual grooming with just any other individual deer, but rather will do so only with family members or the closest of affiliates. Rag Tag was clearly conceding that I was a member of her most immediate family.

❧⸱☙

Our second winter season on the Slingshot Ranch was filled with new discoveries about the local landscape generally, and, in particular, we began to discover secrets about the more personal and individual landscape of the mule deer. Although we were saddened to learn that Rayme would not be joining us for a second season, we were heartened to reacquaint with deer from the previous year and begin meeting numerous new and often surprising arrivals throughout the fall and early winter. One day we quickly observed two new standouts in the crowd as a distinctive pair of twin yearling does took up residence with the local herd. These were yearlings—fawns from the previous year who were around eighteen months old. We noticed that they were obviously separated from their mother, but judging by their relative physical condition, these two had been well cared for as younger fawns. Also, they were clearly accepted among the herd at large, suggesting that their mother had close affiliations with these deer, although there was no question that these two had not been with us the previous winter, for their appearances were so distinctive. There could be little doubt that even after six months we would have still recognized them immediately. The two young does were strikingly marked with shades nearing pure black and pure white, and a skunk analogy quickly came to mind when looking at their beautiful but unusual faces. With the margins of their ears lined in black, and the interior virtually stuffed with snow white hair, both year-lings also sported blackish crowns and pale eye rings, so it was only after a few weeks that we stopped referring to them as "the skunky girls." Soon we began to know one as Cappy—because of a perfectly delineated and uniformly black forehead and crown like a sailor's watch cap—and the other as Flower—yes, a shameless reference to Bambi's skunk friend.

Flower was a gorgeous deer, enchanting but strongly opinionated. Her eyes were almost black, enormous, and widely set, giving her an appearance of extraordinary

⌃ Cappy was a revelation. She was the first fully wild deer to make physical contact in a matter of days.

intelligence—but these eyes were always filled with apprehension. Her proximity to me remained rigidly defined by a safe flight distance no closer than fifteen meters, and there was no question that she was not to trust this humanlike creature.

Cappy, in direct contradiction, was a revelation. Although these two young deer were completely unknown to us and were completely wild and rightfully confused about our strange proximity to other deer, this individual—Cappy—quickly assessed my intentions and initiated direct contact with me in only a few days. In a month, Cappy treated me like a family member, displaying absolute trust and confidence in our relationship. She was the first deer who allowed me direct access into her midst and into her world with complete comfort and resignation. This relationship quickly developed into one of companionship, and, at least insofar as Cappy was concerned, I was probably the safest creature in her environment. Cappy relished being groomed and scratched and would paw my backside for attention if I walked away or ignored her. This deer taught me much about the intelligence of the mule deer and the depth of their abilities to make appropriate discriminations concerning the many complexities of their world. Cappy had assessed me up and down and made a rational choice that somehow included me in her life. Though, like the other deer, if a stranger neared the house, she was gone in a flash. Her ability to convey meaning to me in the form of some unspoken communication that was decidedly clear and complex suggested to me that I was now dealing with a creature of extraordinary potential—perhaps even the potential to reveal the more obscure and secretive nature of the mule deer, the innermost workings of personality, motivation, intelligence, and behavior. Cappy made it obvious if she thought danger could be near or if she was in need of a grooming session.

Clearly, at last, I had my foot in a door—a possible portal—an entrance into the complex universe of another species. Rayme and Anne had stirred my imagination and suggested phenomenal possibilities, but Cappy represented not only the potential but also the means to enter a place I had not anticipated. This one deer represented the irresistible siren call—some small but powerful force of nature that left me helpless to avoid surrender. Cappy casually opened a door, and I simply stepped through. But as this door silently—unknowingly—closed behind, the world was decidedly different than I had envisioned it to be.

I realized that, in fact, these deer had not come into my life, but rather I had been admitted into theirs, and there was no going back. Now in retrospect I wonder—perhaps this was not a door at all but the proverbial rabbit hole into which I had not stepped but stumbled.

Cappy and Flower had filled my life with new knowledge and revelation when I cheerfully bade them farewell at the onset of spring migration. But I was naive and had not yet learned that knowing—even loving—a wild mule deer was a double-edged sword—a sword that would open up a secret world with one edge and pierce your heart with the other. The powerful lesson that I quickly learned from both Rayme and Cappy is that these creatures are simultaneously enduring and rugged but also fragile. The swath that they cut through the world and your life can appear wide and deep—imbued with great substance—but they are also ephemeral, and their longevity is never assured. Although Flower reappeared the next fall, Cappy did not, and it had never occurred to me that such a young, vibrant, and capable force in the world could be so quickly overcome. It was seemingly implausible that Cappy's vitality, intelligence, and wisdom were not enough to sustain her into her third year. However, this was to become a consistent pattern that sadly defines the plight of the mule deer, and all too quickly I came to know that heartache would be an overriding component of any relationship with these creatures. In these times, an early death is not the exception in mule deer reality but the rule. Even though Cappy is only one of two hundred such fragile relationships I have formed, rarely a day goes by that I do not think of her strangely beautiful, inquiring, gentle face and the unexpected vacuum she left in my life. But, after all, I considered myself to be a hunter, a rancher, and an objective man of science—even once trained as a warrior— a man on every level fully acquainted with the inherent and sometimes necessary brutalities of our world—fully resigned to the inculpable and even noble realities of life and death, and not to the childish mythology that life somehow favors and protects the living. In fact, it could be said that, at least to some extent, all living things *persist* in spite of life, not because of it. Now this reality has come to define my life, as I am haunted by so many missing faces.

However, Flower proved to be another phenomenal deer full of surprises, and she, just like Raggedy Anne and others, decided one day during her second winter that I was reliable and safe, and moved into my immediate space and allowed me into hers. Flower appeared that fall without a fawn. Her face was so remarkably similar to Cappy's that on many occasions I thought that the missing sister had been restored to us. But mule deer are completely faithful to their home winter range, and if Cappy had lived, she would have surely joined us early on.

CHAPTER FOUR

Peep's Diary

It didn't take us long to realize that mule deer are under assault, everywhere and at all times. Life is a perpetual gauntlet for this animal, and there is never a time when they are not being compromised or killed by some means—starvation, parasites, disease, predation, human pollution, activity and development, collision with cars, and of course hunting both legal and illegal. The highway accounts for more mule deer deaths than any other single cause. And those are easy to track. It had always been my assumption that mule deer had a relatively free ride during late spring, summer, and early fall, but this is not at all true. Many mule deer die during the warmer months, when they tend to be in more remote locations and thus out of sight and awareness. In spite of the ferocious and protective intentions of mule deer does, younger fawns are notoriously vulnerable—frequently at the mercy of coyotes, bobcats, eagles, wolves, and mountain lions—and, perhaps worse, they must contend with hundreds of unnatural obstacles, including woven wire fences, domestic dogs, and traffic. Mortality of mule deer fawns between birth and four months (before hunting season begins) can be 50 to 70 percent and surpass the numbers of overall mule deer killed annually by hunting. Then, by September 1, fawns and their mothers are legal fodder for bow hunters for most of the month. By the time deer survive one year, they have probably evaded death hundreds of times.

However, we have been surprised to find that fewer and fewer mother does are reappearing in fall—having disappeared during the summer months by mysterious means, and leaving behind orphaned and starving fawns. By about twelve weeks, mule deer fawns eat significant amounts of natural browse, but they still nurse heavily to obtain the high levels of protein necessary to keep up with a growing young body in hyperdrive. Without large amounts of mother's milk that may average 20 percent protein, and with natural browse rarely providing 10 percent, fawns are sure to experience some level of malnutrition if they become orphaned before they are six months old. Some does will spontaneously stop lactating or intentionally wean their young toward the end of November, but most mule deer fawns will continue to nurse into their fifth and even sixth month, with sessions that last for up to one minute and may occur two or three times a day. Does can nurse fawns well into December. The earlier nursing is terminated, the more compromised a young deer will become. Remarkably, Wyoming has continued to allow doe and fawn hunting to occur with a species that has clearly been in decline for decades, and although fawns are shot with regularity, it is more common for the doe to be killed because of her larger and more desirable body size. In addition to malnutrition and a greater susceptibility to disease, motherless fawns will inevitably suffer social, emotional, and physical depression if the maternal bond is broken. Depending on its age, the orphaned fawn may never find its rightful home winter range and its protective maternal clan, and, of course, knowledge of historic migratory routes and the timelines for those migrations are never learned. So, logically, and most important, all the mother's vital wisdom is lost, and a small, uninitiated animal must invent its entire life or perish. The fawn has, in essence, lost everything that can be expected to sustain a young mule deer. In severe winters the mortality of orphaned fawns is almost assured. Never let any wildlife manager or politician tell you that a fawn orphaned in September or October will do fine. That is absolutely untrue. Even a fawn *with* a mother has barely more than an even chance of surviving a difficult winter.

Every year, the orphan fawns that appear in early winter are already so desperate that they will seek help even from a human. As we struggle to save a few orphans each winter, it is frustrating to watch them continue to waste away and die before warm weather and rich green vegetation can save them. Because we never use any sort of enclosure or protection for sick, injured, or starving individuals, they remain exposed and particularly vulnerable to predation. Still, young mule deer can be surprisingly resilient if given any reasonable chance, and we have managed to save a few orphans—both lone individuals and twins.

It is, of course, always impractical to rescue orphaned wildlife and even arguably inadvisable, but any suggestion that there are sound biological grounds for allowing orphaned fawns to starve is a convenient but entirely baseless rationalization. It is circumstance—largely unnatural—that has "selected" these individuals out of the population and not biology. Some of the most robust and perfect adult mule deer specimens that I have known are individuals that I have rescued from starvation. These deer have thrived to become successful, productive does and fine, strong, dominant bucks that are fully capable of surviving a relentless hunting season and a brutal Wyoming winter.

But never have we bottle-fed newborn fawns. That would invite human imprinting, and, as a consequence, fawns would be confused about their own identities as individuals and as members of a species. Human-imprinted deer experiments, unless conducted in the most ideal and unusual of circumstances, can be expected to end tragically for the deer and for the handlers. Many human-imprinted buck deer—especially whitetails—will predictably become aggressive toward humans, and even does on occasion become dangerous, especially around children. The orphans we were able to rescue were somewhat older, starving fawns that were simply given supplemental food and thus a slightly improved chance for survival. The youngest fawns we have rescued were about ten weeks old when they lost their mother.

※

Our third winter at the Slingshot was a tough one, with average temperatures much colder than in previous years and with heavy snows that had accumulated early in the season. When severe winter grips Wyoming range lands, mule deer enter a genetically prescribed starvation mode that may last for two or three months as their bodies naturally anticipate a period of low availability of nutritious forage. In some years this represents a lean time and a mere inconvenience. In other years, it can become catastrophic, and mule deer can starve by the thousands. The owner of a large ranch to our immediate north mentioned finding twenty-seven dead mule deer around his stack yards that spring. By December, I begin feeding a commercially prepared alfalfa "hay cube" in relatively small quantities in various locations to ward off any starvation that may come later in the season. Alfalfa can be a relatively safe and nutritious supplement for mule deer but not preferred, as native browse will always be selected over cubed alfalfa when winters are open and natural forage is available. However, when heavy snows blanket the land, deer will choose hay cubes over starvation. It should be mentioned that mule deer are easily choked on commercial, dry, cubed forage, and the dehydrated feed must be soaked for thirty minutes in warm water to make it safe to consume. Abruptly feeding rough forage to a starving deer can create fatal impactions in the gut. Having watched in the late 1970s large numbers of both elk and deer starve around me while ranching in the vicious Wyoming winters, I can say it is the slowest, most agonizing, and most brutal way for any animal to die. Although technically a violation of the law, I would commonly have to look into terrified eyes and put a gun to the head of a starving elk lying in the snow that was nothing but skin and bones, that had lost all its hair to parasitic scabies, and with nose, udders, and vulva chewed off by marauding coyotes. I do everything in my power to prevent the deer in this study group from enduring such agony and horror. However, the good news is that we occasionally have wonderful success with some unlikely little stray urchin who wanders up desperate and confused. Of course I fully recognize that our "rescues" have absolutely no bearing on the ultimate survival and welfare of mule deer generally but merely represent a choice that we have made and perhaps even an opportunity to make closer observations. That choice is a purely personal commitment and at best can be viewed only as a meager humanitarian gesture that may preserve only one small—and, some would say, insignificant—life.

                                ✍

During the midwinter of 2008, while out distributing feed at first light in eighteen inches of fresh snow, I found myself surrounded by thirty-five exceedingly hungry deer. As I spread well-hydrated alfalfa cubes about in steaming, wet piles, deer began closing in behind me like two intersecting tides. While deer stirred all around in a frenzy of feeding activity, I suddenly did a double-take, seeing a fawn that was only half the size of the other fawns. This was a stranger. Judging by a distinctive face and petite size, there was no possible way this deer could have been from this herd. As I watched the fawn, it ran desperately about the group as if confused and with no understanding of the nutritional possibilities that lay all around. The mature does wanted no part of the little creature and struck and chased the runt, driving it completely out of the yard. As the fawn would again approach, another adult deer would chase it through the snow. After one particularly brutal, hammering attack that left the fawn kicking upside down in the snow, it retreated, and I could see it struggling with mouth open wide, occasionally stumbling and having difficulty getting through the deep snow. Clearly this little one was on its last legs and could be only hours away from death. Judging by how much smaller this orphan was than even the smallest resident fawn, it must have somehow managed to live not weeks but months without a mother. I quickly scanned the herd to see if there might be a strange doe with this young runt, but, as I sadly suspected, there was no new doe in the area—but it just seemed impossible that this little thing had by some means managed to survive so long. We have since discovered that fawns orphaned from a former member of the resident maternal clan are accepted entirely and are exposed to none of the brutality that this fawn was suffering. Obviously emaciated, this fawn had bristling, erect hair with short, stocky legs and miniature shiny black hooves that reminded us of little patent leather shoes. It had a rather dark facial mask with expressive pale eye linings and large oval ears that were droopy, lending her an appearance of even more despair and longing.

As the herd returned for two more feeding sessions that day, the little fawn remained, tagging along, unwelcomed. On the second day, while feeding a frenzied mob of hungry deer, I looked at my side, and there was the little fawn, nervously looking up into my eyes with a heart-wrenching expression. The foundling was shaking with desperation, terror, confusion, and mortal urgency. I reached for a high-protein horse cookie in my pocket, and to my great surprise the pitiful little creature sniffed and took the wafer from my hand. In seconds the wafer was gone and the orphan was at my side, once again looking for another possible handout. Having to actually block the path of several resentful and aggressive does, I shielded the fawn until my pocket was emptied of the nourishing wafers. While desperately taking wafer after wafer, the fawn seemed completely oblivious to my hand as it ran through the fawn's dry, brittle hair and down onto a back that was a ragged ridge of vertebral spines, more like a picket fence than a deer's back. The skin along the sides felt as if it was shrink-wrapped over the tiny ribs. Engorged winter ticks protruded though the dense hair along the

⌃ The orphan named Peep.

edges of the ears. That afternoon when I went out to visit the deer, the little fawn was back at my side in seconds, and this time I emptied two pockets into the starving animal, and a shrunken stomach was partially filled for perhaps the first time in months. These pelletized wafers are made from a vegetable paste and are therefore easily digested. The little deer wandered to the edge of the yard and stood with head down and eyes closed, as if in a hyper-glycemic stupor, while night began to fall and all the other deer wandered out of the yard, away from the house. However, the fawn did not follow but rather sought out a solitary refuge in a dense thicket of gnarly plums, collapsing motionless in a heap with nose down and ears barely protruding above the snow. Even a persecuted fawn's preference for solitude over the safety of the herd is an ominous sign, so it seemed that the likelihood of this little fawn's survival was remote. I feared that by morning I would find it dead where it lay.

Anticipating the worst, I was out standing in the snow before sunrise checking on the status of the new orphan. I was heartened to see that the deer in question was not only alive but actually nosing around in some frozen alfalfa cubes from the night before. The little deer stared at me for a moment and then, with a few words of encouragement, walked directly to my side with tail straight up and took a handful of wafers. While Leslye watched from the back door, the fawn finished an entire pocket full of horse cookies just in time, as fifteen more deer heard us crunching around in the snow and came running. As I walked back in the house, Leslye lamented, "What a poor little peep of a deer!" The little creature had followed me to the back door and stood belly deep in snow, staring at me though the glass with swollen, sleepy eyes and great, sagging ears, obviously confused about the concept of "house." As it squatted to urinate, the question was answered once and for all—this pitiful little peep of a deer was a doe fawn.

We were soon astonished to learn that Peep had not wandered in alone but in fact was somehow affiliated with a rather hefty and unfamiliar three-and-a-half-year-old "loner" buck who chose to stay the winter, becoming known eventually as Rufous, in reference to a distinctly reddish crown. Obviously, Peep had attached herself to this kind and gentle buck as she frequently came and left the yard in his company, trailing along in his footsteps like a fawn would follow a doe. On several occasions we would see Rufous resting across the draw with Peep lying at his side. Although I never observed him grooming his little companion or showing any other maternal-like care, it was clear that he at least allowed this unusual association to occur. Although I would not suggest that this was a potential case of buck-fawn adoption, Rufous's stewardship and knowledge of the landscape offered the only explanation for this fawn's unlikely survival.

Soon Peep was an almost permanent fixture in and around the yard. She made herself available for any excuse to eat, and I began feeding her several times a day. We attempted to offer her a relatively balanced diet of the nutritious horse wafers, along with some cracked corn and mixed grains for complex carbohydrates that might provide some quick but sustained energy for chill resistance as well as a little roughage to keep things moving along. Months of starvation had left Peep's pelage in a shambles of dull, dried, brittle hair that stood erect, especially around her head and neck, in an almost fruitless effort to preserve as much body heat as possible. Starvation had also formed edema in the tissues surrounding her eyes, providing her with a look of complete exhaustion. The only thing that she seemed to have going for her was a lack of a particular respiratory infection that seems to inevitably plague unthrifty, starving fawns in our area.

The common bacteria *Pasteurella multocida* can cause an infection characterized by ocular and nasal discharge and an occasional but not persistent cough. It is a slow, progressing death sentence for a starving fawn, but in some adults it is merely a strangely stubborn ailment that can last for months—or more. In at least two cases, I have known adult does that have persisted with this low-grade infection for more than two years. In its acute stages, I suspect it is a likely culprit of septicemia and pneumonia. This pathogen is normally endemic to the

⌃ The author offering Peep some much needed nutrition.

mucosa of the upper respiratory tracts of many ruminants. Pasteurella is allowed to gain a foothold, becoming pathologic when the immune system becomes compromised by various predisposing stress factors such as inclement weather, elevated parasite load, malnutrition, or some other more primary infection. Peep was the perfect storm of predisposing factors, yet she seemed to have a healthy respiratory system.

At first, Peep was comfortable or possibly just oblivious to the touch of a human hand. But within days I realized that she was not just starved for food and merely tolerant of my touch; she was starved for both food and affection. Clearly she had gone many months without the attentions of her mother and was desperately touch-deprived. Late one morning, in the comfort of the warming sun, I dropped down on my knees and, with one arm across her chest, began grooming her with my hands about the head and neck. Only momentarily unsure about this close proximity and partial restraint, she suddenly went limp in my arms and appeared to fall into some sort of semiconscious torpor as I continued to gently scratch and rub her. It seemed as if her hunger for physical contact had also reached crisis proportions. Each day after a satisfying feeding session, I would hold Peep and remove any engorged ticks that I found and would spend sessions gently scratching along her ears, neck, and chest, searching for small ticks that had become embedded but had not yet begun to become engorged. In a matter of a few days I managed to relieve the little deer of her chronic tick infestation, but she would prevail on me for physical contact two or more times a day. Her need for affection seemed boundless.

Fawns with mothers rarely suffer from winter ticks. Does must have a remarkable ability to rid their fawns of the pests before they can become a bother. Furthermore, deer have places on their bodies that are completely inaccessible with either their mouths or hind hooves and therefore cannot be reached without the cooperation of a family member or close affiliate who might be willing to engage in a little reciprocal grooming. There is a line between the neck and shoulder that cannot be reached, as well as an area around the chest, sternum, or "brisket." And of course, even though ears are totally accessible with the rear hooves, it is difficult to extricate a tick from a floppy ear with a hoof. Those unfortunate individuals without well-established social connections are forced to endure this perpetual frustration. Invariably, if I can convince any peripheral deer without close social connections to allow me to touch it,

⌃ A moment of bliss for Peep, a small fawn in grave danger.

⌃ Offering consolation to a desperate little deer.

it will thereafter identify me as a friend as I act as its tick relief. Although older bucks do engage in mutual grooming on occasion and frequently accept grooming from their older mothers, many never have this opportunity and are grateful to discover that I will be their surrogate family member—if and when they are feeling the need for a little attention or tick removal. It is interesting and often moving to observe that initial awkward moment when caution is suddenly transformed to an instant of recognition that may quickly attain the proportions of a revelation, as perhaps long-lost maternal memories are stirred. With undeniable appreciation, the recipient seems to relax into some state of sensual bliss. It is interesting to note that although gestures of kindness are easily misinterpreted when expressed by a human toward another species, there are distinct occasions when these gestures are recognized, enjoyed, appreciated, and even reciprocated. Clearly, the *expectation* of kindness does not seem to exist as a common experience among most living wild things. However, it does seem that some species have a capacity to care for others and to receive care outside the maternal experience. The mule deer is a species that undeniably harbors an expectation of affection and the nurturing consolation from within its society. It has been a great and unexpected joy to share and understand the importance of that expectation in the lives of these deer.

☙❧

Sometimes, if I was involved with the attentions of another deer, I would feel Peep rubbing her head briskly on my leg, as if prodding me with an imaginary set of antlers, and if that did not gain my undivided attention, she would begin pawing me with a tiny hoof—letting me know that I should be properly focusing on all her needs. And focus I did—for Leslye and I both agreed that Peep was perhaps the most adorable and irresistible creature that either of us had ever known. Although Peep was getting the best nutrition I could provide, her condition was so dire that I felt that her survival throughout the rest of a long, hard Wyoming winter was unlikely. Because her coat was thin and badly deteriorated, it was difficult to resist the urge to bring her in at night when temperatures were well below zero. But finding her suitable accommodations inside a house might be difficult and possibly even terrifying for a wild, five-month-old fawn. On at least two occasions we have had curious deer follow us into the house through a carelessly open door—with no catastrophes—but, still, the possibilities are frightening. The panic/flight response in wild mule deer, once full-blown, appears to be 100 percent nonnegotiable.

Although all the cards seemed to be stacked against Peep, she proved to be one of our great success stories. With most orphans that arrive late in the winter, the best you can hope for is to merely arrest their decline and hope they can hold on until better times. With no place to go but up, Peep actually managed to gain some weight during that winter with constant feeding, but I suspect she deserves most of the credit for having the cast-iron constitution of an unusually tenacious survivor. We have had fawns die during winter who seemed to be initially in much better condition than this little deer. However, Peep was not of this herd, and even after one year, she was not treated with the respect that a legitimate member of a maternal clan could expect. Fawns are rigorously socialized by their mother as well as by the mothers' affiliates, so within weeks of birth, fawns begin their schooling in the proper rules of mule deer etiquette. It was clear that Peep had been principally self-schooled, having no concept of mannerly behavior, and her indiscretions were often brutally chastised.

Once, after swatting a dominant buck on the head for what Peep perceived to be an inconvenient competition for a bite of food, the outraged deer lashed out with enormous hooves in an attack that I thought might kill her. Typically, the larger bucks are gentle and totally indulgent with fawns, but Peep's indiscretion was by all indications not merely rude but a painful assault to the ears of the big deer. Her behavior was deemed egregious and could not be allowed to pass. Gradually Peep learned that there were dire consequences to rude behavior, but it was obvious that her ignorance of the social graces put her at an even greater disadvantage in gaining acceptance in the herd.

☙❧

Life in winter is a strange paradox, where human existence is somehow compressed and contracted in this otherwise vast and unconstrained space. Diagnostic symptoms may vary from extreme restlessness, irritability, or, in the worst manifestation, complete psychosis. "Cabin fever," however, is poorly named, as evidenced by the fact that even working outside

⌃ Peep's unmistakable plea for contact.

every day, snow or shine, can have only a mild palliative effect but is still not a remedy. This strange sense of confinement may in time become overwhelming, but then one day around January, mysteriously, you are rescued by a sudden emancipation of the spirit as life becomes, again, seemingly boundless in the white polar landscape. This welcome liberation may be merely the recognition that time has not actually slowed, space in this case is constant, and it is only existence and the human perspective that is relative. In the dead of winter, a simple trip to the barn can become, under certain circumstances, a complex expedition involving multiple layers of wool and high-tech clothing, an LED flashlight with enough blazing candle power to knock a raccoon to its knees, and, often, a firearm of .30 caliber or better. Ranch life has always been endlessly absorbing, and we are merely the next in the line to serve this place, perpetuating a 140-year-old continuum—no, a tradition—which in large

⌃ Slingshot in winter.

part involves a seemingly infinite variety of demands and the inevitability of, day by day, incrementally falling further behind because of various forces that include the pull of some poorly understood but inexorable gravity. Just like horses and cattle, people also come and go on a ranch. One does not own a ranch—one merely chooses to serve a ranch. No human has ever caught up with the needs and demands of an old, hardscrabble homestead, and many of the good intentions that were never quite realized seventy-five years ago still lie there in a pile, waiting for the next well-intended, ambitious individual to pick up the gauntlet and make yet one more noble try. An old working ranch is the perfect antidote to the futile human expectation of actual achievement. A sagebrush ridge in front of the house bordering the draw is dotted with the caved-in, rock-lined, rectangular depressions of unmarked graves—people who, no doubt, lived hard and died tired. When does the keen knife edge of human ambition dull into a mere quest for survival? Perhaps it relates somehow to those "lives of quiet desperation" that Thoreau was always harping about as he often expressed opinions about the futility of the agricultural lifestyle. I can relate, perfectly. One might ask, "What was the attraction—why would anyone bother—why would these people go to this much trouble in this unlikely place?" Surely, with nothing more than an old wagon, a tired horse, and perhaps a serviceable rifle, someone made a remarkable decision and said, "I think I'll try to make a life here." Here! Imagine—no tractor, no chainsaw, no water at the tap—in what was essentially an un-irrigated desert with any available water frozen hard as steel for four months, not to mention a full three miles straight up a mountain to the nearest house log or firewood. I can only suggest that it has to do with some powerful, spiritual substance that is inherent in this strange and conspicuously hostile landscape. The land is possessed of some quality that inspires us all to confuse our dreams with the actual physical possibilities that our lives can achieve. Each of us is proof that the human capacity for overestimating our own capability is boundless. For some, this land becomes an irresistible siren's call. Finding ourselves run hopelessly aground, we are deaf to the cry of reason, and we are made blind by the magnificence that surrounds us. And although on every fundamental level it always costs more than it comes to, it appears that there is some irresistible romance or some inevitable seduction, and many are inclined to fall perilously in love with a hopelessly brutal piece of this earth. In this part of the West, there is a well-articulated and accepted tradition to live and die for "the brand." Upon first realizing the pervasiveness of this defining cultural concept that still, to this day, resonates in many people's consciousness, I commented, "Really?" Yet here we are—living and dying a little bit every day for our little "spread."

We do not leave home often, and when we do, it is normally with some level of resentment and perhaps dread. Invariably, upon crossing back over the cattle guard, one of us remarks, "Let's don't ever go anywhere again." As we pile out of the pickup to unload supplies, we hear the scolding nicker of abandoned and resentful, overfed but apparently starving horses, and deer rise from their shady, long-suffering daybeds, meandering ever-so-slowly toward the house. Accountability is demanded as we are made aware of our neglect and irresponsibility.

    ⌃ ⌃ Deer seeking rest and asylum in the yard at Slingshot.

CHAPTER FIVE

Anne of a Thousand Days

Spring had finally arrived in that third year, and the first harbingers of true spring were emerging all around, as dandelions began to carpet the yard, creek banks, and meadows in lush green and brilliant yellow. They were a welcome and a glorious sight, replacing the pervading dull grays and browns—the colorless, corporeal remnants of past lives. This ubiquitous little flower is not only a feast for the eyes but a feast for the palate for all creatures. The greens are a delicious addition to any salad, as are the full yellow flowers, and every chipmunk, deer, and bird gathers the first floral bounty of the new season. As spring gradually moves further up the mountain, the fearless blue grouse may be seen gorging on hundreds of the delightful yellow flowers. When backpacking in the high country for days or weeks at a time, I always include a small plastic squeeze bottle filled with balsamic vinegar and olive oil, and enjoy a fresh green and yellow dandelion salad every evening. Spring is always occurring at some elevation throughout the entire summer, and even on the highest alpine slopes, eventually, there is the ubiquitous dandelion mingling among the rare tundra flora. That humans consider the delightful dandelion a plague in their sterile suburban environments speaks volumes.

Although the dark, shadowed, timbered slopes above the ranch were still blanketed in heavy snow, the time for migration was at hand. Ducks and geese arrived by the thousands, the raucous call of sandhill cranes could be heard reverberating from every distant meadow, and all the bucks had shed their antlers with new velvet replacements well underway. A few of the deer started to disappear as their migratory urge became irresistible. The prospect of lush, green, flowering meadows and the sound of rushing snowmelt are the siren's call that must be obeyed. Abundance and prosperity beckon with the recollection of lavish, green mountain meadows blanketed with purple, blue, white, and yellow, while the echoes of bird song and cascading waters speak to the memory of long, lazy days and perpetual cool summer breezes. Ancient reminiscences call to the tired heart of a winter-weary mule deer.

Although accustomed to Raggedy Anne's daily visits throughout the winter, we began to notice that she was spending more time than usual around the house. The apple and plum trees were festooned with swollen flower buds, along with the golden currants and flowering gooseberries. Blood-red box elder blooms had erupted a week before and were now clumps

⌃ Offering Anne some food.

of red and green maple "keys." It was that brief time in spring, when the entire world begins to look like a complex and inviting mixed salad. The tender, purple-green leaves of every lilac shrub and tree created a wall of edible foliage over their ragged and gnarly winter skeletons. Deer enthusiastically snatched at the emerging lilac leaves, contributing a good seasonal pruning to every specimen within reach. Mule deer are ravenous for new green vegetation in spring, so we naturally assumed Anne was just taking advantage of the abundance and variety that the yard could provide. However, Anne rarely ventured far from the yard, and would even remain after her family had browsed off onto a distant sage brush slope, grazing on a carpet of tender emerging cheatgrass or the fresh, tender growing tips of big mountain sage, rabbit brush, and antelope bitter brush. Anne would lie for hours under the protective cover of the hedge rows surrounding the yard, moving only periodically to browse and then find a new protected spot to sleep and chew her cud. Unconsciously, upon leaving the house, I would glance around and look for Anne's head and ears in silhouette somewhere nearby in the dense undercover. She would often stand by the back door as if asking for a deer treat, but we noticed that after eating one or two, she would merely sniff the wafer and, then, as if disappointed, wander back to her small refuge and lay down. In two more days, Anne refused all handouts and we never saw her browsing—clearly something was not right. When deer become injured or ill, they segregate themselves from other deer, perhaps because mule deer society can be taxing, and they are aware of their vulnerability. It soon became obvious that Anne was becoming solitary in a most disturbing way. Her own family members were still in the vicinity, seemingly waiting for her cue to migrate. Anne even became uncomfortable in the relative safety of the yard, and one day wandered down into the draw, seeking more solitude along the creek bank among the thick, scrubby willows. But even though she changed locations throughout the day and night, she seemed to always remain within sight of the house. We would locate Anne during the day or first thing in the morning by walking out on the cliff face and eventually find her lying somewhere below and always near the creek. Once, at midday, I saw her standing motionless just above the creek in an uncomfortable posture with head lowered—leaving no doubt she was in distress. But we were also consoled to see that Anne's family was never far away. She was most often in the company of her most recent fawn, Randy-Dandy, and last year's fawn, Mandy, who would lie with her, along with

Charm, Possum, and Rag Tag, who were usually close by or nosing around in the nearby willows.

One morning I couldn't see Anne from the cliff face and wandered down below. Walking up the creek fifty yards, I immediately saw her lying among the willows, another twenty-five yards ahead. There, under a low, dense canopy, she had found a more solitary place to lie, just upstream by the flowing water in a well-protected, steep-sided, and shady spot. She looked concerned, so I spoke in a soft voice to reassure her who I was, "Hi, pretty girl," but kept my distance so as not to disturb her. The date was May 8, and Anne remained in this one spot for two more days. It was clear that Anne had not eaten in days, and for a time I suspected that she may be trying to abort a premature fawn, but, whatever the cause, she was without

⌃ **Raggedy Anne's daughter Charm.**

⚞ Raggedy Anne, sick.

question deathly ill. Leslye and I, without laying out any plan, just naturally began a round-the-clock vigil, checking on Anne every hour or so throughout the daylight hours.

The following morning at first light we were disturbed to see ravens and magpies feeding on the far ridge above the draw. Thinking the worst, I grabbed my rifle and climbed down through the rocks and tramped a half-mile to the top of the ridge. The birds flushed, and upon arriving at the site I was relieved to find the remains of a cotton-tail rabbit that had been killed by an eagle or coyote. On the route back down I passed by Anne's previous location, and there she lay, exactly where I had seen her the day before. Again I spoke to reassure her, but judging by the swollen and stressed look in her eyes, I saw no way she could survive. If she was in fact having difficulty with a fawn, it was probably not going to abort, and she was at least four to six weeks too early for giving birth to a live fawn.

On the morning of May 10, as the sun rose over the eastern ridge, I could see immediately that Anne had climbed one hundred yards above the creek-run and was now on the opposite side of the draw, on the sunny side of a smaller grassy tributary draw, lying with her head lowered. As I watched, she stood up and walked a few feet and immediately lay back down. I noticed that Anne's older daughter, Rag Tag was lying opposite her, just a few yards across the draw. By afternoon, most of Anne's immediate family had joined her, including Notcha, a close affiliate, whom we had not seen for days, assuming she had already migrated the week before. Obviously, the deer were being "with" Anne and were all standing or lying nearby. As Leslye watched, the youngest fawn, Randy-Dandy, walked over and began licking and grooming Anne on top of the head for several minutes as she lay with head erect and eyes closed.

Late that afternoon, all the deer began to wander away browsing, and as Leslye watched at sunset, Anne began a brief struggle. She tried to stand and immediately fell to the ground kicking. Leslye ran to get me, and just as I arrived Anne made her final kick and apparently lay dead. We watched without a word for thirty minutes, and without seeing any movement or breath of life, we knew Anne had died. She lay on her left side with her head positioned slightly downhill. We chose not to approach her in the unlikely event that she could still be alive and become frightened in her final minutes.

May 11, Mother's Day. I walked out on the cliff face just after sunrise to see Anne lying exactly as we had last seen her. Rag Tag was lying nearby and stood up. She walked over and stood above Anne's body, sniffing and observing her closely. Rag Tag remained with Anne that day, and by afternoon most of the herd was lying with Anne, while several others lay in the willows just below.

Monday, May 12, early morning. I arrived on the cliff face to see Rag Tag, Mandy, and Randy-Dandy standing next to Anne, and then the three gradually began moving up the hill. Rag Tag walked back down to Anne's side, peered down, and seemed to study her intensely. That afternoon I saw a magpie fly up from Anne's location. I then walked to the cliff face to see the does, Crescent, and her fawn Retta in company of four other fawns, including little Possum. The deer encircled Anne with heads lowered, carefully observing with ears pressed forward, but then after several minutes, they began slowly moving up the hill with occasional glances back down. Anne's youngest fawn, Randy-Dandy, suddenly ran back to Anne's outstretched body and cautiously leaned forward, legs extended and neck outstretched with ears canted down towards the lifeless form. Randy was obviously torn between staying at her mother's side or proceeding ahead with the group, but after several conflicted turns of the head, she relented and, with backward glances, trotted ahead to join the group.

By afternoon, most of the deer had reassembled around Anne, including Randy-Dandy, Rag Tag and her brother Frosty, now a mature buck, along with Anne's previous year's fawn, Mandy, and the oldest daughter, Charm. Several other deer lay nearby, including Charm's fawn Possum and even little Peep.

Tuesday May 13. Leslye appeared on the rim of the cliff face shortly after sunrise to find Rag Tag lying close to Anne. Rag Tag remained close for most of the day and was eventually joined by several others in the afternoon. With Randy-Dandy and Charm the last to finally leave Anne's side, all the deer apparently left the area that evening, beginning their belated spring migration. At last the deer had determined that Anne was truly gone, and she would not be joining the migration. She would be left behind. Perhaps for the first time in many generations, Anne would not be the intelligent light that guided their way. Some other deer must now carry her torch to far mountain pastures.

That afternoon I ventured down to the site where Anne lay, and observed that she had chosen a sunny and pleasant location with low sagebrush and spring flowers all around. Holding her head in my lap and stroking her nose and muzzle, I recalled how many times I had felt that warm, soft nose and mouth on my hand and how many times I had run my hand down those big, luxurious ears. The other deer were now all gone, and in that moment it became clear that our mutual obsession with this lifeless form—theirs and mine—was at least in part born of the same need—the need to see these sunken eyes filled again with her kind and ancient wisdom. Even in death, Anne was still offering me her instruction. Suddenly it became clear that this was not just another nameless, faceless dead deer lying on the ground—and surely I have examined hundreds. Now I understood that this was something significant and meaningful—something truly profound—a real life with a real history— something even monumental. This deer had known adventures, adversities, joys, triumphs, pain, and tragedy. She had known the cool, green meadows of a thousand perfect summer days, and the unimaginable hardship of a thousand bitter days of winter. She had been a leader, a protector, an educator, a role model, and a warrior—she was the consummate model for successive generations to follow. Anne's was a rich story written by the ages—she had earned her place among the most fit and exemplary of survivors that had, in some similar way, also blazed a trail for her. Now her family once again bravely wandered up the mountain, quite literally walking in her footsteps and perpetuating a living legacy of more than ten thousand mule deer summers that have come and gone before.

Anne was a powerful presence, and it never occurred to us that we might someday be without her in our lives. How could so much intelligence and substance quickly become so fragile and lost? I carefully laid her head back down on the cool earth beside a big bouquet of dandelion flowers that Leslye must have left earlier in the day. Dandelions were always Anne's favorite.

❧❧

That evening I read back over my daily field notes that I kept during this process—this phenomenon of Anne's passing—in an effort to somehow objectively assimilate the unexpected and moving events of the last several days. Had I just observed and experienced caring, mourning, and grief in a family of mule deer? Had these deer been making a conscious attempt to understand the significance and implications of what had just occurred? How was I supposed to view, record, or interpret these events? Who was I to make assumptions about the depth of another creature's innermost sensibilities? Could I even begin to speculate on the possible breadth of their experience without engaging the inevitable human predisposition to deny them the significance of their complex lives, and the existence of their clearly exquisite emotions? Again, it became abundantly obvious that, as humans, we have no privileged access to reality. Realizing that I could not evaluate or even fathom the significance of what had just occurred before my own eyes, I closed my journal on Raggedy Anne and refused to look at it for three years.

Anne's skeleton still lies exactly where she died, and, interestingly, no scavengers or predators ever disturbed her body. The location is a particularly beautiful spot, so it may be only coincidence that many deer from Anne's family find that location a suitable place to spend hours in repose—or is it possible that they still recall or even long for Anne's powerful but gentle presence? Life is so much more complex than we know, but I seem to grow increasingly helpless to speculate on these things. Ethology, in its pure and most honest form, is primarily an exercise in revealing the magnitude of how little we know about living things— the futile attempt to apply an empirical methodology to all that is abstract, subjective, qualitative, and undeniably mystical.

CHAPTER SIX

Living Among the Mule Deer

It was in the same year that we lost Anne that I discovered I was welcome to join the deer in their various expeditions across the mountain. Late one afternoon in midwinter, after interacting with the deer and feeding them some treats, I began wandering along with little Peep. Peep was at least partially imprinted on me, or at least desperately in need of someone. Without a mother, she knew only that life was not on her side, but she had recently learned that I was the only being who was fully invested in her unlikely and fragile little life. So I unconsciously assumed that she would accept my company under any circumstances. As twenty deer were leaving the yard and browsing out across the north meadow, I thoughtlessly stayed at Peep's side as she browsed along, and in fifteen minutes, I looked up and we were a quarter-mile from the house. I could see that although my proximity was completely familiar to these deer, I was getting the occasional curious inquiry from many, as my company was unusual outside the compound of the house and barns. However, as the well-dispersed herd browsed in a wide, hundred-yard radius around me, it became clear that I was easily identified as an arguably odd but nevertheless acceptable accompaniment to their activities. The sun had set behind the mountain, so after about thirty minutes I left Peep's side, returning to the house. Looking back, I noticed that all the deer had stopped browsing and were attentively watching my progress back across the meadow. For the first time I had suspicions that I might be in a perfect position to begin observing the mule deer under more natural circumstances.

Now, perhaps, I could begin observing and, in some sense, living their life—free of the unnatural effects of the house and ranch.

For weeks I continued to follow Peep or Rag Tag out in the evenings for a little walkabout, and in a month my company went almost unnoticed. Still, I found that if I tried to approach the deer after they had left the compound without me, they would become uncomfortable, and some would start to move away. But as long as I was "among" the deer, they seemed to remain at ease and appeared to be entirely unaffected by my presence. And, interestingly, a few of the deer that had remained suspicious or fearful around the house generally ignored my presence when we were in the field and would now on occasion busily browse around my feet. Logically, they were more comfortable with me in their world than when they had been with me, in mine.

One of our morning excursions took us out toward the wild upper slopes of the mountain, more than a half-mile above the house, and we then dropped over a small ridge

⌃ Heading out with the deer at dawn.

overlooking the draw. Suddenly, we were isolated from any suggestion of human habitation or influence, and we were alone on native, wild ground with fifty uninterrupted miles of mountain terrain above us to the west and more than 120 miles to our north and south. It was as if the umbilical had been cut and some unlikely but more ideal relationship had been born. Although less than a mile above the ranch, I was in wild country with more than twenty wild mule deer that were now actively browsing and alternately scouring the area for possible danger with near supernatural sight and hearing. As they buried their heads back among the sagebrush and snow, I realized that I was occupying no more interest than any other member of the group. I was now living among mule deer.

Stunned, my improbable and privileged perspective became crystal-clear, as with new eyes I began to see the near-impossible beauty of this perfect part of a perfect landscape. Mule deer, sage brush, snow, and mountain became indistinguishable. Where did mule deer end and sage-brush begin? This singular vision of a creature so perfectly interwoven into the ecology instantly transformed the way in which I perceived this remarkable animal, but also forever changed my understanding of its significance as an indivisible component within the landscape.

It is startling to find yourself in a definitively wild ecology, casually mingling with a defin-itively wild creature. After months or even years, you suddenly realize that you are with an animal that under normal circumstances would find your company, even at a quarter-mile, disturbing if not intolerable. Yet, here you are in its midst—not only sharing the landscape but, in essence, being accepted as another member of the herd. Walking and casually browsing, often side by side, you hear the soft crunch of sharp hooves as the deer gently glide down through the snow to the frozen earth below. You hear the chorus of plucking sounds as warm, delicate mouths pull and tear at the tender tips of bitter brush and sage. The perpetual, rhythmic prattle of twenty orbiting mandibles combines to create a faint, almost contented drone in a radius around you. Placing your hand on a strong, well-supported back, and running your fingers down through dense, warm hair, you can feel the sturdy, muscular pull on the rough vegetation that is securely anchored in the compact mountain soil. A liquid black eye watches and comfortably acknowledges your touch, but simultane-ously remains focused on the task at hand. Twenty pairs of large, sensitive ears continuously scan the surroundings, carefully discriminating between the scuffling and munching of the

⌃ How to learn what a mule deer eats.

herd, my own clumsy boots, and the plodding shuffle of six black cows several hundred yards below us in the draw. Alternating heads pop up periodically, focusing with tack-sharp eyes and uncanny hearing. Reassured of no unwelcome footsteps or undesirable silhouettes, they return to the unrelenting business of browse.

In the vicinity of the house, many of the deer will be suspicious, but somewhat accepting of strangers. But when leaving the confines of the house and yard, they become entirely unaccepting of humans. Mule deer naturally maintain a perpetual eye on the horizon, and even while literally in "hands-on" direct contact, they are completely alert and attentive to any unwelcome human or other predatory figure that could appear on the skyline, one half-mile away. On more than one occasion, a silhouette has suddenly appeared on the far horizon as a distinctly human form, and I have almost been trampled by the explosive flight that has occurred. This flight response is one of only two scenarios in which I have ever felt in danger of bodily harm from these animals. The other is the rare occasion when two dominant bucks—one nearly always a stranger—engage in mortal combat. Often with no preliminary posturing or gesturing, an enormous deer seems to come out of nowhere. The power and violence unleashed is unimaginable when experienced at close range, and they are oblivious to anything that stands in their way. I am constantly reminded that the acceptance that I have been granted and enjoy exists only in a small radius around me. And in no way do they consider that my proximity affords them any safe haven.

Interestingly, the innate fear that is hardwired into almost all predators regarding a human presence is disturbingly absent when I am in the company of deer. This is a privileged perspective when the goshawk or the bald eagle perches thirty meters away, but disconcerting when the mountain lion appears. There is an old saying in this part of the West: "You don't have to be faster than the bear—you just have to be faster than the other guy." Invariably, after the deer have scattered, I am left standing face to face with the source of their flight. After more than thirty years of perpetual exposure to these possibilities, it is now my somewhat well-informed policy to never allow any formidable predator the exclusive right to make all the important decisions. When in the field with these deer, I may be seen with a rifle slung over my shoulder—for my protection and theirs—and I have not hesitated to use it on more than one occasion.

Because this is my personal project, it comes with no definitions or expectations. I make my own rules. Even though I adhere to certain self-imposed rigor, I am not one of those detached observers who has been instructed to or will simply refuse to intervene. I never trust nature to just "take its course." There is clearly a time and place for that detachment, but we have a special arrangement here whereby I literally trust the deer with my life, and they trust me with theirs. These deer are not merely the subjects of my mule deer study. They are more like family, and that relationship and that level of involvement alone provide the vehicle for a special access into their lives. And although they have no expectation of my intervention in a time of crisis, I'll go to almost any extreme to protect them. For me, there is nothing to be gained by the death of a deer.

After so many years of interaction, all the deer still remain in every way and in every situation completely wild, and this phenomenon has been demonstrated to me in a thousand ways and in a thousand different circumstances. The terms of our association are clearly and solely defined by these deer. Even though they treat me as a creature who casually shares their landscape, I still must conform to a set of specific expectations. For example, my approach must be indirect. I must not engage in uninterrupted eye contact. My clothing must not vary drastically—no coats or hats with which they are unfamiliar. Furthermore, odd objects such as backpacks and, in particular, any object carried in my hand may create great concern. However, with a little time, most articles become accepted, as their curiosity eventually overcomes their apprehension.

If I attempt to join the deer in a remote location, I find that they display extreme caution at my approach, even at a half-mile. If my identity is unclear, they will become uncomfortable with my presence and will begin to walk away at a quarter-mile. If I fail to identify myself or they have failed to recognize me personally, they will begin to stot and trot in the opposite direction. However, these deer have come to know a particular vocalization and will immediately relax and allow my approach when I initiate the identifying call. With tack-sharp eyes, the deer are fully capable of recognizing me personally at two hundred yards, and often indicate without question that they are satisfied that this is their familiar shadow striding through the sage brush, not a suspicious stranger. Should another person accompany me, even Leslye, with whom they are perfectly comfortable, they are clearly made fearful by the approach of more than one individual. It is only with considerable vocal reassurances that they will allow our approach. Even with our longstanding familiarity, they are still made uneasy by any direct linear approach or uninterrupted and constant stares. Deer etiquette requires an indirect, leisurely, meandering approach, with eyes more often averted. And, rather than barging into the group, I will slowly work my way into their vicinity and then allow them to gradually work in around me, as I am often joined and greeted by a few of the more familiar individuals. Obviously, my direct proximity to any deer is a significant source of reassurance and a consolation to other deer in the distance. After a few minutes of curious stares by a few of the more tentative individuals, I am assimilated into the herd, and my presence is no longer a source of concern. I then seem to be of little interest, attracting no more attention than any other member of the group would receive. Immediately, normal browsing behavior ensues, along with all the various forms of casual mule deer social interaction.

There is absolutely nothing that I could do to compromise the deer's inherent wildness. These creatures are intelligent, entirely cognizant, and totally disinclined to ever jeopardize or betray their better instincts for survival. Above all else, mule deer are survival obligates. I now understand that the suggestion that a human could rob a wild mule deer of its innate will to survive through some form of habituation reflects a naive understanding, or at least an overwhelming underestimation of the species.

❧❧

The following year, as our fourth winter season approached and thirty-five or forty deer began to return home, we were thrilled to see that little Peep had returned. To our great relief, she appeared to be a healthy and well-developed yearling. She was immediately glad to be reunited for some treats and for multiple grooming sessions. Surprisingly, her appearance was exemplary for any mule deer, and although she was relatively short, her conformation was robust, with straight, sturdy-looking legs, her pelage was impeccable, and her facial appearance was absolutely beautiful. Even though she was mercifully ignored when near the group, Peep was still viewed as an outsider.

⌃ Peep, giving the author the head nod.

I anxiously awaited Flower's return as well, but as the weeks passed into winter, I realized, sickened, that, like Cappy had the year before, Flower must have also met with some misfortune over the summer. Sadly my relationship with these two beautiful sisters had been all too quickly ended, and in spite of so many fascinating deer faces and personalities milling about my life, I was all too aware of the empty space that these two losses had left. In a single glance across the herd, their absence was conspicuous.

However, early one winter morning, I looked through a herd of twenty or more deer, and my mind grabbed hold of the specter of two deer I had known so well. There they were—as if Cappy and Flower had somehow been returned to us, not as the mature, healthy deer I had come to know—but as fawns. Although alert to the impossibility of the moment, they appeared—absolutely unmistakable in their appearance and demeanor. Immediately, I realized that these two small deer could only be Flower's two fawns. These were the cookie-cutter image of their mother, and in all probability Flower had been killed and separated from her family only recently, and the fawns had somehow found their way home—perhaps by following some of Flower's affiliates as they migrated to this winter range. It was heartbreaking to think that Flower had been so close and not survived the gauntlet back home, but she had afforded the world, and us, the consolation of these two beautiful, healthy young deer.

Interestingly, both fawns displayed little or no apprehension and both moved into my direct proximity within a day of our first introduction. Just as human infants in the womb come to know their parents' voices, so, too, must the fawns in utero have become familiarized with my voice prior to birth and therefore may have recognized me as some vaguely familiar and safe presence in their ecology. In any case, these two seemed to immediately recognize me as their family member and friend, and in two weeks they both were as casual with me, as if I had raised them from birth. Wanting to honor and help perpetuate the lineage of Flower and Cappy, Leslye assigned the names Blossom and Petal to the twins, and, like their mother, they would come to occupy a great space within my life. The Flower lineage has proven to be a persistent and prosperous one with two more successful generations of offspring. Blossom and Petal thrived in their first winter season. But early one morning Petal wandered in, covered in frozen blood and torn to shreds from a mountain lion attack. She was thoroughly mauled, with scarcely a square inch of skin without deep parallel cuts and scratches where she had been raked by enormous paws. How she survived an attack that was so devastating—how this cat had so completely ensnared this fragile little creature, yet it somehow managed to escape such a vicious grasp—is a mystery. Torn, bloody, and battered, with deep cuts on her rear that exposed the muscle tissue below, she hobbled around the yard for two days, pained and confused. Amazingly, no infections appeared, and in a week her wounds began to close. However, an open gash across her forehead exposed the bone, which remained visible, dry, and bleached white for six months. Petal fully recovered from her physical ordeal, and the visible scars seemed to finally disappear below her luxurious pelage. Now, as you dig down through the dense hair on her forehead, she shows barely a mark.

However, there may have been other, more subtle damages; immediately after that event, she began to display an unmistakable look of worry that to this day has not left her beautiful face.

⌃ Blossom (right) and Petal (left).

Perhaps because of the demise of their mother, the knowledge of historical migration was lost to Petal and Blossom, for they became local resident deer and have since spent their spring and summer in our proximity. Petal has the tendency to become secretive and private during fawning, and only after several weeks will she begin bringing her new fawn up close for an introduction. Blossom, on the other hand, views me as a privileged insider and stays near for the births of her fawns. She even allows me to accompany her in the afternoons as she goes to rejoin and nurse new arrivals, behaving as if I am nonexistent, as she and her fawns call to one another and are reunited each afternoon with me standing at their side. So, too, her fawns seem to treat me as some rightful participant in their lives and are inclined to merely inspect me with a couple of sniffs administered nose to nose, but then casually return to the more fascinating and compelling business of nursing. The trust that this otherwise fierce and protective mother shows me at these times is inexplicable and humbling. However, as darkness nears, I always dread the time that I must return to my world, and they must furtively fade into theirs; then, my often sleepless apprehensions run wild until we are again reunited the following morning.

Because of their relationship to Flower, both Blossom and Petal appear to have been born into the privilege that comes with the status of their high-ranking mother. Blossom in particular seems to have quickly ascended into dominance in the greater herd, and is not shy about aggressively reinforcing her status from time to time. Both deer are larger and more robust than Flower. If any possible threat appears in the area, it is Blossom that abandons all caution and leads a charge of angry deer headlong into the face of danger—to attack coyotes, badgers, and cats, both wild and domestic. When any affiliated deer or fawn has died or been killed, Blossom is the bold one who seeks to tirelessly explore every death and its possible causes and implications. She sniffs and examines the body, and then stays close, revisiting the site many times. I keep an eternal vigil for scavenger birds that indicate any death in the area. Few creatures die in a two-mile radius of which I am not made aware in mere hours. However, now I also keep an eye on Blossom as she wanders about on her various explorations, and her demeanor will immediately alert me to any misfortune that has befallen another deer. Blossom has literally led me to the site of several dead deer.

⌃ **Blossom awaiting new fawn.** Photo by Dawson Dunning.

⌃ **Blossom suffering with new fawn on the way.** Photo by Dawson Dunning.

⌃ Blossom with newborn fawns, just 24 hours old.

One summer, Blossom gave birth to twins but lost one fawn within a few days. The surviving twin, Rosebud, became Blossom's pride and joy. Although born sickly, she thrived and lived for four months as a delightful and perfectly healthy fawn, but she was later again stricken with a mysterious illness that took her life in three days. With Blossom at her side, I watched helplessly as the little one lay sick and eventually died on the creek below the front meadow within a few meters of her birth site. Blossom maintained a constant vigil over Rosebud's remains for ten days. It was only days later that any predator or scavenger dared go near this dead fawn. I had known this fawn since the day she was born. My empathy for Blossom's grief, combined with my own sense of loss, remains a source of great sadness. For weeks thereafter, Blossom revisited the location of her fawn's death and stared from twenty meters away as Rosebud's scant remains were gradually consumed. Along with Rosebud, a certain spark left Blossom's eyes and has never fully returned.

⌃ Blossom's fawn Rosebud with friend.

Because every mule deer is profoundly individual, every relationship I have had with these animals has taught me unique things about their extraordinary range of behavior, about their highly developed intelligence, about their individual participation and experience of mule deer society, and about individual capacities to allow this strange human creature into their lives in a myriad of differing ways. It would be inaccurate to say that one deer is more interesting or extraordinary than another. However, in this ongoing experiment, Blossom represents one true enigma, and is most clearly cast from a mold that is different from that of any other mule deer I have known.

Once in midwinter, after losing two fawns in one week to attacks by packs of coyotes, the deer alerted me to a lone coyote apparently stalking on a sage brush slope several hundred meters away. Becoming outraged, I decided I would fire in his direction, even if the price was terrifying the deer. Slowly, I moved as far away as practical from the herd of about twenty deer without alerting the coyote. However, in her usual bold manner, Blossom chose to follow me, one hundred meters from the others. With only open steel sights, I was far out of range of a pacing predator, but still I raised my Winchester and squeezed off a shot. The bullet hit ten feet ahead of the coyote with an explosion of dust that greatly impressed the animal, and he bolted up and over the ridge as fast as a coyote can run. I looked behind to my immediate left, and there stood Blossom—her complete attention focused on the retreating coyote. The other deer far behind were startled but motionless and attentively trying to fathom what had just happened. I re-slung my rifle on my shoulder as Blossom followed me back to join the herd.

If some predictable "curve" of mule deer behavior exists, Blossom is so far outside the norm as to be at once a delightful source of intimate information and knowledge about this phenomenal species, but also disturbing, in that she is so bold and self-assured that I fear for her terribly. I worry that she may be the one deer I have come to know who is inherently fearless of humans in general. Ordinarily, when these deer leave the confines of our small ranch—and they do every day—I have a general understanding of their wanderings, but the precise destinations and possible interaction with other humans remains a bit of a mystery. We have dear friends who live in the closest adjoining ranch a half-mile away. Colt and Mary are frequent guests and have met many of the deer on multiple occasions. They very readily recognize certain individual deer, and various deer have allowed them to actually touch or handle them on several occasions while in our yard. These deer, of course, find their way to our friend's lush hay meadows almost daily, and may be found around their house, barns, and yard with some regularity. Our neighbors have commented many times that even the familiar deer that they clearly recognize by name—deer that they have been allowed to handle while near our house, are completely unapproachable when visiting their ranch and house. These friends feel very protective and would never do these deer harm, but I am nevertheless consoled that the deer appear to be cautious in other locations.

The many threats to these particular mule deer include a major highway only a mile and a half away. In close proximity to the highway exists a complex and disorganized maze of a dozen or more houses and trailers, grids of driveways, fenced yards and small livestock

⩙ Blossom.

enclosures, a multitude of dogs, and, most disturbing, an array of differing attitudes about the virtues associated with the proximity of a mule deer. Strong opinions may vary from simply the acknowledgment of a beautiful guest, to those who consider this animal to be a "goddamned nuisance" that damages fruit trees, gardens, and landscape plants. And, of course, many simply see the mule deer as a few pounds of fresh meat that may be legally and readily harvested in your backyard from the convenience of your back door. This is all in addition to the presence of large predators, brutal weather, disease, and the ever-present possibility of winter starvation. These are threats that represent a few of the potentially lethal impediments facing every mule deer, every day of their lives.

A local farmer once suggested to me in all seriousness that, as a logical solution to "the mule deer problem," we should go ahead and kill as many as possible and give the meat to the poor, because "they are all going to die somehow anyway."

It is only through an incredible level of intelligence and resourcefulness that any mule deer survives its first year. With so many obstacles, the overwhelming mathematics of probability eliminate any possibility of the existence of a "lucky mule deer." By the time a deer survives one year, it has probably evaded death more times than can be counted. This fundamental reality cannot be overemphasized.

And so I remain mystified that this one unusual and strangely bold deer—Blossom—has managed to elude an early death. As she approaches her fifth year, I cannot account for her continued presence in our lives. I can only guess that my fears regarding her welfare are an underestimation of her awareness of the human threat. But clearly while in my presence, Blossom represents a persuasive mule deer ambassador who will boldly introduce herself to any strange human visitor. Blossom has the power to change people's understanding of a wild animal in ways that would be otherwise unimaginable. Always to their great surprise and delight, Blossom, with complete confidence, readily greets an unsuspecting person who may have stopped by for business or some casual visit with curious sniffs to face and hands. Most of these Wyoming residents only know this animal, if not as a desirable game animal, at least as a dreaded and persistent obstacle on the highways. More than once I have heard someone say with astonishment, as if they had never entertained the possibility, "I've never touched a live mule deer before!" And, more important, after only a brief introduction, I have had these same people—from carpenters to cowboys—ask specifically about this special deer they may have met a year ago, and perhaps for only five minutes. "How is Blossom? Is she still OK?" No one has ever met Blossom who did not immediately fall in love with her, for she is simply an irresistible enchantress. She is adorable in every sense, but, significantly, people recognize some undeniable and powerful substance in this creature, and "cute" would not be the first description that comes to mind. And, far from seeing Blossom as occupying a status of a "friendly and lovable pet" in my life, I admire this remarkable being as one of my greatest teachers, and my respect for her is absolute. I should be half as competent in my life as she is in hers. Because she has been a vital and inspirational part of my life every day for almost five years, I cannot now imagine an existence without this important relationship. I dread the day when I must come to terms with the actual depths of my emotional entanglement with this creature, for she has enriched my world beyond comprehension.

Peep was bred that fourth season, but she failed to produce a fawn the next summer, and we never knew whether she was infertile, whether she had aborted, or whether she had lost her fawn shortly after birth. Her udder showed no evidence that she had ever nursed a fawn, and I worried that infertility might be a consequence of her poor physical condition as a fawn herself. I also wondered whether her early orphan status may have robbed her of her own maternal instincts. In spite of our affections and attention, Peep was still a wild deer and showed every natural need and desire to be a member of a herd. But it seemed that perhaps this was not meant to be, and, sadly, she was always viewed as an unwelcome loner—one relegated to a peripheral and subordinate status. Occasionally, she would receive a cruel and unwarranted hoof to the head or backside when she would come too near, or, as if to remind her of her unfortunate position, she would be once again chased away from the group.

We observed Peep being bred again her third autumn and wished her success as it became increasingly clear that she would never know the pleasures of mule deer social life without producing her own family. That spring and summer, Peep did not attempt to migrate but remained in the vicinity, and we were excited when she finally disappeared, as all mule deer do when they bear fawns. But, after two long weeks, we began to worry that something terrible may have happened to this sad little deer and her prospective family. However, after three weeks we looked at a doe and two fawns browsing in the tall grass of the lower meadow, and the binoculars revealed that it was in fact Peep with two beautiful, healthy-looking fawns. At last Peep had a family, and, judging by the lavish attention that she bestowed on the small, fragile creatures, she was a perfect and skillful mother. In their third week, Peep finally brought the two into the yard for their first introduction.

Of the two fawns, one was slightly larger with a paler face, but the extravagant tuft on the end of his tail unavoidably gave him the name PomPom. The other was shy, and while Peep ate some birdseed at our feet on the front porch with PomPom by her side, this other little one would alternately peer around the corner of the house but, then, when we caught his eye,

⌃ Peep with Boo and PomPom at 16 weeks old. Note emerging dark winter coat.

would quickly disappear. After repeating this several times, the little spotted fawn was stuck with a perhaps even more unfortunate name, Boo. The fawns proved to be bucks with widely differing personalities, but even as their first year came to a conclusion, the three, Peep, Boo, and PomPom, remained inseparable—in every way attached and devoted to one another. Well into June of her fourth year, and even as Peep gestated and grew gravid to the point of appearing uncomfortable, her two young buck fawns, with healthy-looking antlers developing in velvet, refused to leave her side.

Peep embraced motherhood with complete devotion, and she has been a doting and exemplary mother from day one. It is tempting to wonder whether her grueling experience as an orphan, rather than impairing her motherly instincts, predisposed her to be more fiercely dedicated. A few does and fawns seem to lose their close connection after five or six months, but others seem to remain closely affiliated. It's impossible to know whether Peep and her fawns remained completely attached because of a personality characteristic of the mother or of the fawns. It has been a delight to observe Peep—this somewhat heroic little deer—who at last has a real family, although, unfortunately, two buck fawns do not a maternal herd make. And, of course, because they are bucks, the chances of their surviving more than a year or two are remote. Each time I look into those bright, optimistic, and eager eyes, it makes my heart ache. But these unlikely relationships have been entirely of my own choosing, and I am constantly reminded that if you fall in love with a legal Wyoming big game animal, you are going to get your heart broken. Although at times it appears dubious, these deer and I have in fact struck a bargain, and the sadness that is built into our relationship is an unfortunate but at least, for now, necessary aspect of a special gift for which I will always be grateful.

PomPom, although casually familiar and comfortable with my proximity, is aloof and satisfied that I am of absolutely no interest. He is pale overall, with dark eyebrow markings, and we are almost certain that his sire must be the large and beautiful buck that we have known for many years named Boar—an immense buck with a twin brother, Bubba—but, nevertheless, subservient to Babe, the magnificent, dominant buck. Boar chooses to leave the area during the rut rather than stand on the sidelines while Babe gets all the attention. As soon as the rut subsides, Boar mysteriously returns and resumes his position in the herd, and he and Babe seem to remain the best of friends. Boar must have somehow found an

⌃ Peep getting her needs met.

opportunity for a tryst with Peep, however, as the facial similarities between PomPom and this big buck are unmistakable.

Boo, on the other hand, overcame his coy shyness in a day, and in a week became an "in-your-pocket, in-your-face" little deer who comes running with raised tail every time he sees me and pokes around in my pockets until I produce a cookie. And, unlike PomPom, who is rather reserved, Boo overflows with enthusiasm and personality, to the point of

⌃ PomPom (left) in awe of a master buck, Boar, probably his father.

distraction for all of us. In midwinter, Boo's left rear cannon bone became exposed on both sides near the foot, with similar tears in the skin three inches up the leg and an inch wide—obviously from an attack by some large predator. The wounds were so open and bare that the bone bleached out dry and white. Mercifully, the tendons were not involved on the front or rear of the leg, so Boo never became lame, and no infection ever set in. After six months, the skin finally began to cover the bone.

Peep remained totally devoted to her fawns after almost a year, but she had to remind the highly energized Boo of his manners by gently laying a motherly hoof across his back now and then. Still, Boo was not always adherent to the rules of proper mule deer etiquette, and, judging by his cavalier attitude and a certain obliviousness to stern discipline dished out by some other adults, he is tough as nails, like his mother. Boo is smaller than his brother, but stocky, compact, and with facial markings like Peep's—so his father is anyone's guess. However, we know for a fact that Peep had a twenty-four hour fascination with Babe the previous unsuccessful year, so perhaps with this prior history, he might be a suspect for parenting buck fawn number two. Mule deer are not monogamous; in fact, a mule deer doe tends to be quite the trollop for a day or so, entertaining multiple bucks on occasion. Given Peep's overt and varied flirtatious fancies, we have no idea who the real father could be.

Significantly, motherhood—or perhaps age and persistence—elevated Peep's status within the local herd, and she became accepted by all the other deer, and her fawns are treated with all the respect that would be afforded any legitimate herd member. However, because of

⌃ Peep requesting her grooming session.

my obsessive attentions that defined Peep's more formative years, she continues to anticipate my complete availability for the whims of her well-being. She has quite a sense of entitlement. Peep can be willful and manipulative and, with chin raised and ears down, gives me that sad, pitiful, "I'm not getting my needs met" look, which more or less has always defined our relationship. But I am gladly at her beck and call. Although Peep gets lavish attention through frequent grooming sessions from both her fawns, she still expects affectionate attention from me on a regular basis. When I ignore her, I continue to get the brisk, imaginary antler prodding on my arm, and if that fails to produce the desired result, she lays a gentle hoof on my backside.

⯯ On the mountain with the deer—as good as life can get.

CHAPTER SEVEN

And Then There Was Possum

Raggedy Anne had a granddaughter named Possum—
Charm's first fawn, who received her name when she was young because
of her resemblance to a baby possum. She was by no means unhealthy, just unusually small,
slender, and distinctly grayish, with a somewhat narrow and pointed face, jet-black eyes, and
a small, black nose. For those readers who have not had the pleasure of knowing baby
possums, they are irresistibly cute little creatures. Possum was born precocious and playful,
and even though Charm and Raggedy Anne had always been a bit reserved in their interaction
with us, this little fawn was born fearless and overwhelmed with curiosity about her adopted
human family. Charm first introduced Possum to us toward the end of September, between
twelve and sixteen weeks of age, when fawns are already fully alert and in tune with their
environment. By this age, a fawn has already developed rather strong opinions about things,
and even when following a previously habituated mother's example, it may take a month or
so for the fawn to feel fully comfortable with my proximity. The younger the fawn at the time
of introduction, naturally, the quicker it tends to become comfortable with my presence.
When Leslye and I are introduced to a ten-day-old fawn by a familiar doe, often within
minutes we are treated with complete familiarity, which may even include curious sniffs of
the hand or face on first encounter. I have had ten-day-old fawns initiate an introduction,
approaching and allowing physical contact within five minutes. But at the late date of sixteen
weeks, a fawn like Possum would probably not achieve this same level of comfort for

two months or more. It must be somehow significant that no doe has ever displayed the slightest protective anxiety because of our immediate and occasionally hands-on proximity to even the youngest fawns. Of course we would never attempt anything that might be interpreted as restraint by either the mother or the fawn. I would guess that a desperate cry from a restrained and frightened fawn would invite some profound unpleasantness from an angry, defensive mule deer doe. Take heed, for they are all in this way predisposed.

But Possum was extraordinary, and even at the ripe old age of three months, she recognized us as family members and never hesitated to have close physical contact. Perhaps our direct association with Charm late in her pregnancy was a contributor to Possum's familiarity. Possum could be described as a bit of a rodeo fawn. All mule deer fawns are playful creatures and are constantly finding excuses to run and buck, stot (the characteristic mule deer motion of jumping straight up, with all four feet leaving the ground at once), and kick—but not necessarily at three months of age and while in the company of humans. But Possum put on a show every time we approached her. She would easily have become an indoor deer had we encouraged such a relationship. I had a bad habit of entering the back door to retrieve a cookie for a needy deer and then thoughtlessly leaving the door wide open while walking to the feed bin ten feet away. On a couple of occasions, I turned around after filling a pocket and collided with Possum, who had followed me directly into the house with no misgivings. Possum seemed perfectly comfortable with the odd circumstances. The first time she found our tabby cat Nathan, she merely eyed him with a quiet suspicion. Domestic cats, I am quite certain, view fully grown mule deer simply as oversized bunnies, so even a little cat's rather admiring gaze instinctively gives the biggest deer cause for concern. I've witnessed mule deer viciously attacking feral cats in the area. However, Possum always greeted Nathan with open-eyed curiosity as they would stare and sniff nose to nose through the screen door. Nathan always responded to Possum with a soft, inquisitive yowl.

At one year, we were relieved to learn that Possum, like her mother, was not a migratory deer, and she chose to become a permanent fixture and perhaps an undesignated family member on the Slingshot. She would radiate out around the ranch during the day but never seemed to venture far away—then join us in the yard every morning and every afternoon, almost without fail.

⌃ Special time with Possum.

⌃ Possum: a face and personality impossible not to love.

Distinct milestones are achieved in acquiring familiarity and acceptance among the deer, and none are more significant than those that involve the various barriers that define their sense of space. Maintaining a deer's trust and confidence at a distance of one hundred feet is a definite milestone, and with time, patience, and a little luck, that barrier of safety may be gradually reduced to a nervous thirty feet. Eventually a deer may move into the final flight-option distance of perhaps ten or fifteen. Then, at some point, many mule deer make the apparently conscious decision that their lives will be safe with this person, and they may then choose to come into direct proximity. From an ethologist's perspective, you have arrived. However, from this position, ever greater levels of trust can be established and even closer proximity may be allowed when patiently encouraged by the passage of time and perhaps by the provocation of an occasional treat offered quietly from the hand. At first, and in most cases, this level of hands-on interaction is merely tolerated or indulged, until eventually it occurs to a particular deer that physical contact can actually be quite nice. And, treats or no treats, eventually you may become such a persistent fixture in this deer's life that it cannot imagine a world without you. Significantly, when a wild deer actually desires the touch of a particular human, you know that, without question, you have entered a space that is reserved only for the closest of affiliates and immediate family members. Then, perhaps, one fine day some deer may become comfortable enough to lie down and rest in your immediate proximity, which constitutes another important milestone—as of course deer are their most vulnerable to predation or even aggression from another deer while lying down. A resting deer will often feel so uncomfortable by the approach of another deer that it will spring to its feet and move away rather than expose itself to some potential hostility. It would seem that all ungulates are so well designed for their particular efficient and fleet form of locomotion that the need to ever lie down or to stand up was included only as an awkward evolutionary afterthought, merely addressing some unfortunate necessity that had been overlooked. It could be safely said that ungulates appear disadvantaged—the outcome of poor design—when in the act of lying down or rising up. In fact, no matter how much finesse and care is applied by these creatures in an effort to become recumbent, every bed always involves an inevitable surrender, whereby the hapless creature at last and ungracefully plops to the ground with a jarring thud.

Mule deer are aware of their vulnerability, always feeling precarious when resting, and they rarely allow themselves the pleasure of putting their heads down and curling up like a cat or laying their head across their back and going sound asleep. It is only in the still hours of midday and normally only in the company of other resting, but hopefully more vigilant, deer that they enjoy such a respite. When a wild deer remains "bedded down" as you calmly approach and enter its immediate space, you can know with certainty that both deer and human have come far in their relationship, and this may be one of the clearest demonstrations of a complete and unconditional trust. To have a wild mule deer go sound asleep while lying eighteen inches from your side is an even greater achievement—a true complement. Then, for that same pregnant doe to allow you to place your hands on her abdomen, and feel fawns kicking inside her swollen belly only days before birth, is a privilege beyond anything I could have imagined. (However, mule deer are wild animals and should *never* be encouraged to become domesticated and "pet-like." Ultimately no good can come of it for deer or human. Our relationship comes with a price—a controversial price—I have chosen to pay in an effort to uncover what could be vital information about the true and intimate nature of this animal.) I have managed to establish this level of trust with only a few deer in seven years.

Possum was such a deer. Although Possum was from a family clan that was characteristically nervous in our company and slow to become accustomed to my immediate presence, her trust seemed almost boundless, and I was afforded privileges that have been granted only by a few others. I would commonly lie with Possum in the shade on warm spring afternoons and alternately stroke her neck and observe the rather precocious and vigorous kicking going on in her swollen abdomen. As Possum would pant incessantly in the insufferable, seventy-five-degree heat with eyes closed, the rise and fall of her full belly was punctuated with the perpetual prodding of tiny hooves and noses, as two very small mule deer became increasingly dissatisfied with their confinement. Mule deer live in somewhat of a vocally oriented society, and, unlike my interaction with other species, speaking in a human voice has always seemed somehow useful and even appropriate in my dealings with these deer. The strange and unique grumblings of a known human voice can be comforting to a deer, but if they hear two or more voices, they become disturbed. Interestingly, they readily discriminate between a stranger's voice and a familiar person's. But this should be expected, as mule deer clearly know the difference between each other's voices, even at great distances. A doe can differentiate perfectly well between the voice of her fawn and another. And when a mother calls into a group of ten fawns, only her fawn comes running.

Quite naturally I offered some periodic dialogue to Possum while in her presence, knowing that ears other than Possum's were paying close attention to the sound of my voice. Interacting with an unborn fawn in this way may be the only possible imprinting opportunity I have had in this study. Deer fawns are precocial—born fully ambulatory—and their senses of smell, vision, and hearing are acute and active at the time of birth, suggesting that for

⌃ Dialogue with pregnant Possum.

many days prior they are also alert—taking advantage of the opportunity to learn from the activity that surrounds them.

Predictably, Possum wandered off one morning and did not return in the afternoon. We were correct in our assumption that she was in need of some solitude so that she might attend to the delicate and private business of bringing new mule deer into the world. She took up inconspicuous residence in a general area down below the house on the far side of the front meadow along the creek in the draw, and we respectfully pretended not to notice. Here the creek bottom becomes wide and flat, dotted with occasional cattail marsh, with various species of small willows rising above abundant thick, billowing grasses and sedges that thrive on the seepage areas discharged from the slopes above. There Possum strove to achieve invisibility as she browsed for a day or two in a most unobtrusive and circuitous manner. We maintained an almost constant vigil, and occasionally we would look below and see the silhouette of her luxurious ears as she hid in the cover of the cool, shady, riparian vegetation. We were particularly hopeful for Possum's good fortune, as she had lost an adorable fawn, Marcie, the previous December to a mountain lion attack just below the house. During that winter after losing her first fawn after five months of dedication and perseverance, Possum seemed to enter a state of resignation, as the playful joy that we had always known was displaced by disappointment. Now a possibility for some consolation was at hand.

Late one afternoon during the last week of June, Leslye noticed Possum standing among the tall, grassy vegetation close to the creek in a posture that looked odd. Just as we retrieved our binoculars and focused, it appeared that something fell from Possum's backside and disappeared below. Possum immediately turned and began to attend to things on the ground, and as we watched anxiously for several minutes it became clear that Possum was greeting and grooming a new arrival. A few minutes later, we watched a new, wet, and wobbly spotted fawn first stagger to its feet but then fall down struggling with repeated awkward attempts to regain its footing. After several failed efforts, the little thing stood with legs sprawled out like some sort of quadra-pod, with head down, but already sporting those large, conspicuous, drooping ears that seemed to imply some level of disappointment with the new accommodations. Possum spent the next thirty minutes grooming the fawn as it gradually became more skilled at remaining upright and then even managed to take a few tentative steps. As we watched, Possum started moving downstream, away from the fawn, and immediately the little creature attempted to stay close to its mother by following along with choppy, halting steps, droopy ears, and a distinct upward arch to the back.

Here in summer, as water begins to become less abundant, the run of the creek in this rather flat stretch is gradually confined to a widely meandering but narrow grassy channel one foot or more deep and only one foot or eighteen inches wide. Without considering the dire possibilities, the proud new mother stepped effortlessly across the creek, but as the tiny fawn tried to cross, we were horrified to see it immediately disappear in the narrow, ditch-like channel of the stream. Without a word, Leslye dropped her binoculars and ran out of the house, and the screen door slammed behind her with a bang. Across the yard, under the barbed wire fence, and down the lower meadow she sprinted like a mother on a mission. Knowing that Leslye could handle things, and not wanting to create more confusion for Possum and her fawn, I watched closely with the binoculars. Leslye was two hundred yards across the meadow and under the far fence in seconds. As she neared the approximate spot where the fawn had vanished, Possum ran back and observed with wide eyes and canted ears as Leslye dropped to her knees and reached down into the creek. I could clearly see Leslye set the fawn out on the far side of the creek bank in a standing position, then immediately turn around and start walking away. But then, having second thoughts about the fawn's proximity to the water, she walked back across the creek, once again picked up the little wet fawn, and set it back down a few more yards beyond the hazardous water. All the while, Possum stared anxiously from fifty feet down stream, cautiously observing the drama. Again, without looking back, Leslye turned to walk away and I was amazed when the fawn actually began to follow her. In an instant, Leslye was far enough away that the fawn stopped following and stood motionless while Possum began approaching. As Leslye walked back through the meadow, Possum and her wet, trembling little fawn were reunited and, after a little grooming session, continued on down the creek and disappeared through the dense willows. We were never sure which fawn Leslye had handled, because Possum had twins; either she'd already had her first fawn, or there was still one more on the way. Leslye reported that the fawn had been in the water, clearly trapped in the bottom of a narrow and steep portion of the creek with its tiny legs folded underneath and, without her help, probably would never have managed to get out. Seeing how Possum obviously treasured her new fawn and, of course, loving Possum like one of our own family, it was very difficult to watch the fragile little creature wander down the creek with its mother into the brutal wilds of Wyoming, where life is predictably more often unkind to a new fawn.

The following afternoon, Possum appeared in the same general location with two fine-looking little spotted fawns at her side. The new family stayed in the general area of the lower creek for days, and each afternoon we would watch Possum retrieve her fawns for nursing and grooming. After nursing, she would entice the little ones to follow her to a new secure and tidy location for hiding. In this way Possum remained near her fawns but never exposed their exact location until she was ready to nurse, and then, of course, she would find yet a new location in which they could remain safely hidden. Having had experience with her first fawn, Marcie, she was a perfect mother, knowing exactly how to protect and care for her new charges.

Mule deer does constantly communicate with their fawns, who respond in turn with obvious behaviors to specific instructions. Commands to "lie down and stay put" are expressed, and the fawn instantly lies down. Several times a day the mother voices, "You may come to me now and nurse," at which time the fawn stands and, with tail straight up, runs to its mother's side and begins roughly punching the udder before suckling.

Each day, young fawns gain more strength and agility, and within a week they are beginning to go on little excursions with mom as she spends increasingly more time with the little ones in tow. In seven days, fawns start to venture a few tentative feet away from their mother during their periodic reunions, and, at last, they begin actively exploring their new world. Within days, young mule deer become exuberant—bucking and playing. In two weeks they can run like the wind. As mule deer fawns gradually become bored with their mother's more deliberate and dignified demeanor, they become increasingly willful. Twins are a bad influence on one another.

Late one afternoon when the fawns were about ten days old, we watched from the porch as Possum browsed in the willows near the creek below. We could alternately see the tops of the fawns' ears as they milled around with their mother in the lush green grass. Gradually the two worked their way under the lower meadow fence and began a game of tag in the bromegrass, which was already thirty inches tall and a month from the start of haying season. Soon, a simple grab-ass game of tag became an all-out romp, and the fawns went storming, at breakneck speed, across the meadow in a wide sweep, eventually running uphill onto the shallow irrigation ditch hundreds of yards away from Possum. We were a bit outraged at their dangerous behavior and stunned to see this level of carelessness on the part of these poorly behaved babies. We found ourselves further disapproving of an apparently irresponsible mother. I commented, "Willful little sprites, aren't they!" Finally, the fawns plopped down and disappeared next to the ditch, two hundred yards from mom. Possum continued to browse casually, apparently unconcerned with this ten-day-old mule deer behavior. Later, she reunited with the fawns, knowing exactly where they were all along, and they wandered back down the creek before dark.

Two nights later, we assumed our positions on the front porch an hour before dark and immediately saw Possum and her fawns entering the front yard under the meadow fence. Possum swaggered into the yard with the fawns in tow, and, without so much as a glance in our direction, she walked over to the platform bird feeder and started to clear away any remaining seeds. She had been in the yard on several occasions on various days after the fawns were born, but this was their first introduction to Leslye and me. As we spoke softly to Possum, who focused her attention more in the direction of any remaining bird seed, the fawns stared intently but fearlessly at the two of us seated on the porch. I slowly rose out of my seat and went to the front steps and sat down. We always keep a couple of iron rings from old wooden wagon hubs on the edge of the porch filled with mixed seeds for the least chipmunks, and, after clearing the platform, Possum slowly meandered over to check out the seed rings. The fawns followed at her side, and as I sat quietly on the steps, one of the fawns casually walked over and, with apparent interest, sniffed me all over. After this brief introduction, he walked over to the seed ring with Possum, and the three briefly nosed around in the seeds.

Possum and the fawns spent considerable time with us that afternoon before dark, and, interestingly, we had the occasion to watch each fawn urinate and established that one fawn was a buck and the other was a doe. The buck fawn was more robust, with a stunningly beautiful face—even for a fawn. His enormous, dark, glimmering eyes seemed to reflect everything that is good in the world, like receiving a transfusion of light directly into the human spirit. The doe fawn had a more gracile face, with distinct little wrinkles on the sides of her upper front lips while eating. Because of their exuberant behavior two nights before, they became known as Will and Sprite. Each evening thereafter, Possum would bring Will and Sprite into the front yard for treats and visits, and in days they viewed us as family members, as both seemed to display complete trust while in our company. Perhaps the most touching thing about our relationship, besides unavoidably falling in love with these two completely irresistible little creatures, was also observing Possum's absolute trust—her unwavering faith in our good intentions toward her fawns. And so I ask, where in a mule deer's experience and understanding of the world does that capacity reside? How vast is that place within the instinctive and conscious experience of this mortally protective mother? How significant is that place that might allow these confusingly dangerous and alien creatures— these humans—a status of absolute trust with her most precious and treasured possessions? Where in the evolutionary history of the mule deer did that capacity become a possibility, and what were those circumstances? And, yet, remarkably, upon seeing another human walking nearly one half-mile away, this same doe and fawns observe attentively for a brief moment, then cautiously trot away to some safer haven.

When living this close to a relatively large herd of familiar mule deer, and, in this case, so close to a small family of individuals such as Possum and her fawns, each night as the sun sets and your deer family members wander cautiously into the darkness, you find your heart becoming heavy. Most misfortune—and the possibilities are endless—befall a deer in the dark of night. Invariably, when I see any familiar deer wandering away in the evening, I always say a silent goodbye, knowing the possibility of death is, on a given night, not just a possibility but more of an inevitability. Watching two impossibly fragile little fawns wander into the troubled night is an almost sickening experience. A mother doe can expect to lose her new fawn more than 50 percent of the time within the first twelve weeks. So it is better not to give your heart to a newborn fawn, for the odds are stacked against you all. At morning's first light and throughout the day into the evening, we nervously watch the creek bottom and surrounding meadows, hoping that a new pair of fawns survived yet another brutal dark night. Perhaps, then, at last, you see a fawn appear in the tall grass with its mother, nursing, and if sheer luck has prevailed, another spotted fawn may appear at its

⌃ Possum with Will and Sprite.

mother's side, and you briefly acknowledge that all have had at least one more reprieve from tragedy. But, inevitably, as the sun slides low into the evening sky and disappears behind the mountain, the loaded dice of mule deer survival are once again tossed.

The vision of a mother doe trotting through a herd of does and fawns, frantically sniffing each little one, then pursuing further futility as she wanders alone onto the slopes, pleading in desperation—the clear voice of hopeless expectation—calling for a fawn that has been killed and carried away in the night—is for any human still in possession of a beating heart crushing. I have seen grieving does become so exhausted in the quest to locate a fawn—a fawn whose death she probably witnessed—that clearing the top of yet one more barbed wire fence becomes a physical impossibility. As she becomes entangled in the top strand, she is slammed to the ground, and life's cruelty and injustice seems to pervade the world. You stand helplessly and watch her overwhelming and inconsolable grief, and it is only after several days—perhaps a week—that the agony leaves her eyes and becomes displaced by something else. Invariably, in every young doe, the eager, optimistic experience of life's joy is finally overcome by a more permanent state of apparent disappointment. I have watched this almost inevitable metamorphosis on so many occasions that it has become a perpetual dread in my life. Mule deer are born spunky, hopeful, affectionate, and fun-loving, but also so profoundly sensitive that it could even be suggested that they are emotionally vulnerable. Sooner or later, tragedy always replaces the joy in a young deer's eyes.

I always dread the inevitable appearance of disappointment and the scars and anguish that overtake the excited little deer I once knew. I always take note of this phenomenon with the fascinated detachment of an impartial observer, until I am eventually overcome with a heartache that obviously is in no way peculiar to the human experience, and, like the exhausted doe with a foot caught in the wire, I too am slammed to the ground.

In a lifetime of involvement with the lives of so many varied species, and those many particular individuals who represented members of those species, there has been no greater revelation than the recognition that sorrow is a common thread that weaves the lives of all thoughtful creatures into a complex fabric of shared experience. Although perhaps threatening to some, and emotionally inconvenient to our otherwise cold, imperial sense of authority and human dominion over other living things, sorrow—like fear—is clearly a shared trait representing one of our most profound organic commonalities. It is one of the defining *provisions of consciousness*.

And so it was with Possum and her two fawns night after night, as the entire world seemed to hold its breath waiting for the forthcoming safety of the rising sun. Again each day we exhaled the breath of apprehension and inhaled the light that projects the almost miraculous sight of two spotted, willful little deer romping through the deep, wet meadow grass with their noticeably weary mother trailing behind. Their unbound enthusiasm is pregnant with the joyful possibilities of life, suggesting that all is not cruel and vicious, and that perhaps this life should not be indicted and at once convicted for all its apparent and unforgivable cruelty. And so, in my particular version of quiet desperation, I defer to these creatures and their ancient bravery and inherent wisdom—a wisdom that I concede to be infinitely greater than my own.

Over the next few days, our relationship with Possum and her family grew steadily more routine, and each day we could breathe a little easier with the rapid development of the fawns as they began to achieve a strength that decreased their vulnerability incrementally. By three weeks, mule deer fawns are of course still extremely vulnerable, but they have developed enough vigor to avoid some of the minor threats that might overtake a more helpless newborn. On two occasions I encountered the individual fawns as I set about the business of irrigating hay meadows throughout the day. Both times the fawns remained motionless with heads down on the ground and merely eyed me with a quiet suspicion that was only partially relieved by my familiar voice.

That spring, Rodenta had also produced two new fawns, and they were visiting us in the evenings for treats as well. Characteristic of all of Rodenta's offspring, Tom and Jerry were always suspicious like their mother; we have achieved close physical contact only with a couple of Rodenta's fawns in the seven years we have known her. Most afternoons, the four fawns would interact briefly with curious sniffs of the nose, but young mule deer tend to stay close to their mother's side, and it is only several weeks later that they begin to interact socially with others. Rodenta and Possum were close herd affiliates but, typical of new mothers, showed no inclination to join together with young fawns. Rodenta was also hiding her fawns in the immediate area, and I encountered her fawns on a couple of occasions as they lay concealed on the margins of the hay meadows, often near the overgrown shallow irrigation ditches. Fawns, like adult mule deer, have distinctive and individual appearances and are easily identified after only a few introductory encounters. The face of a two-week-old fawn is still entirely recognizable in that same adult deer three years later.

One evening, when the fawns were about ten weeks old, we assumed our positions on the front porch, expecting Will and Sprite to appear with their mother, but by dark, no one appeared. Not wanting to entertain the worst, we merely concluded that Possum was simply being a predictably unpredictable mule deer and appropriately varying her schedule. Possum and the fawns had failed to appear on a couple of other occasions, so that evening was a bit worrisome but not extraordinary. However, the next evening, we had still seen no sign of the family. Then, thirty minutes before dark, we were relieved to hear the fawn's voices calling to their mother as they arrived in the backyard. But as we watched for Possum to wander in behind, she failed to appear. Confused, we watched the fawns as they wandered around the yard, calling with increasing desperation in their voices. Again and again they cried out with one of the most pitiful and plaintiff calls in all of nature, and we began to realize that Possum was definitely not in the immediate area. Perhaps Possum had simply been late in coming to gather up her fawns as they patiently waited for her return. Perhaps the fawns had become hungry and anxious and had set out to find her instead. But as darkness approached, our words of encouragement offered no consolation. The fawns would come in close to the porch but then wander to the edge of the yard and stare out across the meadows, mewing loudly. The inconsolable pleas were heart-wrenching as we sat helpless, waiting and hoping for Possum's appearance. Perhaps she had run far from some disturbance, such as a coyote, stray dog, or mountain lion, and had wisely led the danger away from her helpless fawns. As complete darkness fell, the desperate, mewing voices could be heard as they disappeared down through the lower meadow, and we could only hope that Possum would come charging back to retrieve these lost fawns. We knew that Possum's devotion to these twins was as unrelenting as the preservation of her own life, and she would be making every effort to reunite with them throughout the night. However, the prospects were dire, and this was a scenario that we had never contemplated. Would they know to hide until their mother's return, or would they continue searching and calling until every predator in the area had been fully alerted by their unmistakable cries? Throughout the early night I stood in the driveway listening for the fawns, but by midnight I had heard only the disturbing sound of two distant coyotes as they warned the world of their nefarious intent. Around midnight I entered the house with only faith and confidence in Possum's wisdom that must somehow be at play in this disturbing turn of events. Her fawns could now rely only on her extraordinary integrity and competence. Surely, that would rule the day, for Possum had seen it all in her rigorous life. You don't become a four-year-old mule deer without acquiring the razor-sharp intelligence that comes from the guidance of infallible judgment and one thousand life-saving acts of courage and heroism.

Perhaps the fawns only knew that there was some relationship between the location of our house, the two strange creatures that lived there, and the safe haven that their mother had sought out so many times in their brief life.

But the next day Will and Sprite returned without Possum. They chose to remain in the immediate area of the house, as if somehow knowing that if their mother were to return, she would surely come to this location. They understood that this was a place where they felt some measure of safety. The fawns remained in or near the yard but cried day and night, as we could offer only comfort in the way of companionship and as much nutritious supplemental food as possible. The late afternoons seemed to be the worst for the two fawns—and for us— as the fawns would begin their continuous, desperate mewing. It was gut-wrenching sitting helplessly as the two cried incessantly, even throughout the night, and on the second night we became convinced that some tragedy had befallen Possum, and her death by some means was now assured. As the sun set behind Table Mountain, I sat on the porch feeling sick and angry, and I could hear Leslye sobbing inside the house. It felt as if some terrible tragedy had descended upon the Slingshot, and as I later confessed somewhat apologetically to a friend, I cannot remember a more bitter and irreconcilable sadness than the loss of this little deer and the undeniable grief experienced by her two frightened fawns. She had tried so very hard, and the fawns' expectations and trust in their mother were powerful. Her absence was beyond their understanding—their disappointment immeasurable. No matter how hard I tried, it became impossible to assign any measure of insignificance to the lives of these deer.

Both fawns were of an age where they had begun to eat significant amounts of browse, and with the food that we could provide, they seemed to eat heartily. Of course there was no feed that we could provide that could match the 20 percent protein of their mother's milk. We clearly were affording them some consolation in the way of company as well, and Will and Sprite both seemed to be encouraged by the scratching and grooming that we offered while they ate their grain.

The two were also obviously comforted by Rodenta and her fawns as they would enter the yard for some feed, and it was heartening to see the four fawns integrate nicely while in the immediate area. Mercifully, this wise veteran doe, Rodenta, never seemed to express any resentment or hostility toward the orphans as they interacted with her young. As Rodenta and her fawns would eventually browse away from the yard in the evening, Will and Sprite would accompany them to the edge of the meadow but then soon return to the yard. During the day the fawns would alternately browse and bed down around the house, and I would try

⌃ Getting to know Will and Sprite as orphans.

to find time throughout the day to sit and provide some company and perhaps even some meager sense of security. A week passed, and the fawns gradually stopped calling for their mother, but even after two weeks, one or the other would remember their mother and start calling just before dark.

But, then, one evening we took our positions on the front porch, just as four fawns walked with Rodenta around the side of the house and started eating seeds from the platform feeder and the seed rings provided on the edge of the porch. As darkness approached, Rodenta and the fawns walked to the fence along the front meadow, and as Rodenta jumped over into the tall grass, all four of the fawns climbed under the wire and began browsing alongside the big doe. We watched as the four began gradually working their way down the hill, until it occurred to us

« Young Will as an orphaned fawn.

« Will as a yearling after playing in
the barley hay.

« Will at two years with the author.
Photo by Dawson Dunning.

that Will and Sprite were not returning as in previous nights, but were obviously remaining with Rodenta and her fawns. From that moment on, Will and Sprite were always with Rodenta and her fawns Tom and Jerry, and the five became an inseparable family. Something truly remarkable had occurred. Although I never observed either of the orphans nursing, Rodenta was without question allowing the two to be a part of her family, and it clearly seemed to constitute a rare instance of mule deer adoption. Without Rodenta's protection, and without her keen knowledge of the lay of the land and its many hazards, these two orphans would surely have met with disaster. My admiration for Rodenta is unbounded. Even as yearlings, the orphans Will and Sprite still recognize Rodenta and her more recent fawns, Stella Luna and Fledermaus, as their adopted maternal family and prefer their company. As young bucks are often prone, both Tom

⌃ Possum at the back door.

and Jerry, from the previous year, abandoned their home range in late winter, and have either been killed or found a permanent home elsewhere.

Will and Sprite are now entering their third year and are in every way still attached to one another, to this home range, to Rodenta and her new fawns, and also to the two people who have invested so much time and interest in their lives. In spite of the nutritional challenges of their youth, both deer are exceedingly well-developed, with robust Will approaching full maturity and with Sprite now expecting her first fawn. Sprite's nose still wrinkles when she eats. Will is endowed with those big, magical black eyes and a most beautiful face—even for a deer. Possum still occupies a place in our hearts, and not a day goes by that I do not think of her and expect to see her sweet face looking for us through the door. Possum.

CHAPTER EIGHT

The Babe

Dauby was probably a resident on the Slingshot long before we arrived. She was closely allied with Rodenta, and it was apparent that they might be sisters or even perhaps mother and daughter. Both of these deer are large does, but Dauby looked distinctly tired and I would say distinctly disappointed, and her appearance suggested that she might be an older deer than Rodenta. Dauby clearly wanted and needed our help during the long, hard winter, so with some reluctance she allowed herself in our midst. There was little doubt that her ability to trust had been somehow destroyed—in all likelihood by what she perceived to be some unforgivable travesty at the hands of another human. There was always an irreconcilable fear in her eyes that made me feel ashamed for being the creature that I am. Dauby's ears always hung downward—a result of some former injury or disease—which accentuated the appearance of fatigue and sadness.

During our first winter on the Slingshot Ranch, Dauby produced a rather homely fawn who came to be known as Stinky. Stinky survived to become a mature buck, but he did not live up to his name. Although extremely nervous as a fawn, he eventually became friendly and gentle, allowing me to feed him from my hand and ultimately to give him a welcomed scratch on the head or neck. In fact, even though Stinky achieved rather enormous proportions, he was always kind and gentle but a loner who seemed to avoid any involvement in the unpleasantness of the rut, spending most of his time near the herd but always somehow outside the mainstream. In later years he seemed to gravitate in our direction when other deer were gone, following me around the yard, begging to be groomed and scratched on the sides of his great neck. With lazy, sagging eyes, he was obviously consoled by the affection and would nudge me with his big nose if I stopped before he was properly satisfied. We lost Stinky in his fourth year to hunters just below the house.

During our second spring, Dauby had another buck fawn who came to be known as Babe. A year later, she would have twins, Button and Beau, also bucks, and they were to be her last; however, Dauby's last reproductive efforts were good ones. Button, an engaging personality, was killed in his first winter by lions or coyotes, but Beau and his older half-brother, Babe, survived to become fine, handsome deer.

In our second year on the Slingshot we knew little of Dauby, as she was such a cautious doe, and we would see her and her lone fawn only on rare occasions in the meadows throughout the summer. But by August they had joined Rodenta and her fawns, and once again were about the business of becoming an extended family—a maternal clan of mule deer. It was only Rodenta's encouragement and example that provoked Dauby and her fawn into our presence. However, it wasn't until winter that we began to interact closely with these deer and began to recognize individual fawns by their appearances and personalities. In late October and early November, when deer are returning to their home winter range, most fawns are not only strangers to us but also expressing a little independence, so when thirty deer are around the place for the first time in six months, it is often hard to tell who belongs to whom. I immediately began to see a particular fawn as unique in the herd. This one was conspicuously brawny, unlike most fragile-looking little deer. He looked more like an aspiring Charolais bull calf than a mule deer fawn. The shape of his head was broad and boxy, without the more gracile nose seen on a younger deer. He was darker than most, and his pelage, although quite luxurious, appeared rather coarse and grizzled, and each hair was distinctly agouti, or tri-colored. His hindquarters were truly robust, and from behind the underlying musculature and texture of his coat brought the appearance of a Russian wild boar to mind. He was, nevertheless, only a sixteen-week-old deer, so he got stuck with the name Babe in a poorly conceived reference to the pig character of the movie *Babe*, which Leslye had just seen. We both agreed it was at least preferable to Piglet. In a couple of years, a reference to Paul Bunyan's blue ox "Babe" became more appropriate.

⌃ Babe, a fawn with extraordinary eyes, at five months.

Babe had rather distinctive personality characteristics as well. Although initially a bit suspicious of me—a probable result of Dauby genetics and Rodenta clan conditioning—he was still far bolder than the average fawn, and was possessed of some self-confidence rarely found in any three- or four-month-old deer. His personality could be described as alert and plucky and obviously ahead of the curve in relying on his own wits and judgment rather than waiting on a consensus of other deer responses to various stimuli and situations. He was well versed in all the standard mule deer social graces but was clearly overflowing with self-confidence regarding his status among the other fawns. Self-assured deer tend to be the least aggressive and even when Babe attained his unchallenged role of the dominant "master" buck in this area, he simply seemed to somehow command respect, but never displayed arrogance with any deer willing to be even remotely polite or amiable in his presence. Babe, in spite of all his apparent strength, preferred to avoid conflict.

In just a few weeks, this interesting little deer had sized me up, and was relatively certain I was not only harmless but perhaps even an asset that could meet some of his needs as he boldly came forward for an alfalfa cube. This unusual fawn was engaging, and when little Babe looked you in the eyes, something was conveyed—something transpired from one being to the other.

Babe's eyes were his truly defining characteristic. Strangely enchanting, enormous, and obviously full of intelligence and inquiry, his were wide, almost jet-black, open, and stop-you-in-your-tracks beautiful—not wide like the look in the eyes of a fearful horse, but, rather, wide with an appetite to know all that was in his world. Babe looked at you and before you could avert your gaze, you were spellbound—captivated. The few people who ever had occasion to see—or "meet" Babe—immediately recognized something extraordinary.

As an adult, Babe fulfilled all his apparent promise as a fawn and became a mule deer leviathan—a real "handful," as the cowboys often describe a big, strong horse that possesses a mind of its own. Babe became not just the biggest deer you ever saw but, more important, the most powerful creature who ever cared to look behind your eyes in a startling effort to make contact with you. Babe survived six rigorous and relentless hunting seasons, and, without any exaggeration, there were moneyed-up trophy "hunters" who would have gladly paid me $10,000 for the opportunity to simply kill this deer standing innocently in our backyard fifty feet away.

Babe was completely and definitively wild, cautious, and in maturity—hugely intelligent. His powers of discrimination must have bordered on the supernatural. Even from a quarter-mile away, he could sum up your intent in seconds, but if there was anything of significance residing in the depths of your being, he wanted to know that place, and he would bravely take the time to explore you as a possibility. Babe was willing to grant you your individuality, and it was impossible not to recognize this unanticipated and extraordinary favor with gratitude. Babe would meet you straight on, face to face—eye to

« Babe as a young buck, only a few days into his first quest for dominance.

« Babe, after the rut.

eye—and make an effort to know not *what* you were, but *who* you were. By merely wielding those most powerful but gentle eyes, he would knock you and all your preconceived notions about human superiority and animal consciousness to their knees. And when satisfied that he had discovered and explored the most important thing that you had to offer as a fellow creature on this Earth, those vast, black orbs would soften, and he would look into the distance, lower his head, turn, and then slowly walk away—as if satisfied he had taken away something that was, to him, valuable. On a couple of distinct occasions, I clearly watched this animal forever change people's lives, possibly as a result of standing eye to eye with his massive rack of lethal antlers looming higher than a person's head, and at first incorrectly interpreting the apparent magnitude of overwhelming potential for destruction—some immeasurable power that remained harnessed, but could perhaps unleash some monster hidden within. But Babe confounded with his gentle nature, never causing anyone to feel the chill and discomfort that less powerful and insubstantial creatures project when fear sticks in their throats and binds their hearts. Babe possessed the innocent and authentic confidence that comes with full self-realization.

By his third year, Babe had quickly ascended into prominence, if not total dominance, in part because of his monumental proportions, but also because of a more prominent and indomitable spirit. Babe was that rare individual buck deer willing—eagerly willing—to die that very day and very moment if absolutely necessary to prove his worth as a potential master buck. Even older deer with fifty pounds of advantage and much larger antlers quickly learned of Babe's indisputable prowess, and, often without the need for bloody conflict, surrendered the road to this absolute force of nature. On that rare occasion when Babe was called on to defend his authority, the sheer abandon and power that he unleashed was stunning. Witnessing such an event at dangerously close range is—for lack of more appropriate language—humbling.

Babe was migratory, and of course when these deer disperse in springtime I have no idea where any individual may call home during summer. Mule deer are known to occasionally migrate more than one hundred miles, but I suspect that some of these deer merely disperse up into higher elevations and are not more than five or ten miles away in summer. Babe disappeared in spring around mid-May and apparently began his summer journey earlier than some other migrants did, but he stayed with us just long enough to have a new installment of velvet antlers well underway. Furthermore, Babe returned home later in autumn than many deer, suggesting that perhaps he traveled longer distances than some of the other winter herd members did. This winter herd does not migrate as a cohesive unit at a particular time or in a particular direction, but rather staggers its migration in smaller groups of close family members. Babe also had a disquieting habit of returning toward the end of hunting season, so he must have been in transit during this vulnerable time. Yet, for six years he managed to elude the hordes that flood our mountainsides with unrestricted "general licenses" in a designated "general area"—which means every Wyoming resident and out-of-state license holder can hunt this area with absolutely no management plan or strategy involved in the annual "kill" other than the length of the season. One year I stood on a promontory above the ranch and counted fifteen hunter-orange jackets at one time distributed across the mountainside. With every hunter carrying a rifle and scope capable of killing or at least crippling at one half-mile in this open terrain, it is a rare deer that survives three hunting seasons. In spite of decades of decline in mule deer numbers, this species is regarded falsely as ubiquitous and relatively inconsequential compared to the more economically significant big game animals, such as elk, moose, and bighorn sheep. Management initiatives for mule deer have only recently gained any prominence on the screen of the public, political, and therefore game management consciousness.

Babe usually made his appearance on or about the last day of the regular season, and the only clue I ever had to his whereabouts was that he always appeared with his antlers rubbed on burned and blackened timber, indicating that he lived in a previously burned forest, or at least migrated through one. The nearest burned forest areas would be five miles up the mountain near Wolf Point above the Little Popo Agie Canyon, or ten miles further north on the Middle Fork/Sinks Canyon drainage. Upon his arrival, optimistic bucks would have already begun eyeing the arriving does that would be coming into season in a few weeks. Regardless of any presumptions made in his absence by aspiring young bucks, Babe reestablished the rightful order of things, not within hours of his arrival but within minutes.

It's almost impossible to ascribe a phonetic spelling to the various mule deer voices, and most researchers just resort to poorly crafted approximations; for example, the master buck's rutting threat vocalization has often been dubbed the "rut snort," a totally inaccurate descrip-tion of a phenomenal artifact of the natural world. There is nothing remotely "snort-like" about this voice, unless you are a half-mile away. In reality, the voice more closely resembles a single coughing, growling, territorial roar of the male African lion, or the similar barking roar of a frightened or suspicious bull elk in the wild. The "explosive rut-roar" better describes the stunning phenomenon of a three-hundred-pound master buck announcing his willing-ness to die this very moment for his authority to mate. Rutting bucks also emit lesser threat roars that are perfunctory and uninspired, as well as the occasional long, breathy growl meant to convey growing agitation with some other buck. This more subtle growling voice is nearly always accompanied by an unmistakable threat posture, with every hair standing straight out, changing a buck's coloration from brown or gray to almost black.

Babe began his second year of dominance among this herd by arriving during the dark of night on the last morning of the hunting season. Mule deer season is an anxious time for me, of course, and most mornings I am up long before first light and often out in the yard counting noses, and as the sun rises, I listen to the report of rifle shots in the area. That particular morning I walked out the back door into the yard in absolute darkness (flashlights are considered rude, if not outright horrifying, to a mule deer) and stood there in the October chill waiting for my eyes to adjust to the ambient starlight. Before my eyes could begin to adapt, I realized there was something moving into my immediate space at about eye level and above. Something resembling a large face materialized only a foot from my face, which was somewhat disquieting, considering that walking into the night in a state of near-total blind-ness is never wise in this part of Wyoming. Suddenly I began to make out the shape of an unusually large pair of antlers, and although I had not yet laid eyes on Babe or his new improved antler configuration, I could tell without question that the distinctive shape I perceived in the darkness could belong only to him. Trying to suppress a fear resulting from my obvious, precarious, and vulnerable position, I could speak only one clear but cautious question as my heart seemed to compete for volume in the surrounding darkness. My simple inquiry was, "Babe?" Immediately I could see this great head lower a few inches as Babe relaxed—he then moved forward and sniffed my face. Relief of many sorts vied for signifi-cance in my anxious and confused state. It seemed almost impossible not only that Babe had survived another year but that, after six months and an entire hunting season of relentless persecution, here he was in the pitch black night, casually sniffing my face. I shoved a horse cookie his way, which he first inspected with his hot, steaming breath before it disappeared in his warm soft mouth. With a subsiding heartbeat, I relaxed and became aware of other deer that I could not make out, but were also milling around close by. I headed through the night in the direction of the equipment barn at the back of the yard to retrieve a bucket of grain.

Suddenly, in the inky darkness from ten feet behind, an explosive roar rattled all the buildings, along with my courage and any semblance of my remaining wits. My hair stood on end, and I almost buckled at the knees as Babe declared his absolute authority over this mule deer realm with a resonating muscular voice that was, until that moment, unimaginable. I just had no idea that a sound of that order of magnitude could originate from within a deer—even a deer pushing three hundred pounds. It was the ultimate vocal articulation of physical and emotional volition, and I now knew on a visceral level who Babe was—what Babe had truly become. Although I had always been confident that I could trust Babe—in that moment, in that complete darkness—I feared that if I had been deceived, had been misled, or had misjudged this monumental physical phenomenon and my relationship to it, this moment could be my absolute undoing. One of the foremost evolutionary biologists in the world with many years of hands-on experience with mule deer, after learning of the extent to which I had become involved, had given me a rather stern warning about the dangers of becoming too intimate with this particular creature, and I continue to regard his admonition with great attention and respect. This powerful animal had just issued a challenge to *all* the world—an unequivocal declaration that he would reign supreme or die, and from ten feet away, in the predawn blackness, I had no way of knowing if I had just been included in his world of possible adversaries—just one more rather minor obstacle obstructing his path to supremacy. Both my faith in Babe and any confidence in my good judgment were in that moment shattered. Under the best of circumstances, diverting any malevolent intent would probably be impossible at this close range, and, more disturbing, in this darkness I would never even see it coming. For one fearful instant, I considered that Babe might have already decided my fate.

After two more years of interaction, I realized that, in fact, I was entirely safe with this great deer. I knew without question that I could trust him with my life. There are probably those who would say, "Yes, but then what if his mood and our circumstances fell into some unfortunate misalignment—then what?" I have definitely taken calculated risks with certain wild animals over the years, but I do not have a history of being outright foolish while in the company of those with dangerous potentials, and a level of caution has served me well over the years. I have been naive on occasion—but not carelessly foolhardy. There have certainly been those few frightening encounters with a number of animals in the wild, but perhaps more deadly are those straightforward attacks by dangerously human-imprinted animals, which include three different species of deer, one cougar, one jaguar, a hamadryas baboon, and an eighteen-foot anaconda that was quite certain he could swallow me whole. Whereas some other deer, perhaps even some other mule deer, could prove dangerous under the perfect set of circumstances, I know Babe, and I am completely confident that he would never intentionally hurt me—regardless of circumstance. I have not allowed or experienced that level of trust with many creatures. But, though I speak confidently, there is only one thing of absolute value that I have learned by living—I can be dead wrong about anything.

During Babe's fifth year with us, and after reigning as the dominant buck for more than two years, he was involved in a vicious battle in which his opponent's antler tine completely penetrated his left eye. Although he remained victorious, his cornea was punctured and torn directly over the pupil.

For a month the eye appeared to be a gaping wound that drained day and night, and the possibility that he would regain even part of his vision seemed remote. However, in three months the eye had healed, and it appeared that at least partial function had been restored, but with an opaque scar directly over the pupil and dead center in his field of vision. Babe continued relentlessly defending his territory throughout the rut with total disregard for his injury and without any apparent impediment to his abilities.

The pupils of the mule deer eye, like those of many ungulates, are not circular as in humans, but rather arranged as a wide, horizontal, black orifice, giving a grazing prey animal that is keenly adapted to open space a greater range of peripheral vision and perhaps even a greater sensitivity to any motion within the field of view. Although Babe's vision was

« Babe before the rut.

« Babe was blind in one eye, ragged,
but victorious.

« Babe, exhausted from the rut.
Photo by Sammy Tedder.

obstructed dead center, his vision on either side of the scar appeared to be quite good. Interestingly, during his convalescence, and as the rut began to wind down, Babe was trusting enough to let me wipe away the crusty matter that would build up around the injured eye every day. Although initially heartbreaking and perversely ironic to see one of his defining and magnificent eyes destroyed, Babe seemed to recover with only a quarter-inch milky white spot on the middle of his left cornea but with the interior of the eye still brilliantly brownish-black and crystal-clear. His eyes remained in every way as powerful and engaging as they had always been.

CHAPTER NINE

Making a Case for Mule Deer Miracles

Although not among my few areas of modest expertise, I presume that miracles are not by definition theoretical but rather confined to the realm of the hypothetical. Try as we might, it is hard to uphold or substantiate a miracle with supporting evidence that might lend the phenomenon the credence of theoretical status. It is the paradoxical nature of miracles that they can only be discredited but never empirically substantiated. As a matter of protocol, scientific observation is generally obliged to remain removed from the realm of things theological or mystical, and it relies more properly on a foundation of hard evidence while observing phenomena in nature. I do, however, believe in the apparent magic that statistical probability provides the universe—and, given enough time and opportunity, most anything not only can but, in all probability, will happen. Upon close examination there is nothing arbitrary or ambiguous about probability. You know—enough chimpanzees, enough typewriters, enough time— sooner or later, somebody's gonna write *King Lear*. We won't, for the sake of this silly argument, bring up the complications of chaos theory, entropy, an extraordinary number of dead chimps, and all that. OK, no matter how many trillions of times a tornado grinds through even the most well-endowed junk yard, the outcome will never be a shiny, new jumbo jet. But, for example, let's remind ourselves that in our relatively unremarkable little galaxy of many billions of stars, many planets like Earth must, statistically speaking, exist. Given that there are not millions but billions of such galaxies, Earth-like planets are not just common but abundant—perhaps innumerable in the most literal sense. It appears that even the unlikely and seemingly miraculous appearance of life overflows with statistical probability. When the lone survivor of a catastrophic plane crash tearfully exclaims to the media that God must have been watching over them, is there an insinuation that God was bloody well disinterested in the other 230 people who perished alongside? That would be a pretty shabby miracle and could more rightly be chalked up to some remote but nevertheless statistical likelihood of survival. Winning the lottery is not a miracle. Surely, given other more pressing concerns, a god would not engage in such tacky behavior, even if the recipient could really use a little cash.

However, there are times when something so good and so impossible occurs that it becomes difficult to avoid the divine intervention hypothesis—especially when our more objective perception is clouded by the involvement of those we love. Miracles are one of a few final resting places for all things unaccountable and the unresolved quest for explanation. As a lifelong student of the natural sciences, I am satisfied to acknowledge but one apparent miracle—that of fundamental and elemental existence—no, not "Creation" but existence. I'll give the universe that one, but I once knew a veteran Buddhist monk who, when asked some hackneyed rhetorical question about God, said with an honest shrug, while trying to maintain a weary sympathy toward his inquisitor, "I simply have nothing to say about that."

But to this end, I would like to present and possibly defend the apparently miraculous case of Shady—a remarkable and unlikely mule deer doe. Here, there is no appeal for a declaration of divination and, therefore, no ecumenical council of learned ecclesiastics need convene to hear the merits of this unlikely phenomenon. This is only a simple petition for the unbiased and objective reader to hear her story.

∾∾

Raggedy Anne's legacy is strong, living on and resonating across this landscape with progeny who are both rugged and enduring. Hers is a legacy of strength and courage tempered with wisdom. In our second year on the Slingshot Ranch and our second season with this herd of deer, Raggedy Anne's yearling doe fawn named Charm was bred in the fall, producing twins the following spring. We eventually came to know these fawns as Hue and Shady, in reference to their differences in coloration. Hue, the buck fawn, was bold, of a dark color, outgoing and casual from the beginning, whereas Shady, a smaller, pale doe, was rather shy, much like her mother. Although both Charm and Shady were clearly interested and engaged in our relationship, they were also tentative and fragile in their temperament. But even as a small fawn, Shady displayed a desire to know us, while maintaining an inherent fear of the prospect of some possible betrayal. Fair enough. In such cases, I never encourage or provoke an interaction that obviously creates discomfort and conflict in a deer's motivation to be near or to maintain a distance. Pressing a wild animal's willingness to interact is often counterproductive if not destructive to the development or to the maintenance of a relationship. I never encourage close contact with a deer until she has first initiated or expressed a clear willingness. Mule deer can easily become accustomed to some form of proximity to a human, but the tendency toward flight and repulsion is the easiest of all responses to establish and reinforce in this prey species, and can quickly become the predictable reply to our company. And, besides, the best way to cultivate a curious mule deer's interest in interaction is to ignore it entirely. Mule deer are much like domestic cats in this way—some simply can't stand to be ignored.

Although born into the privileged genetic line of the Raggedy Anne maternal clan, Shady never acquired any of the presumption of dominance that some deer display, but rather chose a more peripheral and subordinate position within the greater herd. Her strategy was to be inconspicuous, to avoid attention from other deer and thus never risk an unpleasant confrontation. Without an unkind look or protest, she would consistently surrender her space to any other doe, buck, or fawn. Shady remained closely attached to her mother as well as to the protective shadow of her esteemed grandmother, Raggedy Anne. The three bore an uncanny family resemblance—although Shady had the most gentle and lovely face of any deer I have ever known—angelic, one could say. It was obvious that she found solace in the safe social space provided by her clan, and as Raggedy Anne lay dying for three days, Shady was one of her most faithful and constant companions.

While interacting with so many deer, it is often easy to overlook or ignore those individuals who remain more retiring, while favoring those deer who aggressively desire direct contact. When some cute little deer paws on your backside and fearlessly sniffs your face, it is difficult to avoid surrendering all your attentions to its affections. However, because of my particular interest in Shady's maternal clan, I was inclined to keep close tabs on Raggedy Anne and her crew. Regularly, I observed Shady watching me from the distance as I interacted more closely with her other clan members. She always displayed a keen interest in my comings and goings, and I sensed that my eye contact was not only clearly acknowledged but desired. Shady seemed to derive some satisfaction from our mutual awareness of one another, and I found that each time I was among the deer, I always found myself searching the periphery for her gentle face. There was some interesting expectation in our familiar exchange. With just a glance and perhaps a kind word, Shady's eyes would soften, and she would look away with apparent satisfaction. Like her mother, Charm, I was certain that our familiarity would eventually build a trust that could withstand the weight of our two profoundly differing worlds, and that one day Shady would afford me the gift of her confidence. One day I would feel her warm, soft nose on my face and run my hands along those plush and opulent ears.

Like most yearling does, Shady was successfully bred in November of her second year. Predictably, she disappeared during fawning season, and, as we had hoped, eventually appeared in the lower meadow one summer afternoon with a fine-looking fawn at her side. She proved to be a doting and exemplary mother, like the does in the rest of her clan, and developed a powerful bond with her rapidly growing buck fawn, whom we began to call Lane and, with more familiarity, Lanie. The two were inseparable throughout late fall and early winter, when some does and fawns began to drift apart. It was comforting to see this shy young doe in the ultimate familial relationship, and motherhood seemed to possess her with a newfound confidence and a security in her abilities as a true survivor. Mule deer mothers are, by definition, warriors. All creatures beware the wrath of a new mule deer mom.

Every mule deer is defined by its many adversarial experiences. No mule deer has persisted a day in this world through good fortune and dumb luck. Every day these animals are confronted with multiple opportunities to die in an almost bewildering variety of ways. Every evening as I watch does and fawns reunite and slip into the inky, foreboding Wyoming night, I find that the analogy of an unarmed combat patrol heading off directly into the path of calculated but unknown danger always enters my mind, and, similarly, the morning often proves that vicious circumstances again prevailed as someone, predictably, has been lost to the night.

Although not often so precarious, there are inherent liabilities in what I do, and regardless of any intention to maintain an objective detachment, I find that deep affection toward these intelligent and engaging creatures is unavoidable. Any treachery that befalls them, at least to some extent, befalls me as well. Often I wonder if there are other people in this part of the world who, at any given time, might actually be grieving for the loss of a mule deer? How odd or even unacceptable would the perception of my personal identification with a mule deer be to the average Wyoming resident? I really have no idea, but, let me remind you, with clear eyes, with detachment, and without undue sentimentality, when you pass that bloody heap of a fresh killed deer on the road, that was not *just another deer*—that is not just the end of something, but rather *someone*, with a real life, a fascinating and complex history, and a purpose, who, just like the rest of us, simply wanted to remain alive in his or her world.

One December morning, as deer entered the yard in a foot of fresh snow, I noticed that Lanie was addled, nervous, and alone. Even though the confusion of the rut had gotten underway, and deer were erratically dispersed with mating activity, something was not right, and my heart sank immediately as I feared the worst for Shady and for this dependent young fawn who was without his mother for the first time. The large predators always descend on this land with the snowfall. I paced around the general area like a cat for hours, looking for some sign of Shady and anticipating the inevitable convergence of eagles, ravens, and magpies at the scene of some bloody mayhem on the surrounding snow-covered mountainside. That day, no scavengers appeared. The following morning, while standing on the mountainside among thirty or more deer, I counted noses and watched for Shady's sweet face. But, as I feared, Lanie returned confused, agitated, and once again alone. My heart ached at the prospect of never seeing that gentle little deer again and at the thought of Lanie being all alone in the world. As a buck, Lanie would not be allowed to remain among the maternal clan but, like many young bucks, would choose or be forced to migrate toward some other home range and only with luck would find some consolation with fraternal affiliations among other similar, lonely young bucks.

A few days later, I happened to pass by a rear window in the house, and the silhouette of a lone deer standing in the snow caught my eye. Immediately I recognized Shady, and I saw that she was in some horrible distress. With ears and head hanging down, and with mouth agape, the deer was bloodied from her midsection back and was struggling to stand. When she attempted to move, she haltered with a stumbling and exaggerated limp. Not wanting to disturb her, I calmly walked outside in deep snow and with a reassuring tone attempted to approach close enough to see the extent of her injury. From thirty meters I examined her closely with binoculars and was shocked by what I saw. Obviously, a mountain lion had caught Shady from behind, and in their struggle the great cat had penetrated Shady's left hindquarter with its enormous "thumb" claw and had, as with a scalpel, opened her up from the base of her tail, down the back of her leg, all the way to the joint of the hock in a deep gash an inch wide and an inch or two deep. Furthermore, the cat had bitten completely through the hock, severing the hamstring (Achilles) tendon at the calcaneus, and the white stump of the tendon was protruding outside the gaping hole. The tension on the severed tendon had caused the other end to retract, and was now hopelessly lodged far up into the more proximal area of the hind leg. The opposing, retracting tendon on the front of the leg had not been severed, so the leg was being held up and was not dragging in the snow. Her hindquarters were covered in dried blood, indicating that she had lost an enormous quantity, but the femoral artery had been spared and most of the bleeding had stopped. Judging by the complete immobility of her lower leg and limpness in the foot, it appeared that she had suffered some catastrophic nerve damage as well, and the leg was probably rendered forever useless, ruling out the possibility of even minor convalescence and recovery. Ungulate locomotion requires that most of their "drive" comes from the stronger hindquarters, even though a majority of weight is carried on the forelimbs. Shady was barely capable of any locomotion at all. Her useless leg required that all of her weight and drive had to be supplied by her one remaining hind limb, meaning that each step required her to lift both front legs simultaneously, balance precariously, and drive the entire body forward with the remaining leg. Her attempts to walk were an impossibly awkward, exhausting, and excruciating exercise in futility. Predators are keenly aware of any unusual gait in an animal, and Shady's attempts to move could easily gain your eye from a half-mile away. She was defenseless prey for even the most poorly endowed predator. That she had obviously survived for two days in this condition seemed all but impossible. Defying all reasonable explanations, after somehow escaping the lion, she must have simply remained motionless in the snow in some hidden location for two days, and no other predator stumbled across her or her blood trail.

Shady looked me in the eyes with desperation, and seeing the fear and pain in her beautiful face filled me with a helpless heartache. Desperately wanting to help, my mind scrambled for options. Should I just help her die with a more quick and humane option than nature and circumstance were sure to provide? And, of course, Shady was never a "hands-on" deer, so no form of medication or treatment could be an option. Confinement or restraint here is never a consideration. In addition, and not that I would hesitate for one second under the appropriate circumstances, it is technically against the law to render any assistance to an injured or dying deer in Wyoming. Stop your car to end the agony of a mangled deer struggling with a severed spinal cord in this state, and you are breaking the law.

But, clearly, no orthopedic surgeon was needed to declare Shady a lost cause. The majority of sound four-legged deer do not survive for long in this country. It seemed obvious that any action I might take not only was hopeless but, worse, could only contribute to her ongoing horror. Cowardly, I lacked the strength of character to go get my rifle, so I simply proceeded to the equipment shed and retrieved a bucket of mixed grain, pellets, and alfalfa cubes. As Shady cautiously eyed me from a few meters away, I broadcast the feed across a sheltered concrete apron in front of the shed and retreated to the house. As I watched, Shady stumbled her way over to the feed and began to nose around, picking a few morsels from the snow. Her limp leg swung in a slow elliptical orbit below her side—like the clapper in a bell that had sounded for the last time. Certainly Shady had not eaten a bite of food in the greater part of forty-eight hours.

This is a perfect example, I thought, of why I cannot continue to maintain this relationship with so many eminently fascinating but also unavoidably lovable creatures, whose prospects are so filled with sadness and treachery, for I lack their bravery and am far more fragile than they are. The natural world is the epitome of beauty and perfection—but only so long as you are a human born into a culture that ensures you will remain entirely removed from its reality. As Thoreau once suggested, "Do not ask how your bread is buttered; it will make you sick."

Mule deer are driven to avoid all contact with other deer when they become gravely ill or injured. This predisposition toward absolute solitude even includes severing ties with their fawns. Shady lingered somehow in the vicinity of the house, visiting the feeding area once or twice a day but completely avoiding all other deer, including her confused and frightened fawn, Lanie. That she interpreted my good intentions correctly and allowed me near was astonishing. But mule deer are intelligent creatures, and there is no doubt in my mind that Shady immediately recognized that I was attempting to be her ally, when, in fact, all her luck and any other option had run out. Each time she visited the area of the house, she would attentively watch for me to exit the back door. With only the occasional reassuring glance, I would, with eyes averted, proceed to the shed to retrieve her ration of food. Nervously, but with eager anticipation, she would inch forward in my direction as I spread food on the concrete apron. As I turned my back on her and began returning to the house, she would immediately move in.

With almost daily visits from multiple mountain lions, large organized packs of marauding coyotes, and a recent wolf sighting out the kitchen window, we knew that death would find Shady in some form at any minute. Each time I looked toward the back of the yard and saw her now-familiar mangled form, and painfully exaggerated ambling gait, I was stunned at how implausible her life had become. It was obvious that her every move was excruciating as multiple claw wounds slowly attempted to knit back together. This deer not only was cut to shreds but also had deep-tissue bruising puncture wounds from numerous bites. However, Shady continued to force herself from hiding, and managed to eat the food I provided, but then would quickly disappear somewhere below the house near the creek and draw. Here, dense thickets of currant growing at the base of the sandstone cliffs provided a labyrinth of passageways and vegetative chambers below a dense canopy covered with billowing snow. I never attempted to follow or discover her secret places for fear of forcing her to some less secure location. Even Lanie was unable to discover her whereabouts, and his sense of loss and confusion over her absence continued. He was a sad little deer, which seemed to compound the tragedy of it all. Some days we would not see Shady, perhaps missing her appearance, and then assumed that the worst had finally happened. But, then, once again, to our relief, she would reemerge and continue to eat the meager food we could provide. Her physical appearance seemed to improve but little day by day, and her movements were still painful for her and painful to watch. She would struggle with a few awkward lunging steps and then stop, as if to catch her breath and retrieve yet another small amount of energy from some internal reservoir, then try again. Almost immediately we could see that the entire upper leg and hip were beginning to atrophy. With no stimulation to the muscles, they began to waste away in only a few days. Day after agonizing day, Shady managed to elude predators, get enough supplemental food in the midst of a hard winter, and, to my amazement, never developed any abscesses or infections. Each morning her arrival in the backyard seemed like an exercise in the impossible, and even now I fail to understand how a small deer who always appeared so fragile managed to survive those first few horrendous days and weeks.

But seeming to somehow defy the laws of nature, Shady must have been making all the right choices, for she did survive. One morning, after several weeks into this ordeal, I looked outside and saw Shady standing on the periphery of a group of fifteen or twenty deer, and then realized that she had apparently let Lanie return to her side. Two lonely little mule deer had been reunited. Shady obviously still felt vulnerable in the presence of other deer and kept away from the confusion of the more active herd but now allowed Lanie to maintain a position nearby. In a gesture of possible consolation, I saw Lanie grooming Shady on top of the head as her tired eyes sagged, enjoying a rare moment of relaxation and pleasure.

Shady would stand off on the edge of the yard and avoid the rancor of any aggressive feeding activity that might be occurring around me, but cleverly never diverted her watchful gaze. We quickly began an interesting little game that involved delivering food to her in such a way that no other clever deer could move in on her special pile of feed. This process involved modifying our strategy each day to a new and secret location within the area of the yard or just beyond. Many other deer were aware of our little charade and would try to circumvent our designs, but by modifying our feeding strategy each day, we were largely successful. She was completely attentive to my clandestine efforts to get her food and would work with me to outsmart the other deer. Eventually she realized that I would never let her go without food, so the best strategy involved her remaining hidden somewhere nearby and then mysteriously appearing the minute the last deer had left the yard. Shady knew that I was always waiting. Her thoughtful cooperation with my efforts was undeniable and completely fascinating. All I had to do was make a certain eye contact with Shady, and, without a word, she clearly knew it was "game on." I found this whole experience particularly revealing by further illuminating, in a most unexpected way, an intelligence and a resourcefulness in mule deer that I already knew were extraordinary.

During the day, Shady began lying in the snow within the protective cover of the plum thickets on the edge of the backyard—further evidence that she was feeling more confidence. Ironically, the atrophy occurring in the useless muscles of her hindquarter relieved some of the weight on her remaining rear leg, enabling her to gain better mobility, and she had survived long enough for the healthy leg to strengthen and start to compensate. She would even join in with her mother and other clan members when they were near, but still sadly found it impossible to keep up with their daily movements out around the surrounding mountainside. It was pitiful to watch her follow her group outside the yard in the mornings, but then become exhausted and stand alone in the snow watching the other deer disappear in the distance. Still, she was managing to find some comfort from the company of her fawn and her family—and, of course, this was encouraging for her and heartening for us. Nevertheless, seeing her pathetic attempts to move about was a constant reminder of her complete vulnerability, and there was never a time when we were even hopeful that she would survive that winter. Given the realities on the ground, it seemed to be only a question of when and where she would be discovered and killed. But just to see that beautiful hopeful face each day represented some distinct triumph for her and some testimony to an unlikely but undeniably powerful young animal with a boundless determination to survive.

Then, early one morning, I looked to see a line of ten deer approaching the yard in the snow and realized that, although lagging far behind the group, Shady was following and bringing up the rear. Then, to my amazement, in an effort to close the gap between her and the small herd, she broke into a smooth, loping, three-legged gallop, and in a few absolutely graceful bounds joined the end of the procession. Shady, with the loss of dead weight on one side and vastly improved strength on the other, was now capable of running with the herd! Of course, when she began to walk, she resumed the awkward, hobbling gait that looked so uncomfortable and strenuous. Shady was never truly able to keep pace with other deer, but she was at least able to spend some time with her protective maternal herd and,

⌃ *Crippled Shady, after one year.*

more important, it was evident that she might now even be capable of eluding certain dangers.

This remarkable little doe managed to survive a brutal Wyoming winter that took the lives of other members of the greater herd with further predation, and some disease that took three fawns—Piper, Elvin, and one unnamed fawn from of a set of triplets whose mother joined us from an adjacent, deteriorating herd that had finally fallen into extinction. But now Shady was again challenged by another obstacle that would surely be life-threatening. The dire question arose: could Shady have conceived a fawn before her injury during the first weeks of the rut? There was no question that she would have completely avoided any deer after the time of her initial injury, and of course she would have been physically incapable of standing for a two- or three-hundred-pound buck. But there could be little doubt that her ability to carry a fawn to term was out of the question. Her pelvic muscles were probably at least partially compromised by such an extensive injury involving all manner of nerve damage, and it was improbable that she would be able to sustain the contractions necessary to deliver a fawn.

As spring progressed, we watched Shady carefully, and by May, as other does began to "show," Shady retained her girlish figure and mercifully had either failed to get bred before her injury, or had quickly aborted as a result of the overall trauma. In any case, we were convinced that Shady had once again beaten the odds, as a pregnancy and birth in her condition would have very likely been a death sentence. Shady began to adapt to her new life, and although she was still gravely impaired, her overall condition seemed to be remarkably good, and with the exception of one useless leg, she at least gave the outward appearance of a systemically healthy deer. Lanie seemed to be all the more attached to his mother and, without being displaced by a new fawn, was allowed to remain in Shady's company, which seemed to provide great comfort for them both. With her young buck fawn sprouting velvet antlers at her side, they gently and politely shared the same feed container as I continued to offer Shady every advantage I could. The powerful bond between a doe and her yearling buck fawn seemed to grow even stronger. And each time Shady and I made eye contact, something truly remarkable transpired as we seemed to offer each other something approximating both gratitude and hope. Then, one morning, as I had always dreamed, I turned and looked behind, and there was Shady standing directly by my side. As I turned and fed her grain from a small container, I felt her warm soft nose, and as she nuzzled in the feed, she allowed me to run my hand along one of her plush and opulent ears.

Months passed, summer came and went, and even though most large predators had moved into higher elevations during the warmer months and would return only with the snow, Shady continued to defy all the odds. And although hunting season was upon us, we had a more optimistic outlook on things. We are surrounded by thousands of acres of unoccupied private ranch lands that separate us from the National Forest and Bureau of Land Management (BLM) lands that lay just above us on the mountain. Our ranch neighbor who borders us on two sides had become somewhat sympathetic to our plight with this mule deer research project. He was disturbed by the uninvited hunters who had been coming onto his land and indiscriminately shooting deer on our property, even alarmingly close to the house. One afternoon four hunters walking on the open hillside across the draw, shoulder to shoulder in blaze orange, opened fire on fifteen does and fawns leaving our yard. The deer scattered across a sage brush slope in terror. As we stood in plain view, the men began shooting into a herd of running deer from a distance of two hundred yards. As if arbitrarily firing into a covey of quail, these people were apparently perfectly content or even hoping to accidentally gut shoot or break a leg on a deer. Considering my state of rage—unlike anything I have *ever* experienced—that they all missed entirely and failed to cripple one of these deer was probably the single luckiest thing that will ever happen to them—and to me. As a life-long hunter, it was the most disturbing act I have ever witnessed with a single group of hunters, and as a former hunting guide with many years involved in the outfitting business in Wyoming, I've run across one or two worthless bastards in my time.

Graciously, our neighbor posted signs and told other neighbors that trespassers and poachers would no longer be tolerated. Our neighboring property was formerly part of a large historic cattle ranch in the area, and, as a courtesy, an elderly member of the original family who lived nearby had been given permission to allow certain hunters on the property at her discretion. However, she was told that this year only antelope hunters could be allowed on the property. Somehow the new instructions got confused by the woman, and she allowed two hunters to come onto the ranch. They drove directly across the property, and within sight of the house and at long range, they shot and killed Lanie standing at Shady's side. Our adjoining rancher was saddened by the misunderstanding and reminded the elderly woman of the new policy, and the two men were unaware that they had made any sort of mistake. They were interested only in obtaining the meat and had merely killed a fine-looking legal game animal in Wyoming. Lanie was not a deer that would warrant even a short hunting story at work the following Monday—he was just a few pounds of meat in the freezer.

An innocent mistake had been made, and it was impossible to be angry or cast blame. All we could do was feel loss for a gentle young buck whom we had come to know and love because of special circumstances, but it was impossible not to feel grief for the plight of Shady, knowing that, once again, she had been terrorized and, worse, that she had lost her only fawn and companion in such a cruel way. How much suffering, cruelty, and misfortune was this little deer going to know in her brief but extraordinary life? Now it seemed fate had further condemned Shady, and she was surely destined to live out her remaining life in the unnatural agony of mule deer solitude.

Shady returned to our yard late the following day, and the disappointment in her eyes was palpable. Her loneliness was now complete and irreconcilable. She had learned to look to me for consolation and hope. That she could still have faith in any personal relationship with a human seemed far too generous, and possessed of some extraordinary virtue that filled me with wonder and with shame.

Historically, with the exception of the length of an official season, mule deer have remained an unmanaged species in Wyoming with near-complete disregard for a population that has been in decline for decades. In an environment where mule deer never live out their potential life expectancy, it would have been asking too much to hope that Shady would be around for many years. There was always that nagging understanding and expectation of the inevitable. But, then, that same inevitability joins and defines us all in a type of biological companionship. If nothing else, we share the inevitability of death with all living things, and, ultimately, I find some consolation in that.

Throughout the following spring and into summer, Shady, like some mysterious ephemeral being, roamed the surrounding hillsides and meadows, appearing with irregular predictability. She would often leave the area of the house in the afternoons with Charm and the remaining members of Anne's maternal clan, but soon we would see her hobbling along in the distance as she fared as best she could alone among rich, new summer browse and the bounty of wet, irrigated meadows dotted with a smattering of purple, flowering alfalfa. Still, she was all too aware of her impairment and that her immobility limited the diversity of browse that she could access on any given day. So, we still had the comfort of seeing Shady every day, and she retained full privileges and access to feed and grain. Shady was not always punctual in her visits—punctuality is not a mule deer characteristic—but she was entirely dependable.

⌃ Raggedy Anne's survivors: Shady, Bangle, and Charm.

Inevitability ultimately rules the day—the absolute prevalence of probability—and around the first of June we were aware that Shady had finally failed to return. First a day, then two, and by the first week we knew that we had finally seen the last of this sad but adorable and inspiring creature. By some means that we would never know, Shady had at last left our world. It was impossible to be bitter. There was only an emptiness in our physical space, our hearts, and our minds—the space that an extraordinary and unlikely mule deer had so richly occupied for so long. That she had survived for a year and a half was simply beyond explanation. She had never been a burden or an imposition, but more like some very complex but ultimately lovable addition to our lives. One remarkable deer had taught me so much about a species, about life and struggle, but ironically had even taught me things about myself. I am still trying to learn lessons from the privilege of knowing Shady, but I'm suspicious that ultimately it all has something to do with integrity.

Finding it difficult to put Shady to rest in my mind, it was the demands of ranch life, writing books, and now even filmmaking that were putting miles and a busy life between me and an experience that was probably going to take years to assimilate and fully understand anyway. That summer, our lives were further complicated and consumed by an inconvenient drought, a plague of grasshoppers nearing biblical proportions, and three teams of draft horses pulling mowers and rakes who behaved more like rodeo rough stock than the docile creatures we had always known. And, to top things off, after a summer engaged 100 percent in irrigation, mowing, raking, baling, and stacking, like every other rancher in this part of Wyoming, we were down nearly 80 percent on our hay crop.

But throughout the summer we were delighted to meet all the new little deer faces that were gradually being introduced among the resident summer herd, and each afternoon a small congregation of enthusiastic fawns would lighten our day and make us realize that life does not hinge on a single crop of hay. It is hard to even be tired when you're watching spotted fawns playing tag in the side yard with cottontail rabbits. Sitting on the front porch late one afternoon, sipping a beer after working with Jack and Robin's teams all day, Robin finally made the observation and commented as a chipmunk ran across someone's boot, "You guys have really got the Disney thing going out here."

Toward the end of July, after the haying operation was complete and all the bales had been gathered from the meadows, does and new fawns would mother-up in the lower front meadow two hundred yards below the house each evening. Leslye and I would pass the binoculars back and forth, watching the new fawns play and interact as they began to establish important social ties that would endure for the rest of their lives. One particular afternoon, we could see a small group of deer below the meadow, and we easily recognized Charm's conspicuous black scar on her flank, along with her two yearling does faithfully following nearby. But then I asked, "Who is that other doe with the dark little fawn at her side?" Leslye grabbed the binoculars and stared intently for what seemed like a long time. Then, in a quiet monotone of utter disbelief, she said cautiously, "It's Shady with a brand-new baby." Without another word she handed me the binoculars, and I immediately recognized Shady's characteristic limp, just as the little fawn ran under her shriveled leg and enthusiastically began nursing.

Shady had apparently disappeared early into complete secrecy to bear her fawn, long before we could discern that she had, by some *mysterious* means, gotten pregnant in the fall. I can safely say that I have never seen a more beautiful sight or known a happier moment in my life. Shady lives—she has a fawn. I rest my case.

CHAPTER TEN

Buck Friends

I have come to know many mule deer under many different circumstances. Meeting newborn fawns who eventually grow into adults is a surefire way of gaining entry into the lives of these deer. However, young mule deer bucks often pioneer new territory as they have occasion to leave their ancestral home range. Consequently, many of the bucks I come to know are fully mature and completely unacquainted with the close proximity of a human. I had known Babe since he was a small spotted fawn, but many, if not most, of the bucks I have come to know have entered my life as young or even older adults and complete strangers. Most mule deer bucks are not inclined to cultivate relationships with an unpredictable and ultimately frightening human. Perhaps my greatest revelation in this entire study and certainly a source of great joy and satisfaction has come from occasionally gaining the trust and establishing a true and intimate relationship with one of these definitively wild creatures.

Many local game birds, such as chukar quail, Hungarian partridge, sage grouse, or pheasants, like most living things, in fact, are horrified by the sight of a human, even at great distances. I am amazed when I see these same creatures running around the legs of enormous mule deer and even merely skirting around a bucking and stotting fawn that is irresistibly inspired to play with these birds. Then, when these same birds see my approach at two hundred yards, they either sprint away through the sage brush or burst into flight and disappear a quarter-mile away across the canyon. All creatures fear the human animal like no other, as if it is hardwired into the genome of most animals, causing me to wonder, evolutionarily, what have we done to become so loathsome to almost all living things? How could this have come to pass in such a relatively short geological time? No other predator on the landscape, regardless of how formidable, is regarded with such abject horror. Even the mule deer possesses the same genetic revulsion to the human animal—with more justification than most—so I am continually amazed that this organic divide—this evolutionary abyss—can be spanned by any means. For a fully mature and wild mule deer buck to somehow possess the capacity to receive my immediate company—or, even more outrageous, my companionship— is always astonishing.

Casper

Casper arrived as a young adult several years ago and earned his name as the palest mule deer I have ever seen. He is truly ghost-like on the mountainside among the sandstones and sage, and I can pick him out of twenty deer a mile away. Casper has struggled inordinately with the various physical ailments that plague so many of these deer, including persistent multiple necrotic lesions that originated in the bone of his maxilla and mandible. These abscesses of the soft tissue and bone first appear as large swellings, and may eventually erupt though the skin. Once the common endemic bacteria *Actinomyces bovis* becomes pathological as a result of some mechanical introduction into the gums, pallet, or bone, and more often exacerbated by a compromised immune system, it can be at least persistent and stubborn, if not ulti-mately and horribly fatal. In addition, Casper was infected with the papilloma virus, which is common in mule deer, causing disfiguring, tumor-like, dark, gray, smooth, hairless growths that may range from a centimeter across to golf-ball-size. These soft or even gelatinous "warts" can occur anywhere on the body and normally represent only a temporary nuisance, as they eventually become strangulated by their own weight and fall off. Then, like juvenile warts in human children, they tend to never reappear. In some individuals with faltering immune systems, such as Casper, papilloma can reoccur year after year, and if occurring within nasal cavities or the tissues around the lips or eyes, it may represent life-threatening handicaps that can interfere with breathing, eating, and vision. Casper has struggled terribly with all these difficulties, and all I have been able to offer is some much-needed, highly nutritious supplemental feed, as well as the occasional unconvincing reassurance that he is still handsome.

This young adult deer immediately sought me out and within weeks of his arrival allowed me to scratch and groom him as if I had known him since he was a fawn. But Casper is clearly a rare mule deer success story, as he seems now to have at last "outgrown" his various maladies, and although he will always be stunted, today he presents a relative picture of health despite some difficulty in breathing because of scarring and trauma within his nasal bones. Nearing five years of age, he has grown a fine-looking set of antlers, and although of a rather small order of magnitude, they are nevertheless impressive, with six symmetrical points on either side. He often bucks and stots playfully around me when we are near,

⌃ The author on the mountain with Casper and others.

shaking his head and ears at me provocatively, and as his excitement builds, his breathing impairment becomes loud like the sound of a big, snuffling dog, alerting me to his approach. Often before I realize it, his big, black nose is in my coat pocket in search of a horse wafer, and as I turn, twelve pointy antler tines are nearly in my face.

Mule deer sustain injuries of every description, including various gunshot wounds that have not proven fatal. With every mature mule deer clearly visible at one half-mile in this vast country, no deer reaches an age of four years that has not been shot at on multiple occasions. Casper was shot in the shoulder last year with a relatively small caliber round at such an extraordinary distance that the projectile arrived with barely enough energy to penetrate the skin and muscle over his scapula but not pass through the bone. The wound began to fester, and in three months the bullet was finally ejected in an outpouring from a cyst of necrotic

⌃ Casper recovering from a gunshot wound.

fluid filled with hair and a .22 caliber lead that was barely deformed. Casper was never made visibly lame throughout the entire ordeal, and now he shows only a trace of a scar.

I don't know for sure if gratitude is one of the many interesting qualities inherent in the mule deer personality, but without question Casper clearly recognizes me as his only invested advocate in this world. But, for a multitude of other, more important reasons, we are pals.

Boar and Bubba

Early one cold December morning, several years ago, I was out with the deer on the mountain slopes behind the ranch, and I looked around to see two rather enormous bucks standing on the periphery in knee-deep snow with wide eyes clearly asking the immediate question, "Why are we not all running?" These were two big wild deer, completely confused that I could be surrounded by thirty-five deer that seemed to be oblivious to my presence. The two stared intently as I pretended to ignore them, but their discomfort became too great, and they quickly moved down the canyon to the draw below and disappeared. These deer were probably twin brothers, about three and a half years old and seemed to have dropped out of one identical genetic mold. Although these deer were in no way inclined to be near me, they did discover that winter had arrived and that I had begun placing alfalfa in the area in a preemptive effort to ward off starvation. Soon the brothers began taking advantage of the opportunities. Gradually the big bucks began to hover on the periphery of the herd and were indulged by the other males not only because of their imposing physical stature, but, more important, because of their deferential etiquette and a complete unwillingness to involve themselves or disrupt the existing masculine order of things.

Although the two bucks shared an uncanny similarity, Boar appeared somewhat more robust, with an aggressive look that Bubba did not share. Boar had the appearance of a true warrior, whereas Bubba was the shyer of the two deer and seemed to project a humble air. For that first year, both of these deer were barely indulgent of my proximity. Boar was and is to this day a gigantic specimen of a mule deer—perhaps the largest mule deer I have closely observed—but, curiously, even after two more years, he never seemed to be a contender in the hierarchy of deer. He never challenged Babe for dominance, though he was distinctly heavier and with much more antler mass than any deer in the area.

⌃ Boar and Bubba—socially isolated, but inseparable twin brothers.

In fact, each year he would mysteriously disappear at the onset of the rut without a trace and then conveniently reappear after the reproductive dust had finally settled. For a couple of years I assumed he was off to visit another winter herd that might not be attended by a creature so formidable as Babe. Although Boar had minor scarring on his face, suggesting he had known mule deer combat, he always returned immediately after the rut with no broken antlers, no visible wounds, and still apparently in the same prime condition that he displayed before the rut.

Evolutionary biologist and mule deer researcher Valerius Geist had observed that, for mysterious reasons, "master bucks" will on rare occasions abstain entirely from the rut, becoming solitary and then perhaps inadvertently preserving precious winter reserves and enduring the seasonal hardships in better condition than bucks that had been rigorously competitive. He suggested that these deer accumulated more imposing size and vigor and then might reenter the rut as more dominant competitors in future years. After three years, I became certain that Boar was just such a deer. I came to know Boar closely, and after so much time, he seemed to consider me an admittedly odd but safe member of his herd. To my absolute delight and amazement, he eventually came to trust me to some degree and cautiously lets me handle him and on occasion hold one of his massive antlers in my hand while I scratch his disturbingly powerful neck.

Brother Bubba always remained suspicious, however, and never allowed me closer than twenty meters, but he was in large measure inseparable from his brother, so if Boar was in the

⌃ Boar, following the author like an affiliate.

area, Bubba was not far away. Perhaps it was the bullet that penetrated his left rear hoof two years ago that convinced him that all humans were equally untrustworthy. Bubba's hoof was a mess for months, leaving him with a conspicuous limp, but surprisingly it did heal in a year, and upon his arrival this summer, he showed bad scarring but with no real deformation, and he walked without any sign of a limp.

Although a most enormous and imposing animal, probably hovering around the three-hundred-pound range, Boar's most conspicuous characteristic is his seemingly contradictory gentle nature. Polite to a fault, Boar rarely makes even the most subtle gesture to any deer—doe, fawn, or buck—that might project a suggestion of dominance or aggressive intent. In fact, on every occasion he will relent to all but the smallest bucks and surrender his space—even when a valuable food source is in jeopardy. For lack of better language, and all visible evidence to the contrary, I have to conclude that Boar is just profoundly insecure. After observing this buck and perhaps one or two similar deer for many years—deer that have displayed somewhat similar personalities—I now believe that these may be individuals that have been physically and emotionally traumatized to such an extent that they were never able to recover. These may be deer that have been thoroughly defeated—and now bear physical and emotional scars that will never fully heal. I am convinced that Boar is a gentle giant who was once hurt badly in combat, and he has grown to be a monumental deer with a powerful body but a fragile personality. All the while growing ever more handsome and statuesque, this unusual deer completely declines to risk life and limb for the opportunity to mate. Bubba occasionally appeared in the area of the herd during the rut, but Boar always vanishes until all rutting activity has ended. At the age of six or seven, Boar continues to grow increasingly massive antlers, although he has begun to lose points and length in his tines. Once sporting numerous small supernumerary or ancillary tines, he now displays a more typical configuration of ten overall points. Boar has passed his prime without ever emerging as a reproductive contender.

The peculiar phenomenon described above may be attributed entirely to personality, as I have watched dominant deer become completely devastated in combat, with perforated necks and abdomens and even sustaining blinding injuries to an eye, and as an opportunity presents itself, these stronger personalities may reemerge to become the unchallenged superior deer in the herd. Ironically, however, it may be the buck with a more sensitive personality who becomes soundly and irreversibly convinced of his inferiority, then one day emerges as that extraordinary deer who makes hunter headlines.

This past winter Boar and Bubba entered the area of the house from off the mountain just before dark. I offered the two big boys some whole corn that I had in a bag nearby, and as Boar ate directly from my hand, Bubba moved in especially close and nibbled on a small pile that I had left on the ground twenty feet away. The two deer finished their treat, and as night began to fall, both bucks slipped away back up toward the mountain.

The following morning the entire herd of deer appeared nervous and fractious in a way that let me know some misfortune had occurred in the night. This behavior is all too common and absolutely unmistakable. Twenty deer climbed the foot of the mountain behind the house, lined up shoulder to shoulder, and stared intently out over the wide basin of the draw beyond. No question—somebody was dead. I stood among the anxious deer staring across a square mile of sage brush and rocks but could see nothing. However, the deer were all staring at a specific location farther out on the mountain. I had heard three or four wolves howling in that direction up the mountain two nights before, so I suspected that they had probably been involved in some mule deer mayhem. A small group of wolves—two blacks and two grays—had been active in the area, and I was aware of one other visitation two weeks before, but I was aware of no successful attacks. In fact, most deer deliberately avoid the wide upper basin of the draw during the night because of the predictability of large predators on that area of the mountain. But after several years, it had been made clear that Boar and Bubba were never true herd members and were always compelled or obligated to spend much of their time in that area.

Very early the next day, I found the deer still nervous, and I soon observed the doe Blossom as she left a group of fifteen deer and headed up the mountain with an all-too-familiar intent—like she was on a mission—and I followed right along. Just as she had once led me to her dead fawn, Rosebud, Blossom led me straight to the top of the first rise a quarter-mile up the mountain. As we reached the crest and stood on the cliff face overlooking the basin, Blossom stared intently, and I immediately saw ravens, magpies, and six golden eagles feeding on a dark spot in the snow and sage bush another quarter-mile out. I bailed off a notch in the cliff, climbed down into the draw, and began striding up the other side. In these instances it is always a highly charged and disturbing sight as large numbers of scavenger birds burst into flight and begin to scatter all around. Panting heavily, I looked one hundred yards ahead and saw distinctive antlers standing above the level of the sage brush. At thirty yards, I knew with certainty that Bubba had been killed. The snow was still deep, but a multitude of scavengers, including coyotes, had been ravaging the remains for more than twenty-four hours. Bubba was completely disemboweled, everything but the contents of his stomach (rumen) had been consumed, both his hindquarters were eaten almost bare, and his ribcage was entirely exposed. I tried to reconstruct what had occurred but could only determine that there had been no combative struggle with signs of mud, blood, and hair typically scattered in a fifty-meter radius that would indicate the work of coyotes or wolves. There was no doubt—two-hundred-and-fifty-pound Bubba had been grabbed and pulled directly to the ground and died on the spot. This was clearly the work of a lion and probably a big one. Although damaged by the various scavengers, the neck and head were still intact, and as I searched for the telltale puncture wounds that characterize the powerful bite of a mountain lion, I looked within the mouth to check for blood that inevitably results from strangulation or a broken neck. There in Bubba's mouth were kernels of whole corn, neither chewed nor swallowed, that I had given him only minutes before his death two nights before.

I observed for days as the herd collectively examined Bubba's remains on multiple occasions. The site began to look quite trampled by all the activity, as more than forty deer continued to inspect the now sparse raw skeleton that was gradually being disarticulated by competing coyotes and large birds.

Two weeks later, a mile from the house, as I worked my way up the mountain slowly browsing, with perhaps twenty deer that included most of the larger bucks, we found ourselves near the site of Bubba's attack. Ironically, as a documentary film camera rolled from the cliffs above, Boar was recorded carefully approaching his dead brother one last time in some seemingly heartbreaking effort to understand the consequences of this incomprehensible development, and perhaps how he was to proceed in a world that would now be unimaginably different. With great intensity and obvious deliberation, Boar leaned forward and studied the remains. After so many years, it seemed apparent that Boar had to somehow accept that his twin brother was in fact gone—that he would now be forever alone, and the only life he knew had also died with his lifelong companion. As three or four does joined this

« Bubba in prime condition the day he
was killed by a mountain lion.

« Bubba, the next day.

« Boar, alone at last.

delicate moment, perhaps some final farewell was offered, for Boar merely looked up the mountain and, without a glance back, moved slowly away.

Having somehow made it my business to observe these strange things, I find a need if not a responsibility to offer explanations. But I am helpless to speculate and simply wonder—is it fair to suspect that only the human heart is left aching?

Shadow

Late during our second winter with the deer, a strange doe showed up one cold day with three fawns at her side. Unusual among mule deer, but not unknown, not only are triplets rare; three surviving fawns of advanced age are truly extraordinary. The two doe fawns were tawny and gray like their mother, who had an unusual head shape that immediately brought the vision of an Australian koala to mind. The third fawn was a peculiar little buck that was distinctive in his contrast to the rest of the family. This small deer not only was somewhat of a runt but was also well defined by contrasting color patterns of dark and light. His head was also distinctive, with a bit of a pug nose and enormous black eyes that were filled with even more fear and insecurity than those of the other members of the family.

At first we saw the family only in the evenings after the other deer had left the area, and we would turn on a back porch light and the four would scatter out of the yard. Soon, they became less fearful and would remain in the yard with a few other deer. Leslye quickly assigned names to the distinctive family, and they became known as mother Koala and fawns Teddy, Bear, and Shadow. I identified Koala as a doe I had repeatedly watched in a winter herd to the east that had been overtaken by a rural housing development and was now nearing complete extinction. In need of mule deer society, Koala and family gradually spent more time in our herd's company but were nevertheless obligated to return to the confusing and dangerous misfortune of their home winter range a mile and a half away—now a tangle of trailers, houses, fenced lots, driveways, backdoor bow hunters, and domestic dogs. Gradually the family left our herd less and less often, preferring to stay in the relative safety and plenty of the ranch.

Koala was an extraordinary mule deer, not only because of her large family but perhaps because the need to care for so many mouths had put heavy demands on her physically, and she was aware that things were not going well for her or her fawns. There was an unmistakable look of desperation in her eyes, and with a facial appearance that was absolutely adorable, she became an irresistible object of fascination. This doe made it clear that she was in need of some help; she knew that strange people were offering assistance, and she was smart enough to take advantage of a life-saving opportunity. In less than a month this deer made a quick decision that I was to be trusted, and one afternoon with the look of life and death in her tired eyes, she walked cautiously to my side and took feed directly from my hand. In that moment, her apprehensions vanished, and she came to me at any opportunity and was immediately glad to be scratched and groomed about her head and neck. However, Teddy and Bear remained more cautious, while the little buck fawn, Shadow, expressed a clear objective to come nowhere near me.

⌃ Koala with the irrefutable look of sadness and disappointment.

Koala's flattering acceptance of my company, along with her delightful disposition and lovable appearance, was more than enough to win my devotion and my heart. Each day at dawn I would look for her arrival around the house with her beautiful fawns and the favor of her enchanting company.

I was looking forward to knowing Koala and her family as an opportunity to further understand the ways and means of mule deer life. But this was not to be. In the midst of the last great snowstorm of that winter, both Teddy and Notcha's buck fawn, Button, whom we had known like a family member, mysteriously disappeared, never to be seen again. Then, that April, I awakened to see deer lined up along the cliff just below the house, expressing dire concern over something below. Arriving at the crest of the rocks, I looked down to

⌃ Koala's orphans after the lion attack.

⌃ Shadow vocalizing. One of the few bucks to frequently display this behavior.

magpies and the distinct dark form of a dead deer in the willows. Within seconds of my arrival, I saw a small, telltale clip out of the left ear of the dead doe and knew immediately that Koala had been killed fifty yards from the kitchen window. The puncture wounds on the back of her neck revealed that a lion had struck in the early hours, and her abdomen had been opened with surgical precision, with only the liver eaten. The lion never returned to Koala's remains, and I considered her death a tragic waste. This lovely deer was one of many mule deer attachments that informed me that this experiment was going to be, among many things, a lesson in the persistent realization of grief.

Koala's fawn, Bear, survived to produce a beautiful buck fawn named Panda, and although stunted as a fawn, he is now a delightful, healthy, but diminutive young deer sporting his

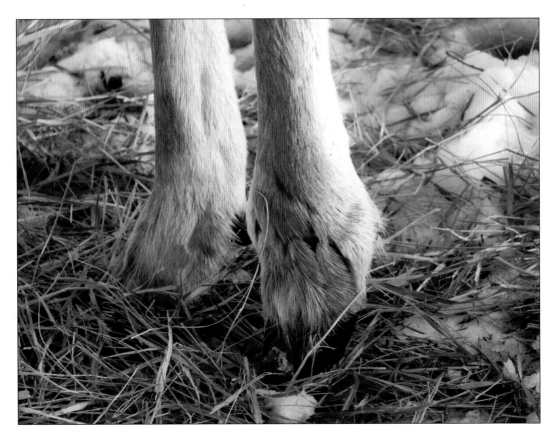

⌃ Shadow's disfigured left front hoof.

second set of antlers. Bear was lost to hunters the following year, but Shadow survived to become a most handsome deer and, at last, a friendly, mature buck. He became one of the few adult deer who would consistently vocalize to me when I was near. Mule deer voices are used conservatively, and to be addressed by a veteran buck was for me the greatest of honors.

To my dismay, Shadow wandered in one morning a few years ago limping horribly on his right front leg, and it was immediately evident that his bloody foot and pastern had, by some means, been completely crushed and raked. After much deliberation, I concluded that the only explanation for this peculiar injury would be a steel trap—probably set somewhere on

⌃ Shadow on the cliffs with the author.

the nearby mountainside by a coyote trapper. Somehow, this deer managed to pull free of the trap in what must have been a violent and explosive struggle. That the hooves were not pulled completely off the bone is phenomenal—yet more testimony to the mule deer's ability to overcome extraordinary adversity. After several years, these wounds, which even involved compounded or exposed bones, have completely healed, but the foot is badly disfigured, and Shadow will always walk with a visible and obviously painful limp.

By five years of age, Shadow was a handsome adult, though stunted, who would appear to a trained observer to be a much younger deer of perhaps two and a half years. His antlers remained well formed but small and without any suggestion of bifurcation. His eyes and face remained distinctly dark, giving him a brooding, mysterious, and somewhat aggressive appearance. But although Shadow was submissive to all the larger, more dominant deer of his generation, he appeared to be regarded with complete kindness and was never bullied.

After observing Koala and similar behavior in several other mule deer does, I think Shadow was a case of partial mule deer adoption. In retrospect, I recall that although clearly included, Shadow never made any effort to nurse, always nervously hovered around his close-knit family, and certainly shares no physical similarity to any of his siblings or Koala.

It is bucks like Shadow, Boar, Bubba, and Casper who have offered the most profound insight, revealing the extraordinary capacity—that "willing" predisposition toward adaptation that defines mule deer behavior most clearly.

PART II

The Essential Mule Deer

⌃ Whitetail doe and fawn. Photo by Marcia Murdock.

⌃ Mule deer doe, Blossom, and fawn Rosebud.

CHAPTER ELEVEN

Mule Deer versus White-Tailed Deer

The mule deer of the American West is one of the quintessential "big game" species, extraordinary on many levels, including an unusual and recent evolutionary development forged from the rigors of their environment—brutal winters, lethal predators, and mountainous terrain. They have a remarkable intelligence, a complex society, and a finely adapted membership in a particularly difficult but magnificent ecology, occupying a vast range roughly corresponding to the often rugged ecology of the Rocky Mountain West, from northern Canada to Mexico. My earliest introduction to this species involved that primal relationship of hunter and prey. But having previously spent years with deer from every corner of the world in a research context, I quickly observed that there was something special about the mule deer, and, like most so-called game animals, they are far more interesting than either the contribution they make to the tradition or "sport" of hunting or their desirability as table fare. Of course, any authentic hunter becomes well aware of these facts and in many cases develops at least a genuine respect for this animal, if not a deep affection. Although this study will probably contribute little to the skills or advantages of the avid mule deer hunter, it is not meant to discourage hunting insofar as it contributes to the maintenance of a healthy, stable population and to the ultimate welfare of the species. But because it is the right thing to do, every hunter needs to know what it is, and who it is, he is actually trying to kill.

It is difficult to describe the mule deer of North America without remembering that they are not merely derived from their distant, white-tailed progenitor; DNA studies suggest that they actually found their genesis as a hybrid between that older species and the million-year-old evolutionary descendent of the whitetail—the black-tailed deer. Their mitochondrial DNA further suggests, more precisely, that the mule deer is in fact the result of unions between black-tailed bucks and white-tailed does sometime toward the end of the Pleistocene. Then, like its black-tailed relative, this new hybrid must have remained in geographical isolation for many thousands of years, dispersing and adapting to the various rugged ecologies of the Rocky Mountain West. Although seemingly convoluted, such reunions with an evolutionary precursor must have happened many times in the prehistory and development of life on earth. And so it could be safely said that the mule deer descended twice from the whitetail. The white-tailed deer, however, precedes the mule deer by at least six million years, whereas the mule deer has probably struggled to distinguish itself as a species for perhaps no more than fifteen thousand. It is still in its evolutionary infancy, a mere newcomer on the grand stage of life, a clever and malleable creature that had the fate of being challenged by a difficult land in a difficult time. Although the DNA of mule deer and whitetails is quite similar, the differences in the phenotypic, or outward, appearance, as well as behavioral differences of mule deer and whitetails, are great. But, then, as we know, chimps and humans are identical within a few percent of genes, so we shouldn't be surprised.

The mule deer is a formidable animal, with males commonly achieving a weight of 250 to 300 pounds, and with occasional individuals attaining 400. The largest whitetails may average 200 pounds, with some individuals weighing much more in some of the particularly robust populations, but most populations would average closer to 150 to 175 pounds for a fully mature, healthy buck. Most deer are characterized by distinct sexual dimorphism, with females of the majority of species considerably smaller than males.

Having spent no small part of my life living with both species, it would be tempting to describe the mule deer as a superior creature in many ways. But it is at least unfair and probably inaccurate to ever compare one species qualitatively to another. Every species, by virtue of its mere existence, has achieved some level of perfection and has in essence found its own perfect means of adaptation and survival. So, in some sense, every species has proven itself incomparable.

The whitetail is supremely adaptable, and the infallible crucible of time has proven this species to be capable of extraordinary resilience. The mule deer could be considered an evolutionary work in progress and a species that has not withstood the ten-million-year gauntlet that forged the apparently irrepressible white-tailed deer. However, much of the ten million years of evolutionary fine-tuning that defines the white-tailed deer still exists within the genome of the complex mule deer. Whereas the whitetail has been described as an opportunistic "weed species," dispersing into every conceivable habitat in the western hemisphere—from the lush boreal and hardwood forest of eastern Canada to the jungles of South America—the mule deer has confined itself to a more rigidly defined set of environmental parameters. Although the mule deer is also a hardy ecological opportunist, it is more vulnerable to various ecological changes or perturbations. This is a creature who may still be biologically constrained by a certain evolutionary specificity.

Perhaps the most telling of the many differences between the two species is the "stocking" and relocation phenomenon. Classically, the adult whitetail can be transported and introduced to almost any new and exotic ecology—desert, mountain, farmland, or prairie—and it can be expected to not only survive but thrive. When the wildlife manager hears the landowner ask, "How do I increase my whitetail deer population?" the answer is always the same—"Just put a padlock on the gate!"

But when a mule deer is relocated from its original ecology into an apparently identical habitat, the mule deer in contrast may halter, become unthrifty, and possibly die. Survivors characteristically have low birth rates and are slow to establish a foothold in a new location. Attempts to reestablish mule deer into ranges where they have been eliminated, or introduce these deer into new but apparently suitable ecologies where none exist, have largely met with failure. Mule deer have adapted to a wide variety of Western landscapes, but once that adaptation is fixed, they appear to be somewhat obligated in a very particular way to a very particular habitat. Even though many mule deer are seasonally migratory—in some cases traveling one hundred miles or more between winter and summer ranges—these often narrow corridors are ancient, and every migrant has been initiated by the previous generation to the various changes in habitat and the specific locations of ideal forage availability along the way. It could be suggested that unlike some bird and insect species that are "hardwired" toward specific migratory behavior, those specific inclinations and destinations of mule deer migration are passed on through successive generations by the example of social affiliates, constituting learned behavior and knowledge that is passed on from one mule deer to the next, perhaps over hundreds or even thousands of years. Learning and transmitting knowledge from one generation to the next is a fundamental tenet of culture and is distinguished from those social systems that are defined by the instinctive obligations of genetically defined social behavior.

The antlers of white-tailed deer are normally smaller than those of mule deer and are structured as individual tines ascending upward from a single main beam. Mule deer antlers are larger and heavier and tend toward bifurcation as each tine ascends from the main beam. The first branch from the main beam on many deer occurs just above the forehead and is often referred to as the brow tine. Whitetails can have very tall and well-developed brow tines, whereas mule deer typically have more diminutive brow tines, and in many cases brow tines are absent entirely.

Another distinct phenotypic or conspicuous visual difference between whitetails and mule deer is the shape and size of their ears. The white-tailed deer has relatively small ears set slightly higher on the head, and are not densely haired. By comparison, the defining ears of mule deer are very large, are filled with hair, and are carried more out to the side. It is impossible to know whether the mule deer's ear represents a larger sound-gathering device, but it would stand to reason that where the ecology is wide open and sound is unobstructed—often traveling great distances—a larger ear may be beneficial. A larger ear may gather low frequencies more efficiently. Mule deer are also creatures adapted to the constant presence of strong winds. A larger ear that is filled with dense, soft, curly hair may serve as a filtering device that may quell or even discriminate past the specific frequency of the continuous high wind passing across the ear—much like the large, furry wind screen devices that cover microphones on windy locations.

Mule and white-tailed deer are generally adapted to different habitats, although the whitetail has proven itself capable of readily occupying almost any former mule deer range, including now the high mountain basins in this area of Wyoming. Whitetails are more commonly identified with the flatter lowlands and river valleys where water is abundant and thus dense cover and trees normally define the ecology. Mule deer in our area are more likely to be found on the dry, rolling sagebrush steppe, the rocky canyons and draws, and the many higher drainages issuing from the mountains. In summer these same deer may migrate up into the higher country and may even be observed browsing along the timberline and occasionally venturing onto the high tundra, momentarily sharing the range with bighorn sheep. While studying bighorn sheep in the northern Wind River Mountains of Wyoming, I briefly observed mule deer near my twelve-thousand-foot elevation campsite on multiple occasions. However, mule deer are more often identified with an ecology that offers rugged and steep terrain, with dense heavy sagebrush, a maze of rocky outcrops, steep draws, and cliff faces. In reality, mule deer and whitetails can survive on the same browse, but both are first and foremost "prey species," so the differences in habitat preference may be defined more by the availability of suitable terrain in which to employ vastly differing escape strategies.

Wild white-tailed deer choose to respond to a perceived danger by running in an unimpeded straight line, at high speeds for long distances on flat terrain, without ever looking back. Indeed, it has been my observation that whitetails even have an instinctive behavioral "trigger" device, whereby a perceived pursuit by another animal will suddenly warrant an involuntary flight response that cannot be switched off until the deer has run for perhaps more than a mile. Whitetails that have been impounded by captivity or circumstance often meet with disaster if this behavior should be elicited for any reason. In mindless panic they may run into any obstacle and will attempt to jump the highest fence. Often the seeming terror doesn't subside until the hapless deer is exhausted and bloody or even badly injured. Eliminating the source that triggered the response will not curtail the desperate behavior.

The study of mule deer escape strategy suggests many things about their complex adaptive behavior and even their extraordinary intelligence. When a mule deer observes an obvious or perceived danger, and in particular if that perception is in the form of a sudden stimulus, the response may be reactive and explosive, much like the whitetail. However, unlike its not-so-distant relative, the mule deer displays a diametrically different response. Although capable of tremendous speed when galloping across open ground, the frightened mule deer does not choose to gallop, but rather turns and bounds uphill into steep, rocky terrain that may be often overgrown in a maze of thick brush. And rather than attempting to gallop through this impenetrable maze of obstacles, the mule deer employs the four-legged bounding gate known as the stot. Springing high into the air, and often with erratic moves to this side and that, the deer expends incredible energy but puts near-impossible obstacles between itself and a confused predator. But, then, after about one or two hundred yards, and if no predator is fast on their heels, mule deer do a fascinating thing—they stop to evaluate and assess the possible danger. They appear to be asking the fundamental questions: Have they in fact reacted to a legitimate danger? If the danger is a predator, is this particular predator actively hunting? If it is on the hunt, is it actually interested in this particular deer? The mule deer appears to employ reason and understanding to dangerous situations rather than blind obligatory instinct. Of course this often constitutes a fatal response when a human hunter is carrying a weapon that can call in an air strike at six hundred yards. Interestingly, the mule deer has become specifically responsive to a human, and, in particular, inordinately suspicious of even the smallest object in a human hand. But throughout their development as a species, the peculiar human predator was the one in mere possession of a bow and arrow, an atlatl, or simply a sharp stick. It is only recently in their development that they have come to fear the mysterious missile that comes at them in silence from one half-mile away. Since their evolutionary genesis during the end of the Pleistocene, the mule deer may have always known and identified the human species as one of their many possible predators. Like the mountain lion, the bear, and the wolf, humans are clearly hardwired into the racial memory of this creature, and we have probably always been at least a marginally predictable feature on their evolutionary landscape. And, therefore, the mule deer, unlike more ancient species, may have always been directly and indirectly associated with humanity. But our relationship may also be unique in that we represent an evolutionary paradox. Perhaps like the grizzly, we are alternately the most deadly of predators and then that creature who may also peacefully share the landscape eating roots, crickets, and berries or perhaps even herding or shepherding other species. As humans we have probably always represented a conundrum of schizophrenic proportions. We are that strange creature who will pull you as a helpless fawn from the frozen water or cut you free from a tangled mass of barbed wire and then tomorrow kill your mother standing at your side and leave her gut pile in the sage brush for you to ponder. So, like their response to any other potential predator, mule deer also ask those confusing fundamental subjective questions: Is this creature human? Is this human in predatory mode? Is this human a direct threat to me today? The mule deer is gradually adapting to the high-powered rifle, and those individuals who survive one hunting season tend to learn that there is no safe proximity to a human, and will quickly abandon the area at a fast, gliding trot without another look back. In dealing with certain other predators, the mule deer will often respond with extreme caution, but may only maintain a safe distance, wanting only to keep an eye on the possible danger rather than making a blind and often unnecessary retreat.

Surprisingly, mule deer will commonly react to a possible predator with coordinated group aggression. Even though coyotes are known to prey heavily on mule deer, which are vulnerable to organized packs, I have often watched individual coyotes as they are relentlessly persecuted and chased by a storming and angry herd of deer with dominant females who I recognize, out ahead and leading the charge. Confused fawns and yearlings cautiously bring up the rear. In circumstances where a perceived danger cannot be fully identified, many mule deer feel a strong urge to cautiously approach and investigate the origin of their concern—overriding fear with curiosity. With heads held high, with ears canted forward, and with slow-prancing, deliberate steps, they cautiously approach a strange object or unidentified animal. It is an obvious display of a well-earned self-confidence, and it is strong evidence that a seminal and definitive adaptive strategy of the mule deer involves the powerful suggestion—for this animal there is no survival advantage in ignorance.

Even though mule deer and whitetails are fully capable of interbreeding, the hybrid offspring inherits specific traits from each parent that are behaviorally incompatible, making survival in much of typical mule deer habitat virtually impossible. Ironically, the hapless fawn inherits the predisposition to elude predators by running uphill into rocks and heavy brush, but is mechanically or behaviorally incapable of employing the stot to pass safely over these impediments.

Another significant difference between whitetails and mule deer is the differing patterns of daily activities. White-tailed deer tend to be creatures of habit and if undisturbed can predictably be found in certain locations at certain times, seeming to conform to a daily schedule of activities. If a whitetail buck visits a scrape or rub today at 4:00 p.m., he is very likely to be there tomorrow at about the same time. If he goes to water or visits a hay field at first light, you can predict with some certainty that he'll be there again at the same time the following day.

In contrast, the mule deer is a circuitous creature, and even though he may be compelled by necessity to revisit certain sites over and over for food or water, he is much more inclined to be in a different place every day at a different time. Mule deer will find different routes to take from one area to the next, and if these deer have moved through a specific area in a specific direction this afternoon, you can predict with a degree of certainty that they will not be moving the same way, in the same direction, tomorrow. Clearly all predators make note of the presence of a possible food source and are particularly alert to the habitual movements of their various prey. It is around the predictable habits of their prey that efficient predators plan their hunting and attack strategies. Mule deer often stay one step ahead of their predatory adversaries by employing a strategy of unpredictability. However, if you think you can depend on this deer to be predictably unpredictable, be prepared to be disappointed, for even the absence of a habit can become a habit, and they apparently know better.

Sadly, wildlife management agencies all over the West have demonstrated many times that once mule deer are in danger of starvation during a difficult winter, they are likely to continue to decline, starve, and die—even after nutritious supplemental food has been provided. This is due in part to a sensitive and complex digestive system that may have already shut down and cannot be restarted, but it is also clear that a hungry mule deer will simply refuse to eat any food with which they are unaccustomed. Indeed, I have introduced palatable, nutritious, and normally desirable food to mule deer under various circumstances and in different seasons, observing their immediate disinterest or even revulsion to a strange food. Often it will take at least weeks if not months to habituate a mule deer to a new but otherwise desirable food source. Apples are a classic example. Initiated mule deer relish the taste of apples—as every apple-growing rancher is all too aware. I personally know mule deer who will mug you if they suspect you have an apple in your pocket! But the deer who has never been exposed to the apple orchard will almost always find the exotic fruit at least uninteresting and, in many cases, will react to the strange smell of an opened apple with apparent disdain, shock, or even fear. Suffice it to say that the mule deer, although robust, resilient, and intelligent, is, nevertheless, a sensitive creature. I personally have always had my doubts about the advantages of sensitivity.

Over time and by various means, however, mule deer almost always eventually become displaced by whitetails. The reasons for displacement are complex and controversial, possibly involving human augmentation to the landscape of which whitetails are more tolerant. Crossbreeding of whitetail bucks to mule deer does is known to be a factor in some populations—accounting for 30 percent of fawns in these populations, which, of course, don't survive. But in many cases, whitetails may simply occupy former mule deer ranges from which the mule deer have mysteriously disappeared. Thirty-five years of observation in this area of Wyoming has lent me an insight into this dramatic and disturbing phenomenon. I have seen complete displacement of mule deer occur in areas where no whitetail existed three decades ago. The whitetail diasporas began in Montana decades ago, and now much of the state's intermountain habitat is entirely dominated by this aggressive relative of the mule deer. In areas such as Swan Valley, the Bob Marshall Wilderness, and even northward, including Glacier National Park, much of Montana's former mule deer habitat has now been entirely replaced with white-tailed deer.

⌃ Typical whitetail buck antler configuration. Photo by Marcia Murdock.

⌃ Note tendency in this large buck toward extreme bifurcation in antler form.

CHAPTER TWELVE

The Essential Mule Deer

All individuals within any species share common physical traits, so the phenotype or outward appearance immediately distinguishes them from any other animals. White-tailed deer and mule deer display very little similarity in their outward appearance, except that they share the same phenotypic traits that define their genus, *Odocoileus*, or the traits that define the appearance of all deer family members known collectively as *Cervidae*—or "the cervids." The same silly lack of distinctions that humans often apply to other races within their own species is the same lack of discrimination that we tend to apply to other species. It's not that the physical stereotype is inaccurate; it just implies a failure to look past the obvious—a failure to pay attention to the details. We may look at a herd of Angus cattle and see one hundred black animals that appear to have been dropped out of a large cookie cutter. But any working cowboy worth his salt gets to know his herd of one thousand mother cows as surely as you can recognize each of your three Labrador retrievers a quarter-mile away. In this way it could be said that every mule deer looks very much like any other mule deer, but with closer examination and a little familiarity, every deer is entirely individual and unique.

Body shapes vary greatly in size and proportions, and the unique physiology of each individual may even give a particular mule deer a distinct way of walking that can be clearly recognized, even at a great distance. A particular doe may be lean and tall with long legs, and another may be short and stocky. These characteristics are almost entirely genetic and represent the normal range of variation that occurs in any population of animals. These same characteristics may or may not represent any particular advantage or disadvantage, but can be responsible for the inevitable "genetic drift" that occurs in populations that become geographically isolated and distant from other similar individuals. So, in this way, to the trained eye, the mule deer of northern Colorado look surprisingly different from a given population of deer in northern Wyoming or perhaps the same species of deer in southern Alberta. The genome may be identical, but recognizable variations in appearance inevitably occur over long distances and over time. A whitetail from south Florida looks vastly different from one in the Wind River Basin of Wyoming. But both races look exactly like a white-tailed deer. Some of this variation is the result of the adaptation to differing ecologies—colder climates may select for larger bodies, or the restrictive nutritional differences in habitat may select for smaller body proportions, or simple arbitrary variation in form will inevitably occur from one region to the next.

But within a local population of animals, and in this case a population of mule deer, most animals display discernible variations in individual appearance. Every mule deer has a distinct facial mask that is defined by differences in coloration, shading, and the unique configuration of these color patterns. The facial mask is most clearly defined during the winter color phase, as summer coats are thin and somewhat reddish and lack much of the distinctive contrast in color. But the underlying skeletal structure of the head is all you need to quickly distinguish one familiar deer from another. Close examination of a mule deer in summer reveals that it could be considered almost hairless, as the skin becomes clearly visible on much of the body through a sparse but even distribution of reddish hair.

In summer months and particularly at lower elevations, mule deer are stressed and made conspicuously miserable by temperatures that rise into the high seventies or eighties. Deer do not sweat like horses, and when summer temperatures occasionally skyrocket into the nineties, mule deer appear gravely stressed, remaining almost entirely immobilized in the shade, usually on bare earth, and panting incessantly as if just recovering from some extreme exertion. Lactating females are especially hard hit, with their metabolic rates already in overdrive. External parasites add insult in these temperatures, with tick and lice populations being a factor in some years. Strangely, tick infestations appear to be much worse in late winter, with multiple species finding the mule deer an agreeable host in the cooler months. These deer are true creatures of the Pleistocene ice ages, and are clearly adapted to high elevations and more at home in cold climate. Twenty degrees below zero Fahrenheit does not seem to bother a healthy mule deer, with single digits above zero more ideal. When daily winter temperatures rise into the high twenties and low thirties, these deer, while not overheated, may be found lying in shady locations throughout the day.

The hair on the ears of mule deer may vary dramatically in shading and coloration, and these patterns are always distinctive. Looking face-on at a mule deer, one might notice that the ears are lined on the outside with pale shades of darker gray and brown, with a slightly contrasting cream-colored or beige hair on the inside of the ear. Another deer may have ears that are rimmed in black, and filled on the inside with hair that is almost white and highly contrasting, bringing to mind a striped skunk. In summer, mule deer ears are completely barren of hair on the outside and feel distinctly overheated to the touch. One function of the oversized ears of mule deer may be to provide a heat-sink cooling apparatus for the warmer months. With copious large blood vessels far in excess to the needs of the ear, clearly heat is being exchanged during the summer. The installment of rich winter hair with perfect insu-lating properties covering the ears obviously curtails the heat exchange, and then the rich blood supply serves to keep the extremity of the ears safe from frostbite.

The crown between the eyes and up over the forehead between the ears may be merely a uniform gray-brown, not unlike the deer's overall coat, but, then, another deer may have highly contrasting lines over the eyes, bringing to mind darkly penciled eyebrows. Others may have a completely black crown, with black, lined ears and pale interior hair, with the end of the ear tipped in white. A white-faced deer is not indicative of an older individual but rather just one possibility in the normal range of variation. The overall coat of a mule deer can also display great variation, with many shades and combinations of darker or lighter gray and combinations of lighter and darker brown. Some deer are tawny and yellow-brown, with almost yellow undersides and legs, while others' hair might be a pale gray with white tips, like Raggedy Anne's fawn, Frosty. Mule deer do not have a melanistic or black phase but may on occasion be quite dark. They are typically white or pale under their chin and often, but not always, have a distinct black dot on the prominence. This pale chin color continues down onto the throat a few inches. Below this throat patch there may be a second throat patch, several inches across, that ranges from distinct on some individuals to almost nonexistent on others. Mule deer have a black nose that is always moist and surrounded by black hair that often creates a black-colored stripe on the distal end of the mandible, behind the chin. Eyes may be completely lined in pale or white spectacles, or, on other deer, completely void of contrasting color.

Whitetails tend to have very pale or bright white underbellies. Mule deer's underbellies are less contrasting but still pale. Mule deer tails are pale cream, varying to almost white, and conform to the color of the pale rump patch that is characteristic of many wild species of artiodactyls—deer, elk, wild sheep, pronghorn, and so on. The mule deer tail has relatively

⌃ Note the distinctions in ear and facial markings between Frosty (left) and Stinky (right).

short hair compared to that of the whitetail, and it is always tipped in some variation of longer, darker hair that on some deer can take on the proportions of a small pom-pom. Mule deer commonly use their tails as a part of their complex repertoire of social signals, but, unlike whitetails, they do not raise their tails in display when running from danger. But a fawn may raise his tail in anticipation of nursing. A raised tail in an adult may suggest the opportunity for a desirable food, or may precede an aggressive confrontation with another deer or some other disturbing threat that is being met with hostility. However, the hair of the entire rump patch and tail of mule deer may become erect—standing straight out when disturbed or running from a perceived threat—probably not at all unlike the hair on the back of our necks at times when we feel spooked.

Mule deer are aware of each other's appearance in the same way that we readily recognize and differentiate between familiar faces and strangers, even at a significant distance. However, I have seen mule deer respond to strange white-tailed deer at a quarter-mile as decidedly unfamiliar and unwelcome intruders, at which time the conspicuously odd interlopers are vigorously escorted out of the area. No such aggressive response is seen when unfamiliar mule deer enter the area. Clearly, however, where mule deer and whitetail ranges overlap, each species becomes habituated to the presence of the other, and all seem to live in at least apparent and perhaps superficial accord.

It could be said that mule deer are possessed of profound individuality in every way. Appearances are entirely unique, but, perhaps more significant, they display a remarkable range of behavior. Mule deer are characterized by wildly differing personalities, which might be expected in a population of intelligent creatures. Indeed, it is probably this continuum of variability in personality that has allowed me my rather intimate contact with the deer.

The possibilities seem endless. Even after almost seven years of direct interaction with these creatures involving more than two hundred individuals, I couldn't begin to characterize or describe a "typical" mule deer personality. I have known particular mule deer every day for six years who continue to be suspicious and will not approach closer than a few yards. Maybe these individuals have experienced some unforgivable horror at the hands of another human, and their trust can never be fully gained, or perhaps this is a particular personality type that can never allow close proximity to such a strange and potentially dangerous creature.

These personality peculiarities tend to run in families. Of course, it is difficult to say whether these characteristic family traits are inherited or they are being learned by example from the mother. However, while in close proximity to other deer, I have encountered presumably wild individuals, both bucks and does, who within two days have been not fearless but rather overwhelmed with the desire to have direct physical contact. I've observed this curious moment many times. A fearful, wide-eyed deer who has repeatedly approached within a few feet—and, again, almost always while I am surrounded by other deer—will suddenly soften its eyes, lower its head, momentarily flip its tail briskly, and then move into direct contact. In some cases these deer are overcome with an almost frantic or desperate need to sniff me all over, with a particular emphasis on the face, which always leaves me grinning. After fully investigating me, some newcomers are comfortable with a gentle hand to the neck and a little scratch; others will move momentarily back from my hand but immediately reapproach. Fear seems to be displaced by the strangely compelling and unlikely circumstances of the moment. This capacity by a definitively wild being is unusual in nature by any standard, and I continue to be amazed. I have observed this behavior often enough that I am convinced it can be explained by an almost insatiable curiosity. One unfortunate scenario would be, of course, that among those seemingly infinite number of personality types, there could be one dangerous buck who may one day choose to do me harm. And never underestimate the physical potential of mule deer does, for they can be formidable as well. Again I am reminded of Valerius Geist's warning about the possible danger of some particular buck, and of the unlikely ability of a human to divert such an attack. I heard him loud and clear. I remain vigilant. I have been scratched, clawed, bitten, gored, trampled, or otherwise injured by at least hundreds of different animals. But after a more cavalier youth and an uncommon measure of dumb luck, I no longer entertain long-term relationships with creatures that pose an immediate life-threatening risk. I have worked with potentially dangerous animals from all over the world—primates, including multiple species of baboons and mandrills; large cats, including cougars, African lions, and jaguars; not to mention at least three species of bears; various crocodiles; alligators; venomous reptiles of every description; and large constrictors—just to name a few. I know what it feels like to be attacked and seized by a cougar, and late one night while alone cleaning out a reptile enclosure at a zoo, an eighteen-foot anaconda tried to make a meal of me—I still wake up screaming in the night on rare occasions from that one. But, still, the animal that I probably have learned to fear the most, the one that is in my experience the most vicious, and will kill you without the benefit of ceremony—is a human-imprinted, male white-tailed deer. Certain "hand-raised" individuals, confused about their own sexual identity and yours, can be the sweetest, most gentle pet you would ever want to know—until they are three or four years old, and until the minute the velvet is rubbed off their antlers. Instantly, and without any warning, your gentle pet will attack you headlong from fifty feet away, running flat-out with head and antlers lowered. There are few weapons in nature more lethal than a white-tailed deer antler. A bottle-fed whitetail buck who one day returns in rut is a truly dangerous creature, and one of the few species that is known in the wild to occasionally, and without apparent provocation, attack a human. While employed at a deer ranching facility in the 1960s, I found that our European red deer stags could also be unpredictable and dangerous, especially when contained in an enclosure and overly familiar with humans. I was once attacked by a completely familiar Manchurian debowski and sika deer cross whom I had fed and handled every day for over a year. We had chosen Elmer as the superior "breeding buck" at the deer ranch, and had sedated and cut all the antlers off twenty other sika bucks in the herd. To prevent injury to the other bucks, we fortunately remembered to cut the tips off of Elmer's antlers as well, or he might have killed me. I have seen films of the North American elk or wapiti as they attacked humans and even cars, but those are cases where humans have a perpetually annoying relationship with individuals in parks and towns—the clearest case of "familiarity breeding contempt." Merely staring at a wild creature can be a disturbing affront, so tourists unknowingly but understandably pester and annoy many species simply by their uncontrollable admiration for an unfamiliar, fabulous animal. While working closely with a relatively large herd of elk at a ranching facility, and even while they were actively in the rut, I never had a bull elk even suggest that he might be aggressive toward me. But we always exercised at least a small amount of common sense, and maintained distances that would not make an eight-hundred-pound animal uncomfortable. You just don't try to scratch a large, mature bull elk on the head while he is visibly aggravated and preoccupied with the rut—even if he was your pal a month ago.

In seven years of intimate interaction with as many as two hundred mule deer, and although I always keep an eye out for that rare possibility, no mule deer buck has ever made the slightest aggressive gesture toward me—even during the peak of the rut. Several four- and five-year-old bucks will approach me for attention, and at this age their antlers loom higher than my head. A five-year-old mule deer is a big boy, and sometimes when one of these large bucks is next to my face, I will actually hold onto one of his antlers to prevent a tine from accidentally finding its way into my eye. At least up to this point in our various relationships, this has apparently never been seen as a provocation. Although there may be an outstanding exception, a relatively safe generalization would be that the mule deer buck is predisposed to have a gentle nature, but not necessarily so the whitetail.

CHAPTER THIRTEEN

High Society: Altruistic Does and Beneficent Bucks

Mule deer, like many herding species, are social creatures, and although they are in no way "herd-bound" like domestic sheep and cattle, they do have a complex social life around which their lives revolve. This deer society is defined primarily by the initial doe and fawn relationship and graduates to a more complex, multigenerational extended family of related or affiliated individuals. Females define the extended family groups, which are often characterized by several generations of does and their successive doe fawns. Buck fawns are initially members of the family groups but are forced away by the expectant mothers the following spring and summer. The yearling does are also forced away shortly before the mothers give birth. These young does, however, are allowed to remain close by—rejoining the mother in twelve weeks or so, as the new fawns become stronger and more independent and begin to follow the doe throughout the day. Related does from previous years may rejoin the maternal group as their fawns mature and the local herd is gradually reunited throughout late summer and fall. Often these herds consist of four or, in some cases, five or more generations of deer.

Although the herd connections can appear loose and poorly defined, they are in fact extremely well defined and strongly identified with a specific winter range. The wintering maternal groups of does, fawns, and bucks seem to be confined to a specific area or range of roughly one square mile. Various individuals from the herd are often dispersed into smaller groups within that range and may come together only at certain times during the day or only occasionally over the course of several days. Winter herd boundaries appear to be rigidly delineated, and although adjacent winter herds never seem to express territorial conflict, it is only under dire emergencies that these boundaries are ever breached, as if they have been drawn as a dotted line on some cosmic map. Furthermore, even though a winter herd may become widely dispersed throughout its range over a twenty-four-hour period, an awareness of everyone's proximity seems to be somehow maintained at all times. About once in a forty-eight-hour period, the entire herd—up to forty deer—will reunite as a group; the means by which this knowledge is being shared is a mystery to me. With the exception of roaming bucks during rut, there is very little social interest or curiosity shown between neighboring winter herds, but there is neither any apparent hostility nor aggression shown between these distinct groups. When on a rare occasion an enclave of strangers are possessed of some over-whelming curiosity with a neighboring herd, the visit is always brief, apprehensive, humble, and cause for little or no rancor. Soon the visiting strangers are satisfied, and off they return to more familiar quarters. These territorial obligations may be inflexible, as in the case of the whitetail, which in southern forests finds it impossible to abandon its home territory, even when the entire range has been decimated by clear-cutting and plowing or catastrophic fire. With fertile green in plain sight, these whitetails suffer or even starve to death rather than abandon their home range. I observed one mule deer winter range nearby that has been gradually overtaken by rural housing activities, and in spite of a patchwork of houses, fences, driveways, and dogs, the deer slowly slip into extinction rather than abandon their territory. When a winter herd ceases to exist, I have found that a sole survivor or two will join a nearby herd rather than languish in the agony of mule deer solitude. Over a period of weeks, these tentative individuals appear to be quietly welcomed without undue resentment or discord.

⧽⧼

Like does, males are largely faithful to a given winter range, and the same individuals will return year after year. Bucks retain long-term social bonds with the maternal herd, and these affiliations are distinctly more complex and interesting than simply the urge to mate. Some older and thus more dominant males may spend their rut in other territories, where there is perhaps less competition, but after the general chaos of the mating season has ended, they predictably return to their original winter herd of does, fawns, and bucks. They are immediately greeted by the other familiar males with only a minimum of ritualized posturing and the obligatory verification and reestablishment of status. Within twenty-four hours they are once again secure members of the herd. Within the winter herd, bucks prefer the company of other bucks. Occasionally, a solitary, mature buck will attempt to become attached to a herd with which he has no prior affiliation, and although he may be allowed to remain after weeks or even months of resentment by the other bucks, he is only allowed a "satellite" status. Most or all overt aggression may subside, but many of these bucks never become fully integrated into the brotherhood of resident bucks. However, with persistence, younger one- and two-year-old unattached antlered bucks may eventually achieve true affiliation with the greater herd.

When predators are active in the area, a winter herd will gather together and "herd" in the truest sense, apparently applying the "safety in numbers" strategy. Once pursued by lions, large packs of coyotes, or wolves, and, particularly if a herd member has been killed, the deer may actually disperse from the home range and take refuge miles away, only returning gradually in a day or two, once the coast is clear. Predator winter ranges tend to be large, so most are itinerate and seem to pass through the area only on a wide circuit. But with a variety and abundance of major predators in our area, it is a probability that some danger is never too far away.

By June, yearling bucks are no longer tolerated by their mothers, and an expectant doe may be seen in aggressive pursuit of her previous year's buck fawn. In fact, all young bucks in their first velvet are eventually persecuted by all the expectant, mature does, whereas the older, mature bucks are ignored or indulged, and even on occasion are casually allowed to inspect the newborn fawns. For a time I suspected that jealous yearling bucks must represent a threat to the mother's newborn. But, after many years of observation, I have never seen a buck of any age ever make an aggressive gesture toward a newborn fawn. It is interesting to observe the gentle and kind interest shown by the otherwise powerful mature bucks in velvet as they cautiously inspect a fragile, wobbly newborn. The little fawns may be seen fearlessly sniffing and examining the bucks with great interest. These early introductions may serve to help the new little strangers become integrated into the herd. But while the new mothers may seem to ignore the older bucks, they continue treating the one-year-old males with great hostility. The doe's pursuits may involve long distances and repeated blows to the young deer's backside as she may be seen chasing the confused juvenile for a mile or more. I have wondered if perhaps this behavior may serve to disperse males into new territory. This is the only possible inbreeding barrier that I have observed among mule deer. It all seems a pitiful development for the confounded young buck who is still entirely attached to his mother and repeatedly tries to return to the comfort of her side. However, if no replacement is born because of infertility or miscarriage, the young buck may immediately reestablish the bond with his mother, and they can retain a close doe-fawn attachment for yet another year. Even though the yearling buck is not always at his mother's side, he will maintain a consistent proximity, coming together with her throughout the day to rest or indulge in the occasional mutual grooming session. Young mule deer bucks are tentative and insecure and apparently derive great solace from their mother's attention.

But, typically, by late June, young males have gotten the message and keep company with other juvenile bucks. Although some of these young bucks will certainly return to their old home range during summer or fall, many seem to disappear into new areas and are never seen again.

❧❧

Most deer are seasonal migrants, and it could be said that by summer there is a somewhat even distribution of deer spread over hundreds of square miles of high country. Here they may raise fawns and avail themselves of ideal browsing conditions throughout the complex mountain ecology, including the rich and botanically diverse groves of aspen that surround the many lush mountain basins and their drainages. Predators no longer have the advantage of large, clearly visible herds of animals concentrated on the open windswept slopes and foothills, as they too are well dispersed and actively about the business of rearing young. And in spite of the migratory predisposition of many deer, there are certainly those groups of related individuals that remain sedentary at lower elevation the entire year and merely represent the predictable distribution of deer as determined by the carrying capacity of that particular habitat. Without the advantage of radio tracking collars, it is impossible to know how far some of the deer in this study group disperse. I believe that once a deer has been born in a particular location, it is biologically obligated and likely to return to the place of its birth to have its fawns, and no amount of encouragement or enticement can alter the urge. The migratory urge can be forestalled, but sooner or later, the deer is compelled to return. Those deer could be considered migratory obligates. But, again, one defining feature of mule deer behavior is that mule deer are definitively unpredictable, and not all mule deer are migratory—and not all migratory deer will be inclined to remain so. Just when you think you have the edge in understanding and predicting this animal's behavior, it will all fly in your face as the deer consistently do the unexpected. However, even a consistent lack of predictability is a pattern of sorts, so I have no doubt that their seemingly capricious behavior is one of their many finely tuned survival strategies. Life for a mule deer is a complex chessboard with no lines, few set rules, and one thousand pieces.

Mule deer are sensual, affectionate creatures, and grooming is an important component of mule deer society and certainly serves to reinforce family bonds and create new affiliations among the group. It is endearing to see two large, fully mature bucks with antlers engaging in this gentle social activity that would seem to satisfy any possible definition of true affection. Indeed, grooming is one of the tools I use to ingratiate myself to these affectionate creatures, and when they respond in kind and attempt to groom me in return, that is the moment when I realize they have come to accept me in some way as a member of their herd or family.

Mothers lavish attention on their fawns, spending much time licking and grooming them in an obvious effort to keep them clean and free of any external parasites. Interestingly, in a matter of weeks the behavior becomes reciprocal, and the fawn may be occasionally seen actually returning the favor to the doe. The grooming process obviously brings great pleasure to the recipient, as doe, buck, and fawn alike may be seen with sagging eyelids, in languid, peaceful bliss, being rhythmically groomed and nuzzled.

It is all too common for fawns to become orphaned throughout the summer, and I have found that even at four months of age, I can quickly habituate a fawn to my touch. Some orphaned fawns, by virtue of their mother's prior status, have clearly been born into privilege and are allowed to accompany other resident deer. But other orphaned mule deer fawns, even orphans from different years and different generations, tend to recognize their precarious situations and band together. Often forming their own family group, they may remain identified with one another for years. In many cases the presence of an unaffiliated orphan is not tolerated by the other does, and even on occasion the helpless fawn is brutally persecuted—possibly serving to keep a sick, unhealthy young animal with little chance of survival from potentially infecting other fawns. In addition, does are often resentful of any other fawn that comes sniffing around their udders looking to be nursed, and sadly a starving fawn will often run to the side of another lactating doe, only to be rebuffed. If an older fawn becomes orphaned, he can survive for periods of time, depending on how much natural browse he has begun to eat and whether he's been lucky enough to avoid a large predator. Mule deer mother's milk can average 20 percent protein, and the richest possible browse might contain 10 percent; however, in most cases, it will include much less. But all orphans become increasingly emaciated, riddled with parasites, and their survival chances decrease daily. Finally, in desperation, these older orphans display an irrational willingness to accept help from any source—including a caring human. Even when under constant persecution and attacks by other deer, these pathetic little individuals will languish on the periphery of any herd of deer in late fall and winter and are thus easily spotted. In rescuing a number of orphans at various ages and in various states of starvation, I have found that not only are they suffering from some lesser or greater degree of malnutrition and a high internal and external parasite load—they have also clearly become desperately touch-deprived. The attentive mother provides nourishment in many forms, and physical contact appears to be vital to the fawn's sense of well-being, both physically and emotionally. In just a day or two, an orphan fawn or twins (orphan twins tend to remain together) may quickly surrender to the touch of a nurturing human, with only the offering of perhaps some much-needed food and a few gentle words of encouragement. Often, within mere minutes of being touched, a fawn will relax in your arms, entering a state of almost unconscious bliss, when at long last it is being scratched and coddled; it is only then that it becomes clear that the little creature is only a walking skeleton, wearing a dry, brittle coat and riddled with ticks. In contrast, when handling fawns who are still associated with their mothers, it is clear that she has managed to keep her fawns immaculate, well filled out, and completely free of parasites. Ticks can be a source of great stress to all deer, and it is with obvious delight and even appreciation that they are removed. Thereafter the orphaned fawns—and even these "rescued" fawns that have grown into adulthood—continue to desire regular grooming sessions. It clearly serves to strengthen and reinforce our bonds over time. Older adult deer who are only rarely or never groomed by other individuals must feel some level of deprivation of this kind of tactile interaction and will now and then "ask" for an attention from me that always seems to elicit great pleasure and relief. If I stop the grooming session before the deer is satisfied, I may be pursued, nudged, or even pawed, and reminded that the deer has not had its fill. On more than one occasion I have seen a mature three- or even four-year-old heavily antlered buck in a semiconscious torpor as his aging mother from several years past once again grooms her very large fawn in the comfort of the warming morning sun. Mule deer affiliations can be strong and everlasting.

The Mule Deer Doe and Fawn

Within all species, certain specific characteristics are inherent, so generalizations can be made about common behaviors and the physiology that are peculiar to that group. Mule deer can certainly be categorized in this way, and, indeed, there are many defining attributes that distinguish *Odocoileus hemionus* from other deer.

And, as with the preponderance of living things, it is often females and the fundamental maternal affiliations that provide the nucleus around which the lives of the members of a species revolve. And, as social creatures, mule deer are most clearly understood in terms of the bedrock that females provide in establishing the family, the extended family, and ultimately the herd that is the foundation on which mule deer life is supported. In most well-organized societies, a structure must be provided, which is often based on a system of social stratification, defined in this case in terms of superior tendencies toward physical well-being and resilience in confronting the environmental stresses of disease, predation, geography, human interference, and weather. This success is most clearly demonstrated by the mere historical persistence of a female and her offspring through time and the consistent ability to produce successive adaptive and prosperous generations of young.

The mule deer doe hierarchy is more complex than the mere physical prowess and aggression that tend to define the social existence and status of the mule deer buck. Although does can be emphatic in expressing dominance toward other females or fawns within the group, it seems that they are not entirely reliant on mere physicality. Dominance can be achieved through more subtle phenomena and perhaps has much to do with the advantages of birthright. Clearly, the fawns born from dominant does are regarded with more respect and deference by the herd at large. In essence, some fawns, it appears, are simply born into privilege. Dominance may even be a poor choice of words to describe the society of mule deer does, as rank based on maternal affiliations may best describe mule deer authority. Even the highest-ranking doe, occupying a position of greatest respect, may not be particularly authoritative in her demeanor or personality.

I've been confounded by the high-ranking status of some females who lack any conspicuous tendency toward hostility and aggression. Furthermore, these individuals tend to go entirely unchallenged. Not uncommonly, when any perceived dispute arises, it is only the most subtle gesture of a raised chin that serves to immediately resolve the issue. Tempers seem to rarely flare toward a dominant female. In fact, with never a need to exercise her rank, it appears that a dominant doe may even become less aggressive over time. However, these same deer seem to be a focal point around which the greater herd revolves. These dominant deer may make decisions about movements and the times for involvements in various mule deer activities—resting periods, feeding activities, or traversing from one area to the next. A high-ranking doe quietly takes the initiative, and others follow. These experienced veterans—females who have throughout their lives encountered violence and terror—will on occasion confront a potential predator, bravely leading the less experienced and more cautious herd on a headlong charge directly into the face of certain danger—into the face of a predator clearly known by all deer to have killed their fawns or companions on other occasions with impunity. I have seen foxes, bobcats, badgers, and the more formidable coyote turn tail and run, as if fleeing for their lives, while twenty angry deer turn on the afterburners. Cases of coyotes being killed by mule deer have been documented. Mule deer are also known to viciously attack domestic dogs and cats. Recent research has helped shed light on these behaviors and even more extraordinary aspects of female mule deer life.

Canadian biologist Susan Lingle conducted an important mule deer study in Alberta. While capturing and tagging a large number of mule deer fawns ranging in age from newborn to two weeks, she recorded the predictable loud, bleating distress calls that were emitted by many fawns at the moment of capture. The high-quality recordings were played back under various circumstances to determine whether mule deer does could discriminate between their own fawns' vocalizations and any other mule deer fawns'. Whitetail fawns were also recorded to test the reactions of both whitetail does and mule deer does to these differing voices. The recordings were played back through hidden speakers, with observers concealed nearby. Mule deer does immediately responded to any fawn in distress and displayed aggressive behaviors toward the hidden speaker. It was also noted that whitetail does responded to whitetail fawn voices but not to mule deer fawns', and that the response lacked the intense aggression displayed by the mule deer. Furthermore, some whitetail does failed to respond altogether after their fawns were a few weeks old. Then, the question arose: were mule deer unable to recognize their own fawns' distress call from any others', or were they clearly going to the aid of any fawn, regardless of whose it was? In subsequent tests, Lingle made a discovery that would prove to be a stunning revelation. Mule deer does standing with their own fawn at their side would abandon that fawn and run to the aid of another fawn who was vocalizing distress in the distance. It appears not only that mule deer cooperate in aggressively attacking predators but, more significant, that the mule deer doe with fawns, or even a barren doe without a fawn, will immediately come to the aid of another female's helpless fawn. She will in fact put herself at great risk in the face of an attacking predator and, by implication, risk the life of her own fawn, should she succumb to the immediate threat she has chosen to confront. Mothers of many species will bravely attempt to defend their own young from danger, but to come to the aid of another parent's offspring is, by any measure, phenomenal, and rarely observed in nature, with the possible exception of elephants and some species of whales and dolphins. This represents true reciprocal altruism and has often been applied as one of the unique qualities used to define highly evolved societies. Human reciprocal altruism may merely take the form of one neighbor gladly helping another neighbor raise his barn, or, in more extreme cases, leaving your home and family and sacrificing your own life by charging headlong at a perceived enemy. To risk death by displacing one's own survival needs and instincts in favor of the welfare of another individual or the group—even at the expense of your own biological family—is an exceedingly rare occurrence.

I have observed bighorn sheep in cooperative pursuit, chasing a large predator down a high mountain pass for a mile or more. From the kitchen window of our ranch house, Leslye and I once watched a pregnant herd of Angus cattle that was spread over a broad hillside in deep snow suddenly band together at a gallop and chase a lone wolf up and across the far ridge and out of sight. And clear cases of other species cooperatively attacking a known predator are a relatively common occurrence. But reciprocal altruism within a herding species such as deer, where one female—even a female with a fawn at her side—is actually willing to abandon that fawn and perhaps sacrifice herself for another mother's offspring is seemingly outside the bounds of ordinary expectation. In our own human society, these extraordinary behaviors, occurring only on the rarest of occasions and demonstrating clear unselfish altruistic behavior, are honored and celebrated above all others.

⁂

Fawns in this area are born in a synchronized event lasting only a few weeks in June and into July. Because so many births occur simultaneously, mortality is limited by the sheer numbers of fawns, overwhelming predators' ability to consume so many newborn deer during this brief time of greatest vulnerability. Many mammals are born blind and helpless—with no knowledge of the world and entirely unable to feed or care for themselves. These species could be considered altricial and are represented by many familiar animals, including dogs, cats, rodents, various common species of birds, and, of course, humans. Although deer and other ungulates could be considered by any measure to be precocial mammals in terms of being born with the benefits of well-developed vision, hearing, vocalization, some innate understanding of the ways of the world, and the ability to walk and even run within hours of birth, small fawns are still essentially defenseless—at least for the first week. Newborns do not attempt to elude danger for the first few days of life and rely entirely on their spotted camouflage, an instinct to remain motionless and hidden, as well as a near-complete lack of any detectable scent. Mule deer mothers hide their newborns, returning periodically to nurse and groom them, but then again hide the newcomers and immediately leave the area. Once or twice a day, after a nursing session, the doe encourages the fawns to follow, leading them to a new location. People often find a well-hidden fawn and make the tragic mistake of trying to rescue an apparently "abandoned" newborn. Invariably the doe is within sight or hearing, and the fawns have actually been carefully abandoned by design. From a human's eye level, a well-concealed newborn fawn can be difficult to locate—even when you know with absolute certainty a fawn is near. With the largest nonhuman predator's point of view less than three feet above the ground, it would be possible to pass within inches of a fawn without detection. On occasion, bears may be seen standing tall on hind legs, attempting to locate a hidden fawn or elk calf. An aspiring predator is forced to "bird-dog" an area and must literally stumble onto a fawn in hiding. Grizzly bears in this area of Wyoming have been observed in apparent cooperation as they systematically crisscross a mountain slope in search of newborn elk calves. However, even with the advantages of camouflage and simultaneous births, as many as half of all fawns may be killed within the first two weeks of life.

Within the first few days of life, while in the more protective proximity of their mother, mule deer fawns are in fact quite bold, actively browsing and exploring their new world with vigor. Week-old fawns are surprisingly alert—they have opinions. They nibble and sample all manner of tender vegetation and investigate an almost infinite array of new sights and sounds. One of the most intriguing and surprising observations has been the acute attention paid by young fawns to any activity in their surroundings, and this even includes visual and auditory disturbances a quarter-mile away. On many occasions I have observed fawns react to an unidentified object or movement in the distance by immediately dropping with their chins on the ground. It could be said that the mule deer fawn is born with an intriguing level of maturity when it comes to recognizing the actual gravity of the life in which they find themselves. Clearly they are born with an almost insatiable appetite for knowledge—young mule deer are hungry to learn.

While in the company of their mother, even the youngest fawns display an independence and willful sense of self that I find fascinating, but also disturbing, as they wander, independently exploring about and occasionally even taking a high-speed romp across an open meadow or along the creek. In three weeks they are tearing about with complete

⌃ Blossom's surviving fawn, Rosebud, at 36 hours old.

abandon—especially when they are being provoked by another equally cavalier and trouble-making young mule deer fawn. Occasionally a doe may be seen displaying fear or concern for a fawn who has left her sight and trot out to corral the little tike along with its overabundant enthusiasm. But most does watch over these excursions tolerantly. Perhaps the advantages of developing phenomenal dexterity as well as an ability to make lightning-quick decisions outweigh any disadvantages such risky activities and exposure may present. Look into the eyes of any two-week-old mule deer fawn, and you may be surprised to find that someone is there looking back—and perhaps even asking far more relevant questions than you. Their intelligent and inquiring faces epitomize conscious expression.

An eight-week-old mule deer fawn is already well informed, bright, knowledgeable—savvy, one could say. By eight weeks, fawns are still not following the does throughout the day but no longer remain entirely hidden and still. They may be observed independently exploring in a more or less designated area, browsing about, and frequently interacting with other deer and fawns. It is phenomenal that by eight weeks, a young fawn not only has survived many life threatening situations but is already relying heavily on his own ingenuity and instincts. By sunset, however, does and fawns are reunited in a rather heart-warming ritual, involving much obvious excitement and vocalization on the part of the doe and the fawn. The mewing fawn responds and runs to the call of the doe with raised tail and is always rewarded by a session of vigorous nursing. Twins may even nurse with enough simultaneous enthusiasm to occasionally lift the doe's hindquarters completely off the ground. Certain does eventually find this aggressive nursing uncomfortable or outright painful, which may occasionally lead to weaning at an earlier age. Many fawns nurse until they are five or even six months old, although sessions become more abbreviated, having more to do with maintaining bonds than with satisfying nutritional needs. A frightened or confused fawn of advanced age often runs to his mother's side and places his head close to her udder in a gesture that implies a need for reassurance. Typically, after mother and fawns have been reunited in the evenings, the family will then maintain a closer proximity throughout the more hazardous hours of night.

It should be noted that fawns younger than sixteen weeks have very little chance of survival without the wisdom, nutrition, and protection of their mother. In a species such as the mule deer, which is in drastic decline all over the West and which has ceased to exist in many former ecologies, the value of a mule deer doe (and, of course, her fawn) is immeasurable. Yet, in much of the state of Wyoming, archery season begins on the first of September and lasts for many weeks. Sadly and inexplicably, the killing of does and fawns is still permitted. And many are killed not by legitimate hunters in ethical pursuit, but rather by "backdoor bow hunters" who gladly kill the convenient doe or fawn standing in the backyard. In the vast number of cases this mortality is never reported, and it is unnecessary to fill out a legal tag if the animal immediately disappears into the barn or garage for processing.

By the first of September, fawns range from eight to twelve weeks old. Most are a mere eight weeks. They are still small, may still bear spots, and are still fragile. These young animals have almost no chance of surviving without their mother at such a tender age. On only the rarest of occasions do any of the fawns of bow-killed does survive. A charitable estimate would be a 90 percent mortality rate for orphaned fawns between eight and sixteen weeks of age. I have closely observed the results of the early bow hunt on so many occasions that it robs me of sleep. I consider the doe-fawn management loophole to be a blind and mindless outrage. Any marginally unscrupulous individual can safely install a mule deer in the freezer as an annual bonus. And I know from direct observation that no rancher or landowner is likely to risk creating a lifelong enemy of a neighbor by "dropping a dime" on them for the sake of a lowly mule deer doe or fawn. Yet this all-too-common policy of turning a blind eye is helping tip the balance of the future of the mule deer. As go the doe and fawn, so goes the fate of the entire species.

⌃ Brizby was a doe killed illegally on opening day of whitetail season. Here she is nursing fawns in late October. Both fawns were dead within a month following her death.
Photo by Sammy Tedder.

The Mule Deer Buck

Most of the research data that has been presented regarding the mule deer as a species has naturally placed emphasis on the buck, because of the financial and sporting significance to government revenues and hunters. The mule deer buck is truly a beautiful and monumental creature, and it is easy to understand how it has achieved the status of "trophy" big-game animal. Unfortunately, however, it is almost unavoidable that the nonhunting public should dismiss this fascination as merely the small-minded male—or, more properly, *human*—obsession with all things large. And in defense of the nonhunting public, they are in many cases absolutely correct. However, the sensibilities that drive hunting in general are much more complex than that. For many reasons, it is easy to admire the magnificent mule deer

⌃ Boar in Autumn.

buck, and, regardless of your motives, I would say that not just many but most lifelong hunters of the mule deer ultimately come to realize a profound affection and connection that is much more significant than the urge to kill and hang the biggest and best on our wall.

Clearly the characteristic of the mule deer that many people initially find most fascinating are the antlers. And I must admit that there is something inherently compelling about deer, elk, and moose antlers. They can be merely interesting to some or an absolute obsession for others. I fall somewhere within the latter demographic. I've always had an overwhelming curiosity with antlers, and even as a small child I felt they possessed some magic when I found them in the field or forest.

In addition to an irresistible aesthetic, there is some indescribable quality, some resonating power that can clearly be felt by any human hand as it instinctively explores the rigidly defined organic shapes and curves of a large shed antler. To firmly grab hold and feel the powerful connection of this remarkable edifice to a living three-hundred-pound mule deer buck standing at your side is life-altering. Antlers are an architectural exercise in perfection, as form follows function, and could be considered a particular buck's most glorious embellishment and simultaneously its most dangerous weapon.

Until more recent times, human weapons were viewed not as mere tools, but perhaps elevated to the level and status of functional works of art, and in many cases even possessed great spiritual and mystical significance. Perhaps it is the paradoxical potential for either good or evil that can imbue an ordinarily functional tool with magical or supernatural properties. Weapons of all human civilizations have often come to represent objects of great beauty, possessing the most profound cultural and even religious significance. Invariably, weapons were made of the rarest and best materials by a people's most highly skilled and revered artisans—consequently becoming objects commonly held in the highest esteem when evaluating any culture's greatest contributions in both technology and art. Visit any world-class museum and observe these classic examples of the perfect objective function, inevitably resulting in the most perfect aesthetic form. Obvious examples include the paleo-hunter's finely sculpted flint blade, the Egyptian or Roman chariot, the ancient and complex art of sword making, and, of course, one of the ultimate artistic expressions combining the best of metallurgy, woodworking, a watchmaker's quality mechanics, and the sculptural symmetry and balance provided by individual artistic expression—the flintlock rifle of the early 1800s. One unlikely and perhaps disturbing example of advanced technological form combining to create one the most ironically beautiful manifestations of fearsome and destructive function would be the P-51 mustang fighter plane of World War II.

To her credit, Leslye is not a student of warfare. In her estimation, movies, books, or even historical documentaries that involve any aspect of human conflict reside somewhere on a continuum between unattractive to outright revolting. If such a film is on a television, she will, without judgment, quietly leave the room. Having always had an inexplicable fascination with the World War II "war birds," I recently convinced Leslye to accompany me to a Lander air show that was exhibiting and flying an all-original combat veteran, fully functional P-51. Leslye, on a whim, agreed to go, even though she wouldn't know a P-51 from an Evinrude outboard motor. We walked up to this unexpectedly magnificent phenomenon sitting on the tarmac in an almost unnerving contradiction of silent potential, and stared quietly with a few other onlookers. I looked over to see tears streaming down Leslye's face. Confused, I asked, "What's going on?" Her only reply was, "I didn't understand."

In this way it could be suggested that the ten-million-year evolutionary battlefield of *Odocoileus* has produced some of the most splendid examples of the "weaponized" aesthetic in all of nature.

After so many years I still spend many days in spring in pursuit of elk and deer sheds, and although I occasionally use antlers to fashion items such as coatracks and door handles, I am always satisfied to view them as freestanding natural works of art. However, this may be the first literary treatment of the deer's antler that does not focus on Pope and Young, Boone and Crocket, or any other fixation involving the rather boring quest for the biggest.

The blueprint for all antler development and structure is said to reside not merely within the growing bud of the antler, but rather as more of an architectural blueprint contained within the animal's central nervous system, and encoded in every deer's DNA. And, make no mistake—all "scientific" explanations notwithstanding—like the regrowth of a severed frog's leg or the development of a fetus from a single cell, antler growth is a truly mystifying phenomenon. Once cervid antler development is completed and the living velvet has dried and been rubbed away, antlers are no longer supported by nerves and a blood supply, and,

⌃ Buck in early velvet.

Velvet growth complete on a buck named Homer. »

⌄ Losing velvet in shreds.

unlike true "horns" that continue to grow, antlers are deciduous and must be shed and replaced each year. Replacement growth "in velvet" begins in late winter or early spring, soon after shedding the old, and is often completed in three or four months. It has been suggested (Murie, et al.) that antler growth in deer—with some species replacing thirty pounds of antler in three months—may represent the fastest development of dense structural biomass in the animal kingdom. Although it has been demonstrated that antler size, symmetry, and particular classic form constitute a visual social expression to other deer indicating the physical prowess and health of a particular individual, antlers are not principally ornamental. It is a rare buck who arrives in spring to shed antlers that are still fully intact.

Buck deer antlers function as large weapons and conspicuous signaling devices, but their size is not necessarily an all-important feature. Although does may see large, healthy antlers as signs of good nutrition and a genetically superior deer, among competitive bucks, the deer with the biggest antler probably garners no more attention than any other similarly large-antlered deer. The nature of the competition for size is probably more peculiar to *Homo sapiens* than to members of the family *Cervidae*. No buck has ever had a concept of how his particular antler might compare to any other, because no deer has ever seen the particular device that resides on his own head and how it may compare to any other. Mule deer bucks are much more interested in the magnitude of the indomitable spirit that animates a potentially great deer.

Frequently people observe bucks sparring and shoving each other around with antlers engaged, and then mistakenly assume that these deer are "fighting" and being aggressive. To the contrary, this familiar interaction is in fact an integral component of male mule deer social life and could be said to be more associated with recreation, brotherly bonding, and even affection. In every case, these bucks are herd members who have had longstanding relationships, and the dominance issues involving superiority or competition were probably resolved in previous years as fawns and yearlings. Sparring is normally a courteous, almost gentle affair that involves a degree of deference and respect, as two familiar bucks may be seen carefully engaging their antlers so that neither is in jeopardy. Commonly, some strenuous pushing may eventually be involved, but when either buck begins to feel uncomfortable with the escalating hostility, one or the other will disengage and, then, in a gesture of courtesy, look away. More often than not, any escalating emotion is playful, and disengagement may result in both males bucking and

A subordinate buck, Crusty,
asking Boar to engage
in some brotherly sparring. »

Massive Boar agrees. »

Sparring concludes and bonds
have been gently reinforced. »

stotting around in gestures that look like the two are having great fun. Bouts of sparring are often the result of a solicitation or request by one individual and the acknowledgment and acceptance by the other. Sparring sessions often occur between differing ages of bucks and among bucks of differing social standings. It is endearing to see a yearling buck or even a buck fawn solicit the most powerful dominant deer and receive the kind and indulgent favor of acceptance as the master buck ever-so-gently allows the young deer to engage with his great head.

❧❧

Buck deer have a perfect sense of the exact locations of the tips of their antlers and will occasionally employ an antler tip delicately to an itch on their rump or gently remind nearby fawns or does to respect their space. On occasion, a buck will quietly approach me from behind, and I will feel an almost delicate touch of an antler tip against my back as a 275-pound leviathan lets me know that he wishes his presence to be acknowledged.

Most male deer have a desperate desire to breed females. However, most of those bucks draw the line at the possibility of grave injury or death to fulfill that goal. But there is that occasional full-grown master—and, yes, probably even one without the largest set of antlers—the one great individual with an indomitable spirit who is, without any question, willing to die today—this minute—for that one opportunity. The vast majority of buck deer or bull elk, upon encountering a willing spirit with that level of commitment, immediately realize that, while reproduction is a wonderful thing, today is probably not the day. That is the revelation that is repeated in a thousand minor deer and elk skirmishes every day. However, on that most rare occasion when two uncompromising personalities collide in battle, the unmitigated power discharged gives the more reticent human mind pause. So, as humans, we are humbled in the midst of our own inevitable and definitive ambiguity, and left only to admire or even envy this unfamiliar resolve—a resolve unleashed with absolute moral authority.

❧❧

⌃ Bucks showing true aggression.

With massive body proportions, a rut-swollen neck, and a magnificent head literally crowned in a lethal weapon, it is easy to incorrectly conclude that the mule deer buck is not just a formidable and intimidating fellow, but possibly an altogether violent and dangerous one as well. Indeed, on occasion, the mule deer buck is capable of a physicality and brutality that is almost unimaginable to most of us, in both the sheer power unleashed, and the unambiguous and immediate willingness to die. Lasting for only three tedious weeks, the rut is relentless, exhausting, and, for the most part, no damn fun for anybody. Bucks are rarely killed in fights but often suffer serious puncture wounds, and blindness is a common occurrence, as a sharp antler to the eye is nearly always unforgiving. Broken antlers can be seen on almost every competitive deer, and broken bones can even occur now and again. During the fall of

2012, we had three dominant bucks who were at least partially blind in one eye. Needless to say, an injury to both eyes is a death sentence.

Bucks are driven to distraction and can easily lose twenty hard-earned pounds a week as they struggle for days without food or rest. Does are pestered and aggravated. However, when actually settling on a mate, a buck and doe occasionally spend a congenial day or so together before the male is off to the next exhausting obsession that could be waiting somewhere out there in the sage brush. Mule deer bucks do not maintain a harem as bull elk do; rather, they just try to keep competitive males confined to a more peripheral status. During that period when a dominant buck is attending to a particular doe, various other does in the herd may become receptive simultaneously, and the rut then becomes more democratic as other males have opportunities to mate. Sometimes a doe may favor a certain male who has no seniority or authoritative status among the other males. He may just merely suit her fancy. Although the final preliminaries to mating can be somewhat flirtatious and coquettish on the part of the doe, with much pawing and head rubbing, the consummation appears to be a perfunctory affair, lasting less than a second.

As we observe the complex and convoluted reproductive behavior of many species, it is hard to see the biological advantages, and often these behaviors even seem to possess elements of the absurd. What can possibly be gained by the finest specimens of a species fighting to the death or achieving a state of irreparable and often fatal malnutrition and exhaustion? Why would we continually lose our finest bull elk and finest mule deer bucks as they become more vulnerable to the elements of starvation, disease, and predation? It is a well-substantiated fact that mortality is disproportionately high among those fine bucks and bull elk who have had rigorous and dominant breeding seasons, and they are much more likely to succumb to the hardships of winter than are females or subordinate males. The unavoidable but seemingly illogical message appears to be that the opportunity to mate once or, better yet, to be dominant for a single season is a fair biological exchange and worth the price of one's life. It is easy for us to look at these bizarre and apparently maladaptive aspects of reproduction with sad fascination as we remark on the apparent waste and foolishness of a thoughtless animal. But, of course, in this case, the most applicable of all anthropomorphic analogies is human sexuality—it is the one thing that makes fools of presidents, kings,

⌃ Babe visiting the doe Brizby.

religious leaders, politicians, judges, and common folk alike: it is perhaps the ultimate source of all our undoing, regardless of species. Replication is the strongest and most powerful imperative in biology, often transcending both the instinctive and the conscious will to survive. Ultimately, it appears that we are all primarily obligated, like the salmon, to swim inexorably upstream toward the individual fate that awaits us.

However, even though the mating and procreative experience is vital to mule deer, it occupies only a brief window of time in the life of these creatures, and the vast majority of their lives is spent in other pursuits and activities. Historically, observers may have overestimated the significance of the reproductive process as a component within the social life of this animal; there's a lot more to mule deer society than their simple need to procreate.

Mule deer mating season lasts just three weeks, and by mid-December, they've put an end to it and moved on.

In contradiction to all the frenetic activity of the mating season—all the aggression and hostilities—the mule deer buck is in fact a stolid and placid individual who is conservative in his activities, wishing only to live a peaceful and quiet existence among a few agreeable affiliates, and for most of the year, in fact, bucks are much less inclined toward rancor and hostilities than are their female counterparts. Bucks are quietly respectful of one another, perhaps because they have learned difficult lessons about the expense of violence and the disadvantages of animosity. Commonly, an enormous deer who was soundly defeated in battle and suffered severe injury will never recover emotionally from the trauma and thereafter will always abstain from hostilities with any other deer. All mule deer bucks bear the physical and emotional scars of enmity.

By the first of March, if mule deer bucks have survived the rigors of breeding and the subsequent exhaustions of winter, they begin losing their antlers. Older bucks tend to shed

⌃ Observing the rut. Photo by Dawson Dunning.

antlers slightly earlier than younger bucks do, and the suspected initiators of shedding include factors such as physical well-being, length of day, and the reduction in blood levels of certain hormones—especially testosterone. Having observed the shedding process and recorded specific shedding dates of particular deer over successive years, I have found it interesting to note that a particular shedding date of a buck is not a predictor of shedding in any other year. The date may vary by as much as a month. A buck in physical distress may shed earlier or retain his antlers weeks longer than other more healthy deer do. Reduced blood levels of testosterone and slow protein anabolism encourage resorption of bone at the zone between the cranial protuberance called the pedicel, and the actual antler, creating an interface that eventually separates the antler from the skull. Antlers rarely drop simultaneously, and it may take days for a second antler to fall. Large buck deer and especially large bull elk experience severe discomfort and disapproval with the loss of the first antler, which often comes as a great surprise, startling the animals when the drop occurs. They are immediately made aware of the strange and awkward asymmetry as powerful muscles are suddenly sent into spasm with the new and sudden imbalance. Veteran older bucks or bulls may immediately set about dislodging the remaining antler to relieve the stress. This is often the case when both shed antlers are found lying close by. Some individuals, usually younger males, may endure and adjust to the imbalance for hours or many days. Bucks are profoundly aware of their antlers, which, beyond mere weaponry, serve as prestigious visual reinforcements to their well-earned positions of status or authority. Bucks recognize, respect, and even fear the sight of a particular deer, not necessarily because of the size of his antlers, but because of *who* might be wielding them. Upon dropping his antlers, a buck's relative status within a group of other bucks may hit the ground simultaneously, and clearly bucks are made resentful by their sudden vulnerability. With heads lowered and ears back, they become visibly worried and unhappy, and without question they are experiencing a grave disappointment that appears almost pitiful on occasion. Vendettas and old grudges that may have been percolating for months are now expressed as a subordinate buck with a lower status may grab the opportunity to express a little dominance and "herd" the recently humbled affiliate around for half a day. It is not uncommon to see a young spike or fork-horn showing a little arrogance to another buck who is two years older and heavier by fifty pounds. But this same

≽ Chip suffering the price of enmity.

spike may eventually get a sound and probably well-deserved trashing, even from a dominant doe, when he sheds his antlers.

However, dominant herd bucks—master bucks—although normally characterized by a gentle nature are, nevertheless, prideful creatures, loath to relinquish their superior and hard-won positions of authority. On one rare occasion, I observed such a master buck, with fresh blood dripping from the sockets of newly shed antlers, as he responded to the aggressive confrontation of a large but subordinate buck who was still sporting a full complement of well-developed weapons. With no possible protection, the master buck roared and initiated a full-blown death charge, hitting the deer broadside with such power and abandon that the subordinate buck was slammed backward and completely upended. The master buck was unharmed and walked away without an apparent scratch—unlike his unfortunate but heavily antlered opponent. A visible shudder of recognition went through the small audience of attending bucks, myself included, and no other attempt was made to question his absolute authority. Humility reigned supreme that day.

I have directly observed the shedding event on only two occasions—in other words, actually saw an antler hit the ground. On a third occasion, I happened to see a drop or two of fresh blood at the base of an antler belonging to Babe, then a four-year-old dominant buck. With a horse cookie in one hand as an inducement, I grabbed hold of the bloodied antler and gave it a little tug, and, to my great surprise, with a slight "click"—not a snap—it fell off in my hand. Babe found this sensation disturbing, and he ran a few feet away and looked back with curiosity and perhaps a certain level of disapproval. As he methodically shook his head and remaining antler

⌃ The author giving Babe's antler a tug.

« Shedding the first antler.

« Shedding both antlers.

« Stumpy examining his shed antlers.

slowly from side to side, I held out the antler, and after he assessed that nothing untoward had occurred, he came over, gave it a sniff, and casually walked away with apparent disinterest.

On multiple occasions I have tried to elicit some level of recognition or any indication that a buck might find a freshly shed antler interesting or possessed of some significance. Mule deer bucks commonly view a shed antler—either theirs or another's—with complete indifference. In contrast, I have seen antlered elk attempt to spar vigorously with a shed elk antler lying on the ground.

The following morning, Leslye noticed that Babe was completely antlerless and was able to recover the mate by backtracking his path up to the house through the snow. She walked to the bottom of the draw and followed a few splatters of fresh blood, and there was the antler.

When antlers are shed, they typically leave bloody sockets perhaps a quarter-inch below the level of the hairline. Blood may dribble down the sides of the buck's head for an hour or so, and occasionally a deer's bed may be found, either in snow or open ground, with a significant puddle of blood. But within six hours the sockets are completely dry, except in freezing temperatures, when fresh blood may freeze bright red until it can thaw and dry. Initially, however, the holes left by the shed antlers look like gaping wounds, and it is a little disconcerting to look down onto a deer's skull. In a day or so, the sockets have scabbed over level with the hairline and no longer look like nasty injuries. In a matter of weeks, and corresponding to an increased level of testosterone in the blood, the antler bud begins to swell. In another month, the tender velvet antler has grown a few inches, and the buds of branching divisions become visible. At this time the antler feels warm and "velvety" in the truest sense. As the antlers begin to branch and bifurcate, they are already surprisingly rigid, although they are at all times vulnerable to disfiguring injuries. Older bucks in particular seem to be aware of the growing antler's vulnerability and are noticeably guarded and protective as they navigate carefully around trees, rocks, brush, fences, and other similar bucks. Naturally, each successive set of antlers reflects the original, individual architecture of that particular deer, and a comparison of sheds from previous and successive years are clearly identifiable as belonging to a specific buck. But there may be significant differences in form beyond the predictable addition of mass as the individual matures and grows larger. Surprising differences can still occur from one year to the next, and an individual who had typically symmetrical antlers but with many incidental ancillary (or supernumerary) points in his fourth year may have predictably larger antlers the following year in the same "typical" form, but with no smaller ancillary points. Small mule deer brow tines have a tendency to come and go from year to year as well. So, a perfectly healthy buck may have a total of twelve or fourteen points one year and the following year have much larger antlers, but with only the typical five on each side. Often, however, some small peculiarity on an antler may be evident on a particular deer year after year.

The aging process and antler development in deer have been studied in great detail, and all healthy deer seem to experience a progression of larger and better developed antlers as they achieve adulthood. Antler growth and development tend to reach a peak in size and symmetry as the animal reaches his prime, and may then begin to wane in size and symmetry as the animal starts to age. In many populations of mule deer, the prime years may vary between seven and nine years, although in populations under ecological stress, this peak in development may occur as early as five or even four years. Indeed, it appears that some individuals in this population are starting to show some regression in overall antler development by their fifth year. However, it has been suggested that mule deer bucks can continue to grow throughout their entire lives, so antlers may continue to become more robust and massive, especially around the base, even though they may have less length in the beams and may have begun to lose some of the more distal bifurcation, resulting in fewer points.

Typically, yearling bucks will either grow a pair of "spikes"—an unbifurcated antler in the first year—or display a single bifurcation, known commonly as a fork-horn. Perhaps a third of yearlings will include a minor third tine on one or both of their first antlers. Contrary to popular belief, this initial configuration is no indicator of future antler growth in any individual, and absolutely no predictor of a deer's possibility as a future "trophy." Some landowners or hunt clubs "cull" their yearling spikes in a mistaken effort to improve their gene pool, when in fact they may well be culling out their potentially best deer. Indeed, long ago

⌃ Panda as a yearling. He's now an older deer, but still continues to shed his antlers in early
October, a month prior to the rut.

I was involved in an ongoing nutritional study in a large sample of five different species of deer that demonstrated that the configuration of the first antler was no predictor of future development.

Additionally, there has been a misplaced emphasis on selecting for genetically superior deer based on "apparent" antler size, when in fact an overwhelming body of research has demonstrated that "trophy" deer, elk, red stag, and so on are far-and-away determined by, and the result of, outstanding nutrition, with less correlation to so-called "superior genetics." That rare trophy deer, in most cases, is not a genetic anomaly but merely a healthy deer who, through ingenuity and luck, somehow managed to live into his prime. I would suggest that

❧ Stinky.

many lifelong hunters in this area of the West may have never actually seen a fully mature mule deer who has reached his prime. Most of the "monster" bucks that people report are simply those few individuals who have defied the odds and lived to be fully mature four-and-a-half-year-olds. If the superior genetics approach had validity, all deer would be exceedingly small and inferior, as the *apparently* finest deer are always selected out of the gene pool based on their trophy characteristics. In any given population, world-class nutrition will produce a world-class deer almost every time.

Three years ago, two gentlemen of advancing age who had received permission to hunt the adjacent ranch every year for more than two decades killed a deer just below our house. Hearing the shot, I walked with heavy heart to the location and introduced myself to the two. Brothers from out of state, they seemed like nice older men. Strangely, my only real recollection of the two, as they carved away on this deer, was how delicate and soft their hands appeared to be and how incongruous that seemed in this context. They politely asked if they might drive through my property to retrieve their deer, which was by now gutted and cut in half just behind the ribs. I saw that the two were already shaky and exhausted, and might not be able to climb out of the draw with a large deer, much less drag it to their distant vehicle. I said that they could drive around through our property and offered to help them load the buck. In an hour they were backing their pickup through the sage brush and in close to the deer. As we heaved the two halves into the truck, they described how they were lucky to break his pelvis with the first shot at three hundred yards, and then one of the men commented, "In twenty years this sure is the biggest deer I have ever killed. How old do you think it is—five, six?" I said, "I have known this deer since he was a spotted fawn. His name was Stinky. This was only his third set of antlers—I have all his previous antlers at my house."

CHAPTER FOURTEEN

The World as Perceived by a Mule Deer

Making Sense of Scents

Scent and olfactory reception are among the most ancient and highly evolved biological systems, as molecular information is transferred from one individual directly into the central nervous system of another. Scent is an important component of mule deer social life, and it could be considered another means of communication involving a complex vocabulary, as vital information is conveyed and received throughout the herd. Both bucks and does have similar external scent glands that are used to express individuality and social status, as well as physical well-being, sexual prowess, and reproductive status. Of the mule deer's many glands, the most conspicuous are the tarsal glands located on the inside of the hocks and the metatarsal glands that run longitudinally outside and below the tarsal gland over the rear cannon bones. Both tarsal and metatarsal glands are covered with hairs that trap pheromones and convey information from one individual to the next. Although conspicuous, the longitudinal metatarsal gland may be largely vestigial but retains the specialized hair. In both sexes, the tarsal gland is "urine-rubbed," meaning that the deer crouches and urinates on the hocks, which undoubtedly serves a significant role in mule deer sexuality. However, the tarsal gland also serves to express information throughout the entire year, even among fawns, so the significance appears to be much more complex than for mere reproduction. Glands are also located between the toes, known as "interdigital," and may serve to mark certain geographical pathways and perhaps even the individuals who have used those pathways. Small, gender-specific

glands located along the base of a buck's antlers are useful in disseminating information, as the whitetail delicately leaves his mark above his "scrape" on an overhanging twig the diameter of a toothpick, or the mule deer may leave his mark on a well-rubbed trunk of a small tree or shrub. I have often noticed that freshly shed whitetail antlers have a distinct musky odor around the rosette—the burr or base—where it intersected the hairline, and this scent lingers for about twenty-four hours after shedding. Having retrieved hundreds of freshly shed mule deer antlers, some within seconds of falling, I have never been able to detect any noticeable scent.

The various external glands of mule deer may be expressed individually or in concert. The tarsal gland in particular can be quite pungent and strong, even to the human nose, especially during the rut when bucks are making their most overt olfactory displays. However,

⌃ A buck urine rubbing his tarsal glands during the rut.

females also emit strong tarsal gland scents at other times and in other social settings that have no apparent reproductive significance. It even appears that, on occasion, these scents can be mysteriously expressed in an instant, and then in another instant the scent disappears, almost as if an aerosol had been emitted that was not captured in the specialized hair surrounding the glands. Although all deer are fastidious and constantly lick the tarsal gland clean, mature bucks in rut allow urine to remain on their tarsal glands and therefore can retain a more pungent scent for the duration of the breeding season. Fawns are inclined to urine-rub their tarsal glands, and does are careful to constantly groom the fawns' hocks to reduce scent. Young bucks also keep their tarsal glands spotless. Though their scents can be quite musky and distinctive at certain times, they're not as strong as those of a buck in rut. Most of the time mule deer emit no detectable scent to the human nose. And if the unlikely opportunity arises to bury your face between the ears of a friendly mule deer, you will discover that, like most healthy wild animals, the deer has a very pleasing, clean, warm scent, bearing no similarity or relationship to the musky scent glands.

Located at the inside corner of the mule deer's eye, where the lachrymal gland would be located on a human, there exists a small slit that runs down from the eye toward the muzzle and forms the opening to the pre-orbital gland. Common to cervids and other artiodactyls, this gland is found on both sexes of mule deer and may be opened or "expressed" in an array of contexts, including various states of excitation involving curiosity, fear, aggression, and perhaps even pleasure. Although clearly related to a broad spectrum of important emotional states and social functions that have been explored by many observers, the true significance of this organ remains poorly understood, if not altogether misinterpreted. With the provocation of some stimulus, an almost invisible line at the interior edge of the eye opens into a roughly oval, pinkish orifice an inch in diameter that can correspond with fright and caution, or, on another occasion, may precede and accompany a bout of violent, aggressive hostility. When in the company of dominant bucks, especially during the rut, I always keep an eye on the pre-orbital glands of nearby individuals to assess the mood of a possibly agitated deer. When competing bucks engage in serious fighting, the pre-orbital glands of both combatants may be seen widely flared, and it could be inferred that these "glands" probably have some profound visual significance and act as signaling devices in addition to any transmission or reception of olfactory information. Unlike the glands of bighorn sheep, the pre-orbital glands of healthy mule deer do not seem to produce a scented discharge. In fact, by rubbing my finger down the hairline covering the opening to the pre-orbital gland, I can detect no significant scent on my finger, either before, during, or immediately after the gland is open. And, by the way, never attempt the same experiment on the tarsal or metatarsal gland, as a mule deer may "cow-kick" you in the face with tooth-shattering force if your touch comes as a surprise! The pre-orbital glands in bighorn sheep clearly serve as true secretory glands that produce or express a readily discernible waxy, scented discharge that is used for marking. However, this gland on wild sheep is entirely superficial, confined to the thick hide, with little or no apparent involvement with the bone below—not even a small vascular foramen. In stark contrast, the underlying skeletal structure in the nasal bone and maxilla directly beneath the pre-orbital gland of mule deer provides a large, almost gaping access to an extremely complex sinus labyrinth connecting directly to the sensitive membranes surrounding the convoluted nasal turbinates, as well as direct pathways to the olfactory bulbs of the brain. These glands must be important, considering the extraordinary risk of severe cranial injury and infection that this opening presents on the face of an animal that fights with penetrating weapons on its head. Indeed, on numerous occasions I have observed bull elk and buck mule deer suffering persistent necrotic infections of a pre-orbital gland after a foreign body or pathogen had been introduced during combat. Once established, these infections may persist for years or even throughout the life of the animal.

It appears that the pre-orbital glands in deer may serve as more of an information receptor than a true secretory gland of expression, implying that they are not true glands at all. It should also be noted that both does and bucks may flare their pre-orbital glands when experiencing pleasure, as, for example, when an otherwise inaccessible itch is being scratched. Rather than facilitating mere primitive responses to stimuli, these functions may pertain more to abstract communication and expression, involving those subtle elements of emotion, including fear, aggression, insecurity, pleasure, or the recognition of individuality. Because of the difficulty in studying this type of elaborate animal communication, it may be impossible to quantify the more conscious experience of a species. We humans are often left only guessing.

Dogs literally "see" the world through their noses and gather a similar degree of complex information about their surroundings. But dogs not only smell in the same three dimensions that we enjoy with human vision; they can probably also smell with great temporal accuracy into the past and simultaneously explore a fourth dimension of time. We can only clearly see that a deer track is not fresh, whereas a dog probably knows without question whether a particular track is two hours or two days old. Perhaps in imagining the significance of scent in the lives of other creatures, we would be better informed by looking toward the science of linguistics for encouragement and understanding.

Deer Speak

Many people are surprised to hear a mule deer's voice, but in fact these deer are quite loquacious. In any ordinary mule deer herd, you may hear frequent vocalization. However, these voices are ordinarily quite subtle and can only be heard from a few meters away. Mule deer have an interesting repertoire of vocalizations, and it could be safely said that they in fact have a vocabulary of sorts.

Most mule deer vocalizations are variations of a simple nasal-sounding "wheh" that may vary greatly from one individual to the next. Some voices in does may be a deeper "uhhh," and, although seemingly of a modest volume, they send a fawn running to its mother's side from a great distance. Or, the same sound might be from a frustrated but optimistic buck repeatedly pleading to some despondent doe for attention. Mule deer have hearing that clearly borders on the supernatural, but often these calls are emitted at what seems to me to be a relatively low volume, yet the fawn may respond from a distance of a quarter-mile. Often the simple "wheh" is an expression denoting the need for acknowledgment and perhaps a solicitation toward some need that is not being met. It could also represent some mild level of frustration. If I am known to have a deer wafer in my pocket, which is often the case, and I fail to acknowledge or return eye contact to an individual who would like some recognition, either fawn, mature doe, or buck may suddenly make a frustrated plea of "wheh," accompanied often by a brisk upward nod of the head—as if to imply, "Hey—can you not clearly see me?" If this fails to gain my attention, I might get a gentle hoof to my backside or a good nudge and rubbing from a fuzzy head on my hip.

⌃ The buck Stumpy greeting the author with a nod.

Many vocalizations have to do with various levels of discord that often arise in the group. Trespassing on one's space is cause for some level of censure, which may involve a few brisk whacks to the backside, accompanied by a few staccato grunts that help reinforce the gravity of the perceived trespass. When individuals stand and face one another on hind legs with violently striking hooves, their voices can be exceedingly loud and seem to correspond in volume and intensity to the level of anger and violence. These events, whether between bucks or does, always remind me that this level of viciousness could be devastating if directed toward a human. Often bucks in territorial conflict will emit similar huffing barks like the does, but the larger, resonating bodies and the degree of anger can make the vocalizations much more impressive, but these sounds should not be confused with the territorial rut roar. The bellowing, roaring voices and the savage aggression of an all-out confrontation between two dominant, warring bucks, with mud, snow, and fur flying and with the ear-splitting crack and clatter of massive antlers, make for a spectacle of truly monumental proportions. These mercifully rare fights are testimony to the true power of this animal. I am always inspired to just stand back and move away slowly.

The fawns are the most predictably vocal of all the deer and often may be heard calling to their mothers when they suddenly feel vulnerable or abandoned. They will vocalize repeatedly with one of the most heart-wrenching sounds in all of nature. With an almost irresistible, high-pitched, pleading "mew" that would soften the most hardened heart, they plaintively and repeatedly call until mother returns with her "come-to-me" call, and the pitiful little waif runs to its mothers side with tail raised high and wagging. One of the most

≽ Elvin, always a sick fawn, seen here vocalizing with the author.

heartbreaking experiences of my life has been listening to the inconsolable calls of a fawn or pair of fawns as they cry for days and nights for a mother who has been killed. It is most horrible when the fawns are still young and spotted, but fawns often continue nursing and remain completely attached to their mother for many months after spots have disappeared. Even these older fawns in fall and winter will wander for days calling and searching for their lost mothers. Furthermore, a fawn in mortal distress, whether somehow trapped or captured by a predator, will discharge a bloodcurdling, shrill cry that can be easily heard for half a mile. When I hear that sound, I always instinctively grab a rifle and go on the run, and there is no room for negotiation.

As a human observer who has in essence made himself a member of this group and interacts in close—even hands-on—proximity, I am constantly, and by design, pushing the possible boundaries of human and wild mule deer interaction. The deer let me know when I have gone past their obligatory boundaries, and I quickly correct my inappropriate behavior—so far with no apparent cause for resentment in any individual. In previous relationships with other species, I have made a concerted effort to avoid ever using my human voice, but not so with mule deer. I do find that they have the capacity to comfortably relate to my voice in fascinating ways. For example, I have always found it interesting that mule deer clearly learn and know their names.

As soon as we named the first deer, Rayme, she recognized it and responded. We soon realized that others had the same predisposition. They clearly had some capacity for this form of individual recognition and identification. So, I began to demonstrate over and over again that within a browsing group of thirty deer, I could call, "Rag Tag!" or some other deer's name, and, in almost every instance, Rag Tag or the other individual in question would look up inquisitively and amble over to my side, at which time I might offer her a little grooming or perhaps a cookie. In a few minutes she might lose her fascination with my company and begin browsing at my feet. Another strangely interesting and mysterious observation that occurs without fail is the response to my voice in times of fear. If one deer suddenly startles for any reason, all the other deer will respond with some level of panic, and the deer may all run and scatter. This response is rarely from the stimulus of a charging mountain lion, for example—but that is always a possibility—so the level of response is obligatory and completely appropriate as an important survival strategy. No deer stands around questioning why another deer is so upset. But, more often, it is merely a reaction to someone—deer or human—accidentally slipping on the ice or some other clumsiness that created an involuntary stir. If I perceive that the source of the fright was not caused by a real danger, I can actually quell their fear and stop their flight with a few words. A simple "it's OK, girls" will often conclude the drama, and everyone will immediately reassemble and relax, as they clearly recognize that their reaction was not based on a real threat. And not uncommonly, of course, I was the sole source of the clumsy or awkward thing that created the turmoil in the first place. Similarly, if I approach a particularly shy deer who has always been uncomfortable with my proximity, and this individual is clearly starting to become disturbed and bordering on panic, I can simply say something like, "It's all right, girl, it's just me," gain her eye, and then look away—and immediately it has a calming, reassuring effect. In almost every case, the deer will turn and face me, and the eyes will soften. Then, to show that she is convinced, she also will look away. Of course, deer do not understand human language, but, without a doubt, they tend to derive some meaning from the context and tone of my words. These deer are clearly consoled by my voice, but, more important, they are attentive to any possible meaning and appear to make associations with specific words. In our interaction with dogs, for example, we find nothing extraordinary about associations and responses to the human voice. However, dogs have been bred for thousands of years to pay attention in this way. Accounting for these traits in a wild mule deer is an intriguing mystery as I question the origins or advantages of this obvious ability.

Of Space and Species

Most social animals possess a clearly defined sense of space, and even though instinct often demands that these organisms remain in close proximity, that proximity may be rigidly defined, and each animal is expected to respect the individual space of the other. When any deer's space is violated, she becomes noticeably uncomfortable, then, often with a raised chin, perhaps with ears pinned back, she warns the offender. If this gentle reminder is insufficient, a lurch forward with a raised front leg will often send the offending deer back into its rightful space. Any deer's butt in your face is deemed unacceptable and regardless of status is cause for a brisk whack across the offending derriere. And, in almost every such instance, regardless of rank, the offending doe, buck, or fawn always politely and with a sudden leap surrenders that space without a resentful glance back. Clearly, it is an innocent mistake and not a deliberate affront. Young, unsocialized fawns are constantly reprimanded with a stern hoof across the backside or between the ears as the herd passes the rules of mule deer etiquette from one generation to the next. However, when two deer of similar rank seem to find their proximity in dispute, and often when a desirable food is in contention, hostilities may escalate into a frontal assault resolved with only a couple of well-placed hooves to the head or shoulder. If this confrontation is complicated, perhaps by hostilities involving previously unreconciled disputes, both deer may rear up on hind legs, with ears pinned, and with loud, staccato, grunting vocalizations, hammer each other violently. Usually in short order, one deer submits, and then may be pursued with one or two more obligatory and humiliating blows to the backside. These rare disputes can be violent and frightening, as sharp hooves send surprisingly powerful blows resonating through a body cavity, sounding more like the blow from a baseball bat than from the hoof of a deer. And, once in a great while, one will be slammed violently to the ground, becoming vulnerable to injuries more serious than mere bruised dignity. Fortunately, these fights rarely escalate to such viciousness, and mule deer society remains, in large part, one of apparent harmony and accord.

The Touch Factor

The deer love to be scratched and groomed. It's an essential aspect of our interaction. One day, while standing among twenty deer and interacting more directly with a deer that I had known for several years, she became resentful of a nearby deer. This is a predictable occurrence with many deer, and I cautiously suggest that it appears to be some sort of jealous behavior. As she pinned her ears and began to charge the intruding deer, I wanted to forestall some unnecessary rancor and thoughtlessly grabbed the 150-pound deer with considerable force, using one arm across her chest and holding her tight with another arm over her back. She was suddenly stopped and completely restrained! To my great surprise, rather than being instinctively resistant or even terrified by her confinement, she simply relaxed in my arms and gave up on her attack, but continued to focus her attention on the retreating doe—and not her apparent captor. I released her, and we resumed our interaction. I have repeated this intervention many times with particularly familiar deer to prevent hostilities, especially when the hostilities are directed toward a smaller yearling or fawn. And, so far, we have never had any misunderstandings, resentments, or fear—so, I ask: How can a wild deer calmly accept physical restraint from a human? Why would it have the capacity to allow restraint by an alien species, when the only restraint a deer can possibly know is on the occasion of being seized by a large predator? Who can account for such unexpected behavior in these extraordinary creatures? Of course, I would never be so foolish as to intervene with two mature bucks expressing hostilities. In these cases, I am strongly inclined to move in the opposite direction.

Occasionally I will find an engorged tick on a deer's ear that needs removing, and, interestingly, in most cases, there is no doubt that the deer is completely aware of the tick and is

⌃ The author intervening when Will displays "jealous" behavior toward another young buck.

eager and delighted for me to remove it. Often a deer will want to sniff and examine the dreaded creature to make sure that I have in fact successfully dislodged it. The deer's gratitude at this time is unmistakable. However, some deer, like some horses, are sensitive about having their ears handled, and although they don't actually try to move away, they simply try to pull their head away when you grab at the tick. Many times I have literally had to restrain a deer with one arm as it tries to pull its head away, but, again, there is no real resentment or fear associated with this restraint, and never any response that would approximate an escape attempt, and certainly no hostile reaction. These behaviors are outside the realm of things that I could have anticipated, and to my mind often border on the outrageous, appearing to defy a logical behavioral explanation based on models of predictable responses having possible survival advantages and evolutionary significance. After several years, I am left without explanation, and although these observations probably have no real bearing on understanding the true nature of the mule deer as would be appropriate in a more rigorous and strict ethology, this predisposition to communicate and interact far outside the boundaries of what might be expected from any wild species is fascinating. These qualities may at least denote an animal with extraordinary ability to understand and adapt. Perhaps it is the plasticity and malleability of this creature that is so remarkable, and my only possible explanation is founded in the mule deer's obvious predisposition to be reasonable.

Working in and among so many individuals, often in direct proximity, I occasionally get the entire weight from the hoof of a two-hundred-pound deer on my toe, which can hurt, and I just shove the deer off. Occasionally a sharp-pointed antler will accidentally poke me here or there and can also be painful under just the right circumstances. And, of course, on a few occasions I have moved or turned suddenly and inadvertently struck a deer on the leg with my heavy boot, or perhaps jabbed someone with my sharp elbow on his or her tender nose or face. These deer have never taken any kind of offense based on such a misunderstanding, nor reacted with fear from what they clearly interpret as an accident, not the result of my intent or any anger.

Also, I must mention that mule deer appear to be profoundly sensitive to pain. These deer are constantly receiving minor injuries from altercations or accidents with other deer or objects in the environment such as sharp sticks, rocks, barbed wire, or cactus hidden beneath the snow. Although obviously a fine design for a fleet, athletic prey species, these digitigrade, even-toed ungulates have managed to concentrate an unimaginable amount of stress on the smallest possible bones in the smallest possible space, and every mule deer spends much of its life suffering and recovering from chronic and predictable hoof and leg injuries. Hoof injuries are a perpetual plague in all mule deer. And of course there is barbed wire everywhere, which is always a source of injury, both minor and horrific. There has never been a more perfect and deadly fawn trap ever devised than the common "hog wire" or woven wire fence. By the time any deer reaches one year of age, she is covered with scars from wire cuts. Deer show suffering with gestures that can be interpreted only as dramatic responses to injuries. A blow or wire cut to the leg while crossing a fence may result in a deer's holding the injured leg up for a few minutes and trembling in some unmistakable expression of agony. If the pain is unusually severe, the deer lowers its head in a particular posture, then often opens its mouth wide in a manner that looks, for all the world, like a silent scream. It is a heart-wrenching sight but, in most cases, subsides in a few minutes. Mule deer will also on occasion respond to an immediate injury with various cries and whines—particularly when the injury arrives from their own mistake or misstep, and therefore is not accompanied by fear.

All of this suggests to me that mule deer are sensitive creatures with far more complex capabilities than we know, and perhaps there are subtleties in their behavior and interaction that are outside our immediate ability to understand. This ability to apply reason and then adapt in unexpected ways is clearly phenomenal, and it is difficult to speculate on how deep this understanding and intelligence runs.

With an unexpectedly wide diversity of personality and character types, I find that I anxiously await the next intriguing individual, the next remarkable possibility that may show up in my life. And then, perhaps, together we can explore ever greater levels of communication and interaction—for me a deeper understanding of the mule deer but, more important, a deeper understanding of one another. Now, when I look into the wide, open face of some strange deer who has suddenly entered our midst, or when a trusting mother brings her young fawn to me for that first meeting, I look into those bright, intelligent, inquiring eyes and see only the possibility of the inconceivable.

⌃ Mule deer and wire fences—a perpetual plague.

⚔ Dare to look into the eyes of this animal.

On Eye Contact and Trust

Mule deer are immediately made suspicious by any admiring gaze, however—even if the intent is entirely innocent. A predator's eyes are its most efficient and highly evolved weapon. The eyes initiate the pursuit—they lead the charge. The eyes are the tips of the talons, the leading edge of the arrow, or the spire point of the bullet. They are first and foremost the author of destruction and death to any prey animal. It is no wonder that any cautious creature is likely to view the intense, well-focused eye with suspicion. It is also an irony that trust can be established down the barrel of this same gun. It is testimony to this deer's ability to reason and discriminate, in essence, to evaluate a possible predator's actual intent. The mule deer has survived as a species, in part, by these finely tuned powers of discrimination. So, in building trust, we must be careful how and where we point our weapon.

I see the deer on the mountainside, casually browsing, as if unconcerned with my presence, a quarter-mile away, but, in fact, I am being watched—not just my every move, but also, more important, my purpose—my intent. But, then, I am the watcher—the observer—the one who with eyes averted obsessively attends to their every move, their every nuance. Our subtle but distinctly common interest is separated by rocks and sage brush, but our familiarity—our gaze—divides the intervening space into decreasingly smaller increments, until our mutual inquiry connects us in an almost intimate embrace of shared curiosity. Our eyes connect again, as if to say simply, we are here now, I see that you exist, and I acknowledge and allow your space, and you grant and acknowledge mine. We have, by all these simple definitions, established a particular relationship. By averting my eyes, I am acknowledged in my willingness to share the companionship of this moment. The deer's eyes are averted in a similar gesture of acknowledgment and acceptance. An etiquette has been observed, and we have granted one another individuality. By no means has trust been established, but a respect has been granted. Some meager foundation has been laid, and, now, a bridge could possibly span the distance between our worlds. Our bridge is based on suspension—the suspension of arrogance, of superiority, of presumption or judgment, and, by these definitions, a most fragile relationship is upheld but is now remarkably freestanding.

And if we acknowledge this connection day after day, those threads of acceptance become lines of trust, and eventually the span is lessened, and our bridge is reinforced and strengthened. The forces that draw on this bridge are grounded merely in the symmetry of mutual consent that teeters precariously on an unspoken edge of honesty. Even the suggestion of betrayal will send this fragile edifice crashing into ashes. But, as long as this perfect balance is rigorously maintained, we are now free to bridge our worlds and explore one another as two creatures who share the prospect of greater understanding.

PART III

The Mule Deer in Crisis

⌃ Maternal clan in Red Canyon—a great herd now down to a precious few.

CHAPTER FIFTEEN

The Predators

Mule deer, like so many herding, flocking, or schooling animals, are considered to be "prey species," and it could be said that all such species are, in terms of both physiology and behavior, forged and in many cases ironically sustained by their predatory adversaries.

Predictable cycles of feast and famine—population boom and bust—always define the natural world and the existence of every species. Animals respond to abundant resources with lower mortality and increased survival. However, as the carrying capacity of the land is reached, increased consumption eventually degrades the habitat. Predators respond to increased populations of prey species with a corresponding tendency toward population increase. Resources are eventually exhausted, predators abound, and, of course, prey populations begin to decline in response. The equation is very simple. As with small rodents or rabbits, these cycles may run their course in only a year or two. In the case of the largest mammals with lower birth rates, these extremes in population may take a decade. But, make no mistake, the inexorable decline over many decades in mule deer, bighorn sheep, and moose populations threatens to result in the virtual disappearance of these species from the landscape.

Ironically, predator species in this part of the West appear to be thriving. Coyote populations have been increasing steadily for decades, mountain lion numbers appear to be at historically high levels, and the newly introduced gray wolf is dispersing and proliferating in numbers that were never predicted by even the most optimistic prognosticators. This powerful predator may work wonders as a management tool for the elk that have prospered into a state of near irrepressible numbers for half a century, but for the many other large game species that have not fared well in recent decades, it is only another devastating factor in the lives of creatures already facing seemingly insurmountable odds. The wolf may be the perfect animal in a perfect world, but that is not the one we live in. For the species in decline, this reintroduction could not have come at a worse time. Even if its impact is modest, the wolf could have the direst implications for the possibilities of any long-term recovery in these animals, who are actually the ones who are in a truest sense endangered. Packs of wolves have been described as capable of killing mule deer with near impunity, although not yet a significant limiting factor in our area. Cases of mature mule deer bucks successfully fending off attacks by lone wolves have been well documented, even when such attacks lasted for hours. But this would be the rare exception involving heavy, well-armed bucks.

Coyotes kill mule deer, especially fawns, but an adult mule deer may have better than a fighting chance when confronting a lone coyote. However, it is well recognized that organized and cooperative packs of winter coyotes kill mule deer adults and particularly fawns with regularity. I have reconstructed this struggle many times in the snow, seeing the chase, the animal surrounded, the initial capture with frantic yaps and growls, and bleating deer with dashes of blood and handfuls of hair outlining the struggle. The deer is dragged to the ground and continues to be slashed and torn by hundreds of relatively small teeth, the nose is torn off and eaten, and then, at long last, the abdomen is ripped open, and the deer is disemboweled. Finally, the still-beating heart or major artery is exposed and severed, sending several great spurts of brilliant red blood spilling out onto the snow. Only then is the horrendous agony ended. The pack continues to tear and fight over the carcass, and by first daylight, there is barely a scrap of meat left for the ravens and magpies. The detachable parts have all been hauled away, and only a bare rib cage and the distended paunch remains, containing the vegetative contents of twenty-four hours of hard-earned browse. It has been my observation that the majority of coyote kills involve fawns who are already somewhat encumbered with snow and ice, and in almost every case a nearby fence has been involved to slow, redirect, or ensnare the inexperienced deer. Furthermore, thawing and melting create large

⌃ Coyote.

ice dams that then form frozen ponds up and down the creeks and drainages. These ponds then become covered with a light skiff of snow, creating the look of level ground. First-year fawns appear to be completely unaware of this hazard, and once forced onto the ice, deer hooves are entirely useless, and trapped fawns are killed almost 100 percent of the time.

Mountain lion populations have soared throughout the West. The success of game regulations and citizen compliance is the key factor in the population surge in many predator species. Historically, Wyoming had working cowboys covering thousands of square miles of backcountry, moving cattle from one range to the next throughout the spring, summer, and fall. Every cowboy carried a rifle on his outfit and customarily shot, or at least shot at, every mountain lion he saw. Clearly not the best management tool, but, needless to say, lions became rather reclusive and very difficult to get a look at. Sadly, for many reasons, a working cowboy on horseback is an exceptional sight in Wyoming backcountry today. Encouragingly, game laws with teeth bigger than a mountain lion have persuaded folks not to shoot every living thing they see, every time they see it. Now, however, we may be confronting a little too much of a good thing as the pendulum swings in favor of the cougar, which some say has now reached population levels that are hovering at historic highs, and is even described by some as an "infestation." A local outfitter who merely trains his dogs to hunt, but does not kill the lions on the adjacent ranch, has "treed," identified, and photographed eight distinct individuals—all within sight of our house and ranch. I have always been a romantic about the awesome big cat and relished every sighting and confrontation that I have had—including a disquieting event wherein I was momentarily grabbed by a large male. Fortunately, I was in the company of another person who intervened, or I surely would not have come through it without a scratch! But now I find that the old equation "familiarity breeds contempt" is changing my view of this powerful presence on the landscape. I have seen and encountered more lions in the last five years than I had seen in the previous forty.

Mule deer are the preferred prey of mountain lions, who for tens of thousands of years have apparently maintained a healthy balance. It has been observed that a lion may kill as many as one mule deer a week, so one lion taking fifty mule deer in a year is undeniably a sizable dent. If mule deer were proliferating as they should be, this could represent the proper stabilizing force in maintaining mule deer numbers in a steady state of equilibrium in a given habitat. However, mule deer are in a steady state of decline for many reasons—the cougar is now just one of many contributors. Mountain lions are a legal game animal in Wyoming, and quotas for lion harvest are rigidly defined and enforced. To my knowledge, only two have been killed in our Table Mountain area this year, but already the annual quota for the greater area has been met. In six years I have come to know the mountain lion, not with the same degree of familiarity as the deer, but our observation of one another has been at times quite personal. I observe the lions' comings and goings almost every day, which often includes their surveillance of me and my yard, my house, my horses, my automobiles, and, of course, the deer. There is rarely a time in cooler months when all of our activities are not being keenly observed by this somewhat arrogant predator. They regularly pass through the yard and don't hesitate to inspect the house up close, as we commonly find fresh tracks around the back door, the out buildings, and even the parking area. Early one morning, as the sun shone across the side window of Leslye's car, a perfect paw print came into view, representing clear evidence that the big cat decided to actually take a look inside the driver's side of the vehicle.

Cattle appear helpless to protect their newborn from this powerful cat, but then domestic cattle represent an unnatural and readily available food source. I've observed dozens of kills during spring calving season on the surrounding large ranch that prefers not to actively "calve" but rather let cattle rely on their own wits and ingenuity—proven historically to be a bad idea. It seems that lions are so competent that it is only the flood of multiple births that allows some calves to survive. Unlike the kills of the coyote or the wolf, lion kills appear to be relatively efficient, and death comes swiftly most of the time, but the unfortunate fact is that in most instances, lions will merely open up the abdomen of a freshly killed calf or deer and eat only the heart and/or the liver and then are off to the next easy kill. I find this behavior increasingly hard to admire. I have observed and kept an eye on one hundred or more individual lion kills, often for many days, and even employed as many as five infrared, motion-activated trail cameras on these sites. I have but rarely documented a return visit to a kill site by the lion. Yet the bold lions leave their telltale blood-stained scats every night under the cliff face that falls just below our house. It is my suspicion that lions often "scent-mark" their kills, thus persuading the smaller scavenger species such as coyotes to stay clear, so the remains are gradually picked away by scavenging birds, and the majority of the animal is wasted. There is a rare exception to this rule that is often romantically documented as "typical mountain lion behavior": the mountain lion with cubs will often cover her kill with brush and debris and revisit the site many times. But without the desperate need to feed hungry cubs, that rarely happens—at least in this ecology.

In the past, I labored under a common presumption and misconception about this remarkable cat. After hiking and riding horseback for many decades through thousands of miles of Wyoming backcountry, I regularly surprised and observed every wary species of native wildlife, but, with only a precious few exceptions, I never saw the mountain lion in spite of abundant tracks and signs. My logical assumption was that the lion was possessed of near supernatural powers and managed to slip away long before I could come within its proximity. Now I know for a fact that lions are not overly wary, and if they are, they do not choose to slip away before the rider or hiker arrives, but merely lie low as you pass close by. Mountain lions will "flush" from your immediate approach—more like the response of a covey of quail at your feet than any behavior you would expect from a robust, predatory mammal.

But then the mountain lion is what it is, perfect, tried and true—and could care less about my judgments and opinions. Just like our own species, the mountain lion knows much of want but knows and cares little about waste when the illusion of abundance abounds.

When out on the mountain with the deer in winter months, I always carry my old .30-30 Winchester slung over my shoulder. After so many decades, it is more like an extraneous bodily appendage, of which I have no awareness. Living every day for months and even years in the wild with various prey species, I have discovered a curious and now disturbing common denominator. If I am standing in the immediate proximity of my wild associates, every aspiring predator species, seemingly without exception, appears to forgive my otherwise terrifying humanity, or I simply become invisible and lost in the crowd: a paradoxical and somewhat disturbing privilege. As a result, I often find myself standing only meters from large birds of prey, such as red-tailed hawks and golden eagles, as well as formidable predators,

⌃ **Mountain Lion just above the ranch.** Photo by Sammy Tedder.

such as coyotes, wolves, and mountain lions. I, of course, stand with a silly look on my face while I watch my various companions flee in abject horror. At that point a predator may well choose to continue a pursuit after its prey or on occasion decide that my presence has interrupted its hunt. To date I have never actually been confused for prey, but I keep it high on my various lists of possibilities and expectations. I have literally had wild turkeys killed at my feet. Even though I honestly never expect a situation to arise that would call on me to shoot a mountain lion, a bear, or a wolf, it is foolish to let a formidable predator have the only vote on who lives and who dies today—regardless of how remote the possibility.

Canadian evolutionary biologist Valerius Geist—a lifelong and true backcountry "field man"—suggests that any human in a wilderness-like setting that supports populations of large predators should always carry a defensive weapon. His theory is that an armed

⌃ Bears in the neighborhood. Leslye's hand for scale.

⌃ Photo by Sammy Tedder.

individual unconsciously walks and moves more boldly and is unknowingly less likely to project an air of inferiority and vulnerability. Predators make their living keenly observing and interpreting body language, and I think there is validity in his observation. Having allowed myself to become exposed to a couple of situations where I was clearly in peril—helpless, in fact—with my fate resting entirely on the disposition of a vastly superior and overwhelming force of nature, I vowed that in the future I would always operate on a more level playing field. It may be only Samuel Colt that makes us equal.

To many people's surprise, we do not live in a 1950s Walt Disney fantasy, and, sadly, all the stereotypes about the concepts of "wilderness" and the "balance of nature" are largely theoretical and mostly theatrical and literary fantasies, perpetrated by the desire for some meaningful order and even some element of kindness and generosity in our vision for the natural world. Order, predictability, and the notion of an overriding virtue are attractive ideals and may have certain validity in a truly natural state, and perhaps may be validated statistically over thousands of years, but definitely not decades or even hundreds—and definitely not in the world in which we live today. The wolf does not cut the sickness from the bone, but merely kills the thing in front of him—good, bad, or indifferent. In fact, it has been well established that wolves kill injured or infirm animals in about the same percentage as they occur within the population in general. In other words, if one in ten animals in a herd is compromised, about one in ten kills will involve these individuals. In large part, Mother Nature is simply not a nice lady. She holds little regard for logic and conservation, and definitely not for compassion. That which is "natural" needn't be presumed to be somehow righteous or confused with the distinctly human concepts of good or bad. There is extraordinary order in the natural world—that order is often achieved by way of a paradox that can be profoundly chaotic. Nature, although exquisite, magnificent, and somehow ultimately elegant, is likely—perhaps even predisposed—to be messy.

If you want to get biologically brutal, the truth is that we are all prey species, and whether the agent of death is a saber-toothed cat or a prion-induced encephalopathy, sooner or later most organisms will die by the designs of some other. This is the most fundamental, if disquieting, premise that defines and ultimately unites all living things. If it so happens that you are eating your fellow organism with regularity, by conveniently assigning the hapless creature to the category of all things merely edible, it becomes easy to rob it of any significance outside a possible meal, thereby relieving the dining patron of any possible responsibility or consideration. Whether scientist, hunter, consumer, or predator—we are all guilty of robbing the other living creature of its significance as an individual. It's not that biology dictates that by consuming other living things we are necessarily behaving in some evil manner—I am not a vegetarian—but it could be logically inferred that every living thing should be regarded with at least a modicum of respect for *who* it is. Regardless of your particular relationship with another creature, it is still an individual—it is still *someone*. If we are thoughtful—even caring—beings, it seems the very least we can do is avoid robbing any other being of its "oneness."

Because many prey species are also game species—and in the case of mule deer, a big game species—they have become an economic institution—a source of revenue, however meager. So, a government biologist must spend his valuable time and our tax dollars collecting 320 "eviscerated carcass weights," to put some seemingly mathematically relevant figure on the annual "kill" and "hunter success ratio," rather than actually finding out something significant about a deer species in decline. It is the bane of every wildlife management agency and every wildlife biologist that wild creatures are principally defined and considered in primary terms by their relative economic contribution to state governments. Either a thing is a "resource," natural or not, or it is deemed to be of little value and thereby possessing little significance. But, at the very least, it is the means by which a creature may "buy" its way into the minds if not the hearts of our citizens—this is the nature of the beast as seen through the lens of our civilization.

❧

I am thoroughly and deeply rooted in the tradition and culture of hunting since my earliest recollection, and the process was never considered a mere interest or hobby—and certainly never a sport. For better or worse, hunting appeared to be an obligatory component of my DNA, just as surely as a cat has a specific response to a mouse. As an objective observation and without a note of pride, I must readily admit that I have been a deadly proficient hunter. I don't know if my history should warrant praise or condemnation, for I am a true hunter, and I have surely killed them all. But, now, disturbingly, I have an internal conflict that is becoming irreconcilable.

I see humans in orange clothing scouring the landscape in $20,000 ATVs, "tricked out" with advanced electronics and transporting hunters equipped with extraordinary high-velocity rifles with laser, light-gathering, range-finder scopes, and I feel something sickening and visceral churning inside. In this day and time, it seems an animal is likely to be killed not by a real hunter but a "sportsman" launching an incomprehensibly expensive and highly technical "special ops"—or a laser-assisted airstrike that may come silently from a half-mile away. I am appalled as hunting becomes defined by big money, which has successfully ingrained the notion that for any ordinary hunter to actually kill an animal, in addition to some version of the aforementioned vehicle, he or she now requires advanced combat technology—preferably of "tactical" quality (an important buzz word in sporting goods these days). Often, hunters must be further provided motivation and inspiration in the form of the abundant hunting videos that occasionally descend to the level of snuff porn. Watch as your beautiful game animal is struck by a two-hundred-and-fifty grain bullet traveling at 3500 feet per second. Then, as the film slows the motion down and repeats the moment of bullet impact over and over and over again—staring transfixed at the monitor—satisfaction visibly washes over the hardware store clientele. Watch the strange, almost hypnotic delight, as again and again the hydrostatic shock ripples through the body with a devastating force fully capable of stopping a tractor-trailer. Finally the film advances, and as the creature kicks on the ground, a cheer goes up from the crowd celebrating the "kill" with jubilant high-fives all around—like their team just scored a goal—like the rival has been defeated. They then line up to buy products with names such as "The Devastator," "The Terminator," "The Eliminator," or, one of my personal favorites, "The Guillotine." The sporting industry has drawn on modern civilization's most important technical and tactical advancements in off-road transportation, electronics, and weaponry, providing hunters with hardware and software that would be suitable in modern warfare. Now, as our Wyoming legislature voted to allow the use of silencers on these same weapons, the once-definitive concept of "fair chase" has become a preposterous ideal. These overwhelming advantages being directed toward any unsuspecting wild animal has veered so far out of perspective as to become not merely outrageous, but just another perverse human phenomenon. Tragically, these attitudes have become so pervasive in hunting "consciousness," that after more than a decade, we have a whole generation of hunters that don't know any different. Because of the obvious economic advantages, government has become entirely complicit in this mentality.

As in the consciousness of ancient hunting societies that always recognized their relationship to their prey as noble and even sacred, today I know many hunters who still pursue animals with respect and ethics—individuals who rightfully enjoy and take pride in the *process*, but also recognize, acknowledge, and honor the enormous sacrifice an extraordinary animal has made. I continue to view the hunting tradition—this process—this primary relationship of predator and prey entirely correct within certain ethical boundaries. I consider hunting infinitely superior to letting someone else kill your animals for you and placing the remains in hermetically sealed packages at the grocery store. If you are going to kill and eat an animal, you should first have to look it in the eye. And, of course, I recognize the role of hunting as a vital and necessary tool in the management of many species. Still, I have become in large part ashamed to be identified with a new and more pervasive culture and the economic interests that seem to have hijacked the remaining integrity from an admirable tradition.

While living in the company of so many unsuspecting animals who have become the objects of complete neglect and, simultaneously, the targets of Western civilization's most advanced and lethal technologies, I wonder how many times the crosshairs have brought me into view as some distant hunter scans the herd that surrounds me in his quest for the mythical trophy ram or buck. For this reason and for a multitude of others, I am beginning to identify the various creatures with which I live not as the game animals I once studied and pursued, but rather as defenseless victims. I recognize that much of my perspective and the apparently irreconcilable dilemma in which I find myself is a departure from what some would describe as a more detached and objective point of view. But my keenly objective point of view is from the mountain looking down, and I am clearly beginning to observe distinctions between the many possible predators with which we share the landscape—and the incontrovertible enemy below.

⌃ A brief acknowledgement from mighty Homer.

CHAPTER SIXTEEN

The Trouble with Mule Deer

Mule deer are under assault at this time in history in ways that are unprecedented. An animal that has the potential to live twenty-five years in captivity, but in the wild might ordinarily expect to live an average of nine to thirteen years, will now rarely survive six. This troubling statistic is equally true for both does and bucks. The possible reproductive life of a doe has been cut in half, and the recruitment of new fawn-bearing does is diminishing each year. Population numbers are down in much of the West, and in many habitats that once represented an ideal historical stronghold, mule deer numbers have plummeted by a staggering 50 to 70 percent in the past twenty years. And in many ecologies in Colorado, Wyoming, Idaho, Nevada, and Montana that once supported vast numbers, mule deer are absent entirely. We should be asking, "Why?" The irony of this particular statistic is that once an animal has vanished, its population numbers vanish from any census count and therefore from public awareness.

This Table Mountain herd has slipped by 30 to 40 percent in seven years, and two adjacent herds, which I have also monitored closely enough to recognize individual deer, have ceased to exist entirely, with the few survivors now joining our group. A fourth herd to our immediate south diminished to only a few individuals and then ceased to exist entirely during the 2012 hunting season. Only one doe with two fawns survived, and in lonely desperation they have now joined our herd. We watched the attrition occur daily as they were irresistibly drawn to illegal bait sites to the east.

Mule deer sex ratios tend to slightly favor bucks fawns over doe fawns, but bucks tend to have an especially high mortality rate over the first two years of their lives. Bucks are always stressed by the rut, and for reasons that are poorly understood, they are less likely than does to recover vital nutrients in summer when better browse is available. However, does will manage to become impregnated even when does outnumber bucks, even in the extreme. Buck-doe ratios of mule deer two years and older commonly vary from 40 percent bucks to as low as 10 percent bucks. Moreover, there has been evidence suggesting that does who have been physically stressed will tend to have higher ratios of buck fawns. Bighorn sheep are known to have the same response to stress, but in both cases, the result is always the same—poor recruitment of new replacement females to provide future offspring for the herd. This herd has been experiencing inordinately high numbers of buck fawns for several years, with 2011 skewed by a particularly lopsided ratio. In the fall of that year, with only ten fawns surviving among this herd of approximately forty deer, eight were bucks and only two were does. Such a skewed ratio of doe fawns to bucks can hardly be attributed to random variation. Although both doe fawns survived their first winter, neither apparently survived to return to their home winter range the following fall. In other words, there was zero recruitment of replacement does for an entire year. This represents a hole in the breeding population that will reverberate through this herd for many years. If this trend is representative of mule deer populations at large—and there is ample evidence to suggest this has been a trend, not for years but for decades—the continuation of doe/fawn hunting permits is poor management practice, to say the least. Furthermore, migrating does should be returning to their winter range in autumn fattened and happy from a summer spent in the most ideal forage conditions. In recent years these migrating deer have been returning to winter ranges in September and October in a progressively malnourished condition. Does with twins are especially hard-hit, of course, from the added stress of two hungry mouths. In early October, summer coats are shed, and winter coats should be fully installed. But in the past few years, winter coats have not fully emerged, and we see ribs and vertebral spines when healthy deer should be plump and ready for the rigors of a long winter. Their dire condition becomes even more apparent as I run my hand down their backs and sides. Not only are they emaciated; they are sick. Returning does in wet years and in dry have persistent low-grade infections that are passed directly to fawns, who then have poor survival rates, and often these survivors remain impaired throughout their lives. With some does looking like concentration camp victims, I shake my head and remind myself that, beginning September 1, she and her underdeveloped fawn are still legal game animals in the state of Wyoming.

The recruitment of deer who have become isolated by the gradual disappearance of other adjacent herds began four years ago and now appears to be complete. So, although this group has been steadily composed of around forty deer, our actual losses have been merely replaced by these few survivors from surrounding herds that have slipped into extinction. Causes for the adjacent herd disappearances are many and complex and include factors such as urban sprawl and rural housing development, which subdivides the landscape into small lots or acreages with fences, yards, and dogs. As it turns out, and by no surprise, the habitat in which humans invariably prefer to live in the West is precisely the same habitat that best supports mule deer in winter. We prefer and they require the rich variety of browse along the fertile diversity of the canyons, creeks, and rivers. We have chosen their ecology—and now, after so many thousands of years, they must attempt to coexist and adapt to a radically changing world that is not of their making. The many so-called "urbanized" mule deer who appear so oblivious to the humanity that surrounds them are, in fact, profoundly stressed by the company they are forced to keep. They are desperately trying to survive in spite of a thousand unnatural impediments and boundaries—to an ecology now unrecognizable and incomprehensible. They are not domesticated; they are not tame—and they are in no way "habituated" to the teaming mass of human urbanization that surrounds them. The habituation that has occurred is our own, as this beautiful artifice of the natural world unknowingly fades past the veil of irrelevance into invisibility. Furthermore, owners and occupants of forty-acre "ranchettes" can be resentful of sharing their landscaped yards or meager pasture land with deer and antelope, who are occasionally compared to an infestation of grasshoppers. And, of course, such a tract of land when subdivided into five-acre lots is more lucrative than all the hay grown in several lifetimes. Struggling small-time ranchers often find the opportunity to make the easy dollar irresistible.

A dramatic increase in highway traffic with more frequent encounters with cars and trucks is a devastating force impacting mule deer all over the West. There is a single eighteen-mile stretch of road north of the Wind River Canyon that averages well over three hundred mule deer kills a year, or about one every day—year in and year out. In 2007, twenty-nine white-tailed deer, four antelope, and 340 mule deer were killed on that one road. It is estimated that as many or more deer are killed by drivers as by hunters. These numbers, of course, reflect only the individuals who were killed immediately and do not include the vast number of mortally injured deer who made their way off the right of way before succumbing. While attempting to give mule deer mortality actual meaning by putting it in some ridiculous economic vernacular that voters and politicians can understand, someone in government was recently quoted by the Associated Press as saying that "$7 million 'worth' of deer are killed in a year on Wyoming roads." And, of course, the resulting damage to vehicles, including injuries and even occasional fatalities to humans, comes at an enormous price.

In addition, oil and gas development continues to subdivide the land with a grid of roads constantly rumbling with heavy trucks lacking maneuverability, which increases the likelihood of traffic mortality. And all of this human activity places a multitude of obstacles and obstructions in the path of historical migratory corridors of mule deer, as well as other species such as pronghorn and elk. There are well-meaning people in private, state, and federal agencies, as well as the oil and gas industry, who struggle to find solutions to these escalating problems, but problems arise at a faster rate than solutions.

As we lose mule deer territory, opportunistic white-tailed deer seem to be willing to irreversibly occupy former mule deer habitat when given any opportunity. The Red Canyon south of Lander during the decades of the 1970s and 1980s represented some of the most ideal mule deer habitat in the state. In those years, while working horseback every day in that canyon and more than fifty thousand contiguous acres ranging from desert to mountain, I never laid eyes on a white-tailed deer. Nor did I see a whitetail in all of Fremont County, although I would occasionally hear of a sighting on one of the river valleys east of Lander. Today, the whitetail is the predominant species of deer in all of our river valleys, and it has become an abundant occupant of former mule deer strongholds such as Red Canyon, largely displacing or at least reoccupying former mule deer range land. The environmentally rich historic Slingerland Ranch, lying at the mouth of the Little Popo Agie River at Red Canyon, historically supports a typical winter herd of fifty or more mule deer, as of the winter of 2013, supported six—six! Disturbingly, the tenacious white-tailed deer has even begun to occupy the high mountain basins throughout the summer—a habitat historically known to support and encourage prosperous populations of mule deer.

In cases where a species is clearly threatening to saturate or surpass the carrying capacity of a given habitat, doe-fawn and cow-calf seasons are entirely appropriate and one of the best management tools for balancing and sustaining a particular population. White-tailed deer, elk, and pronghorn are flexible species that can reach or in some cases even surpass sustainable population levels in many areas. However, the doe/fawn hunting concept was always strictly intended as a management tool and not an economic or political device to provide more hunter opportunity, revenue for state coffers, or votes for politicians. But, mysteriously, as mule deer struggle and continue to decline, you can still post your nine-year-old daughter's photo on Facebook, as she proudly holds her first dead mule deer fawn up by its ear for all of us to admire. Do we actually want to pass this message of callous ignorance and greed directly from our highest government officials to our children? Even though I no longer hunt mule deer, I would like to see this tradition continue, based on the continued prosperity of the species, but to allow doe and fawn hunting in the light of the decline of this monumental creature is revolting. Aldo Leopold and Olas Murie have both long since rolled over in their graves. The educated public and wildlife management agencies are bewildered as Wyoming wildlife policy becomes increasingly political and, worse, an economic cash cow.

Perhaps most disturbing is the flood of ongoing research indicating that the entire web of life in the Rocky Mountain West is being impacted by the effects of local and global changes in soil chemistry caused by atmospheric pollution. As the pH of mountain soil—particularly granitic soil—continues to become dramatically acidified, and powerful nitrate compounds steadily accumulate, life is becoming difficult or even in some cases intolerable for many plants and animals alike. Tree death within forests throughout the Rocky Mountains has currently gone far beyond mere epidemic, with many areas already approaching 100 percent of trees dead or dying. The Medicine Bow forest of southern Wyoming is said to be 90 percent dead, but a recent twenty-mile drive I took through the forest indicated that there were, in fact, no survivors. Mountain ranges all over the West are now experiencing tree mortality of 50 percent and greater. As pH cascades into more acid ranges and nitrate accumulation skyrockets, bark beetles find the weakened trees easy prey, so beetles proliferate by the trillions as our forest trees succumb by the billions. Climate change and drought are certainly contributors, but this intensively studied global trend began in eastern Soviet Europe in the 1950s with the complete destruction of many northern European forests from the unconstrained discharge of dirty industries, primarily in the environmentally unregulated Soviet Union. Trees began dying in epidemic numbers in eastern North America with the death of the boreal forests of Appalachia during the 1960s and included the sterilization of many lakes throughout eastern Canada. Global and local pollution from urbanized and industrial areas to the west arrived in the northern Rockies in the 1970s but became truly catastrophic starting around 2000. Now these effects are reverberating up and down the chain of life, until many plants and animals from the largest to the smallest are in decline— from ground squirrels, marmots, pikas, and bighorn sheep to mice, moose, and mule deer— from the high alpine tundra to the river drainages and basins. Both state and federal agencies tend to avoid acknowledging the hard science that has verified this phenomenon from hundreds of different research approaches for nearly half a century—failing to mention the underlying causes—merely focusing on the more economically and politically palatable secondary factors such as drought, "climate change," and bark beetles.

For decades, universities and institutions have studied the effects of acid rain, nitrate deposition, and now extreme levels of ozone on wildlife and forests throughout the West. Even researchers in Yellowstone Park recently admitted that the primary culprit in tree mortality was the effect of atmospheric pollution in the form of nitrate deposition and resulting free nitrogen in an ecology normally defined by limited availability of nitrogen. Soils of higher elevation and colder temperatures are always characterized by slow decomposition of organic matter, resulting in a predictably low availability of nitrogen. Sudden introduction of high levels of nitrogen can become outright toxic to plants normally growing in ecologies defined by slow nitrogen exchange. The effects on the soil's micro fauna and flora are far-reaching and complex.

Our problems are in essence global, and have been occurring in every mountain range in the world for more than half a century. Tree death in the Rocky Mountains is entirely predictable and merely follows a pattern that began in earnest fifty years ago but actually had its genesis with the Industrial Revolution. The problems began to be identified and understood by scientists all over the world in the middle of the last century. These tragic phenomena have been explored and documented globally, producing a veritable mountain of the finest research exploring cause and effect. The causes are clear, and the effects are obvious and well known. However, our own Department of Agriculture still fails to acknowledge any correlation between air pollution—in particular fossil fuel pollution and the resulting acid rain, composed of nitric and sulfuric acids in the form of nitrates—and the death of forests in the West. Scientists, both in the West and in a multitude of ecologies around the world, continue to illuminate these problems with ever greater clarity as they pertain to issues of the effects of worldwide and source-point pollution. To suggest that our problems in the Rocky Mountains somehow differ from the identical problems that have been occurring in mountain ranges all over the world for more than half a century reflects a neglect of good science and common knowledge that is difficult to explain.

One effect of acidification that has been studied worldwide in ecologies suffering similar problems is the sudden absence of certain obscure minerals that have bonded with elements such as iron and oxygen in the soil. These elements—often vital trace minerals, such as selenium, become chemically bonded—sequestered—in a form unavailable for uptake by plants. While studying the decline of bighorn sheep, my colleagues and I spent many years exploring the causes of nutritional deficiencies in many of our resident species of the northern Wind River Mountains, particularly those species living at high elevation and on more granitic soil.

After years of relative prosperity, suddenly, bighorn sheep began a steady decline in populations throughout the West during the 1990s, resulting in formerly successful herds suffering drastic reductions in numbers, or in many cases, declining into complete extinction. This perfectly followed a correlating rise in nitrate deposition and cascading pH values due to acid rain. Mark Williams of the University of Colorado at Boulder has followed this trend in excruciating detail for more than two decades.

Here in the Wind River Mountains of Wyoming, lambs appeared to be suffering from various ailments, which could be caused or exacerbated by possible mineral deficiencies that occasionally result in a form of nutritional muscular dystrophy known as selenium responsive disorder. Our evidence gathered over a ten-year period suggested a clear correlation between the high annual rainfall that was accumulating in the very wet years of the late

1990s and 2000 and low lamb survival. The wettest year of 1999 correlated with a complete collapse of the bighorn sheep population of the Whiskey Mountain herd, and, in essence, no lambs survived from a herd that was estimated to number in excess of 1,500 individuals. This herd saw a 50 percent drop in overall population in about five years. Then, as this same ecology began to suffer from one of the most severe droughts in recorded history, starting around 2005, the lamb population predictably began not to prosper but stabilize. As of 2012 this herd of bighorn sheep has not yet begun to recover, and the disturbing correlation exists—the less polluted rainfall accumulates in mountain soil, the better the survival rates of bighorn lambs as well as various other species of plants and animals. But there is no doubt that we have clearly reached that point in human history where our precious rainfall may now cause living things to die.

Deficiencies in selenium may ultimately manifest in some degree of selenium responsive disorder, fostering a complex of progressive pathologies that leaves any young animal predisposed to health problems, including poor neuromuscular development and a damaged immune system. Death often results from predators because of impaired mobility, as well as secondary infections such as pasteurella-born pneumonia and necrotic infections of the mouth and cranium caused by an endemic bacterium—*Actinomyces bovis*. Pasteurella and actinomyces are both part of the natural oral, nasal, and upper respiratory flora of many ungulates, much like streptococcus bacteria in humans. It is only when the immune system becomes compromised that these bacteria finally establish a foothold and at last become truly pathological. Even though these various infections may become the final agents of death, in most cases they are still secondary to more insidious primary causes. There are, however, differing genetic strains of pasteurella peculiar to domestic animals that can be more virulent and consequently devastating to wild populations.

One important study of particular relevance to mule deer was conducted by biologist Werner Flueck, in conjunction with the University of California at Davis. The close genetic relative of the mule deer, the black-tailed deer, was in a catastrophic decline in the area of Shasta County in northern California, with doe-fawn ratios at an all-time low and populations plummeting. Flueck had strong suspicions that, just as in so many other places in the world, years of heavy atmospheric pollution with acidic characteristics could be to blame.

He then set out to conduct an unusually exhaustive and rigorous study to determine whether changes in the availability of certain trace minerals due to changes in soil pH could be the problem. Flueck published his seminal report in the *Journal of the Ecological Society of America*, titled "Effect of Trace Elements on Population Dynamics: Selenium Deficiency in Free-Ranging Black-Tailed Deer." The research revealed that black-tailed deer were suffering from a nutritional deficiency in selenium, which appeared to have seriously limited fawn survival rates for several years. Flueck's team trapped and implanted nondigestible boluses in 1,695 female deer estimated to be of breeding age, several months prior to the spring birthing season. The boluses were designed to release 1.3 mcg of selenium per day as a supplement, and each deer was marked with a radio transmitter for future observation and then returned to the wild. Of 1,695 deer sampled, blood tests at the time of capture revealed that 80 percent were deficient in selenium, according to official livestock standards. Another 15 percent showed at least a marginal deficiency. The study group and subsequent fawns were carefully monitored throughout the spring and summer and into fall. The test results on recaptured deer indicated that selenium supplementation had dramatic effects on fawn survival rates and on blood levels of selenium. On average, selenium blood levels were 3.1 times higher in females when compared to levels measured prior to treatment. Flueck writes, "Productivity (fawn survival rates) due to Se supplementation was increased by 2.6 times . . . over un-supplemented deer (a staggering 250 percent increase) and resulted in an *additional* 51 fawns per 100 females" (italics added). Flueck further reminds us of the growing body of data that now strongly suggests that "anthropogenic manipulation of ecosystems, in the form of acidic atmospheric precipitation, has now been widely demonstrated to reduce the bioavailability of selenium in free-ranging herbivores." References were also made to several authors who have "described a world-wide increase in the incidence of selenium responsive diseases in animals." In this same study, Flueck points to research substantiating our suspicions regarding the relationship of the acidification of soils by atmospheric pollution and a corresponding reduction in plant selenium concentrations. Flueck concludes his discussion by warning, "This implies that the impact of large-scale anthropogenic activities may alter Se or other trace mineral cycles in remote areas, which would reduce the effectiveness of small, isolated areas (i.e., Wilderness Areas, etc.) for protection of biodiversity."

It is important to note that the capture of even thirty large ungulates and the installation of radio collars is an expensive, labor-intensive, and even dangerous effort that could be considered a heroic accomplishment in any wildlife study. To capture, take blood samples, install boluses and tracking collars, and then attempt to recapture 1,695 deer is an accomplishment of a magnitude almost unprecedented in wildlife biology. The result, of course, is a truly definitive study with overwhelming scientific and statistical acumen, leaving biologists everywhere humbled and with little room for the grumblings of the Monday morning academic. Hats off to Flueck and UC Davis! At the time this book went to press, Flueck was conducting similar research near Bariloche, Argentina, where he has been studying the conspicuous role of selenium-iodine deficiency in the twenty-year decline of the endangered Patagonian huemul deer.

Considering the overwhelming body of evidence suggesting that plants and animals are being uniformly harmed by anthropogenic effects of pollution in mountain soils, it would be illogical to suggest that the conspicuous and unexplained nutritional problems plaguing our mule deer are not in some measure the result of these same effects. However, it's not merely through "game management" but only through the funding of legitimate research that these problems can be illuminated. And clearly it is only the loud and persistent voice of an informed and caring public that can stir a political environment ensconced in the very industries that create the toxic substances that ultimately rain down on the land. Only by intensive studies provided by significant funding will answers and solutions emerge. Our window of opportunity is rapidly closing on the mule deer.

The mule deer's future rests in the wise decisions that we make and, to a great extent, the ethical values that we hold dear. If we let reason lead our way, this remarkable animal still may have a fighting chance to remain an icon on the Western landscape. But the mule deer has in essence run out of options—ecological, biological, and evolutionary. Fate has not dealt these deer a good hand, and the question is, are the hands in which they now find themselves caring and competent? The choices are no longer theirs but ours.

⌃ **The hardest part of my job.** Photo by Dawson Dunning.

CHAPTER SEVENTEEN

Updates on Old Friends

Babe

Babe surprised me in fall 2012 by showing up earlier than usual, and his appearance coincided with the onset of the regular gun hunting season, which this year would last for nine days. Immediately upon his arrival, he was called on to set things right by engaging another enormous affiliate of the same age, whom we have come to know as Homer. Having arrived two weeks earlier, this imposing buck had incorrectly presumed that he would be the dominant deer at last. Poor Homer instantly received a sound thrashing in a true battle of titans that, among other humiliations, broke a large piece off the main beam of his right antler. Babe went unscathed. Because he was a lifelong known affiliate, Homer did not choose and was not forced to leave the area but simply resumed his position in the regular hierarchy, and although remaining a little sullen, made no more of his new arrangements.

Sadly, I quickly observed that Babe's damaged eye had continued to deteriorate throughout the summer, and he was, at last, completely blind in his left eye. He was now distinctly more vulnerable to predation, and of course this hunter-savvy deer who had survived so many seasons would also be completely blind on that side to the approach of a distant human. However, PBS had begun to film a documentary of these deer, and with their help this year we had succeeded in securing thousands of surrounding acres from hunting. We felt reassured and could breathe a little easier knowing that Babe had a reasonable chance of surviving the hunting season yet one more year.

As the hunting season wore on, I remained constantly vigilant as in previous years, but with more confidence that we would not experience the heavy losses of prior years. We had become aware of several kills that had occurred just to our south on a small property that is hunted heavily, but none were individuals from this winter herd. On the last night of the hunting season, as I worked near the house and while Leslye was involved with chores at the corrals, we both heard two distant shots just as night began to fall. Neither of us was in a position to know the exact direction of the shots, but we were both disturbed and suspicious that they may have come from the protected land above us on the mountain. Because of the dark conditions, I made no effort to hike back up the mountain to look for trespassers or illegal hunters. However, the following morning at first light I stood on the cliffs behind the house and glassed carefully up the mountain. Then, a mile and a half in the distance, I saw the dark shape of a pickup truck in an area with no trail or vehicle access. My heart sank. Quickly I grabbed my rifle and took out at a run as Leslye watched from the cliffs and called the Wyoming Stop Poaching Hotline. I had run barely a mile when I stopped to glass a dreadful sight another half-mile ahead. There were three people dressed in hunter orange who were dragging a large deer slowly across rough terrain toward the waiting truck. Obviously, someone had killed a deer the night before, and he had returned with reinforcements to help drag it out. Only one of the men appeared to be armed. I continued running through the sage brush, up and down steep ravines, until I could get a better view. Again I stopped to glass, and at one quarter-mile, there was absolutely no question about the great deer who was being pulled along the ground. Even at this distance, Babe's antlers were unmistakable. I immediately began preparing myself for an encounter that was going to be at least disturbing if not outright dangerous. The three were so consumed with the task of dragging this big deer across rough land that they completely failed to see me coming in the distance. I popped up fifty yards from the men, who quickly viewed my unexpected presence with astonishment. I do not consider myself a particularly imposing presence, but it was probably clear by the look on my face that this was not a friendly visit. I reminded myself over and over again to exercise all possible restraint.

Fortunately for me, all the hunters were polite and distinctly contrite as I introduced myself. I explained that the land was completely off limits to hunting and that no one had received permission to hunt here in two years. They had in fact trespassed, not on one posted property but two. And, I explained, this deer was an important player in an ongoing research project and was intended to be prominently featured in a documentary film on mule deer. The individual who had actually killed Babe apologized for what he said was a misunderstanding, and I advised him that the game warden was on the way.

I hurried back to the ranch, and Leslye screamed in anguish as I passed and told her that Babe was dead. Jumping in my truck, I met the game warden at a predetermined location on the highway, and he pulled the hunter's truck over as it went by and then made the arrest. Feeling sick and angry, I thanked the warden and just walked away from my old friend and companion, Babe, now just another dead deer lying on the back of a flatbed truck. I felt strongly that Babe's remains deserved to come home, but in all poaching cases, the carcass is confiscated, the meat is processed and donated to a needy family, and the antlers are retained as evidence to be presented in court. I notified the two landowners of the violation and never inquired about the outcome of the case. I was later advised by the warden that the hunter was not going to contest the trespassing charges. But, whatever the outcome, I could find no consolation in any of it. After going to such extremes in an effort to create a somewhat safe haven within such a vast area, that this one particular deer was killed among so many other possibilities appeared to be a cruel irony that to this day seems strange and irreconcilable.

It has been some months since Babe was killed, but his death shook me to my core, and the depths of our longstanding relationship have become apparent as I miss his powerful but gentle presence every day. Now I realize that, for me, Babe had come to represent a profound and important figure—not just some enormous deer that I had closely observed for six years, but more like a wise and exalted brother—one that willingly offered and contributed so much to my life. I will always be richer for having known this extraordinary, intelligent being, and humbled that he allowed me to share in the intimacies of his existence. Babe had a favorite place near the house where he often chose to rest, and now when I look at that location, I still expect to see his statuesque silhouette in elegant repose. Babe was many things, but among a long list of perhaps more significant superlatives, he was also just a big, gentle tough guy who was impossible not to love. I have never regarded another living being with more respect and admiration.

⌃ Babe approaching for a visit.

Shady and the End of Miracles

Not wishing to diminish the significance of Shady's triumph, I will say only that in biology or the individual experience, if triumph actually exists, it is never a prevailing state of existence, but rather always transitory and conditional, if not ephemeral.

Shady's fawn was not only unexpected, but practically inexplicable. I have never observed such maternal devotion in any other living thing, and unlike other does that traditionally leave their fawns well hidden throughout the day, Shady was determined never to leave her fawn's side. Employing no small effort and determination, I concluded that this deer simply refused to abandon her fawn for any period of time, and was always faithfully hovering somewhere within a fifty-meter radius. I must admit that the daily sight of this unlikely mother and fawn was not only amazing; it was also an inexhaustible source of joy. Clearly, this crippled little deer had been made whole. At last the fire in her eyes was rekindled, and she was again fully invested in the business of life.

Four full weeks into the unlikely life of her fawn, I awakened early one morning and immediately saw Shady frantically running with her distinctly awkward gait from one location to another in the creek bottom just below the front meadow. This was the all-too-familiar heartbreaking scenario played out as some mother deer tries in vain to somehow turn the tide on a fate that has already swept away the most passionate and motivating experience known to living things. Of the various possible stages that might describe mule deer grief, acceptance is the most difficult. Shady's fawn was surely dead, and in desperation she was attempting to find a way to set things right. Within minutes I knew the exact position of the fawn as she repeatedly rushed to its location, examining its remains, and then would once again frantically run out in some futile attempt to prove that it was not in fact dead, but lost. Shady was forced to jump across two fences as she rushed back and forth across the creek and meadows in a state of near panic. At one point she jumped the fence in the front meadow and hobbled over to several does with fawns who were browsing tender alfalfa. Pathetically, she limped first to one fawn and then to the next, sniffing each in hopes of somehow disproving the grim reality in which she was now bound. Then, again, she hurried down the meadow, across one fence, then another, rushing to her fawn that she clearly knew was dead.

I have seen this desperate behavior displayed by does who have lost their fawns on more occasions than I would want to recall, but somehow the observation of this crippled doe in such agony for having lost the only kind thing that had happened to her in two years was almost unbearable. Throughout the day she ranged farther and farther from the site of the dead fawn, scouring the countryside and calling with a longing voice that I could distinctly hear two hundred yards away—then, remembering, she would go shuffling back yet one more time to the fawn's location. That evening she became increasingly exhausted from running constantly in a crippled condition with no rest, food, or water, and then made one more attempt to jump the barbed wire fence by the lane. As if the universe had conspired to heap even more insult and agony on this gentle creature, her front leg caught the top strand of wire, and she was completely upended—rear end over front—flipped and cruelly slammed to the ground with such force that I could hear the thud from the house, causing me to worry that she may have broken her back. By some convoluted means, she landed under the bottom strand of wire and lay there momentarily, as if the life had been knocked out of her with one final crushing blow. As I stood on the porch with bolt cutters at the ready, she raised her head and with a struggle managed somehow to drag herself from under the fence. As she stood trembling with her head low and her lifeless rear leg touching the ground, it seemed all the verve and spirit that existed in this remarkable deer must by now be completely destroyed. Shady appeared dead on her feet—I had just observed the thorough unmitigated breaking of a deer's heart. There could be nothing left.

The following day I wandered to the site of the dead fawn, and there among the willows along the creek bottom lay what would otherwise appear to be a perfect healthy little spotted fawn. Shady had done her job well. The big cat had only removed her heart and liver through a neat incision in the abdomen just below the ribcage. It appeared that the fawn had been killed for a mere morsel. My heart ached as I saw the site trampled by Shady's anxious hoof prints.

Throughout her many ordeals, Shady had been one of the most innocent and hopeful creatures I will ever observe, but as I watched the bright light of joy and optimism leave the eyes of this brave little deer who had struggled so desperately, I feared that in that moment, the light may have left mine as well. And as this tragedy unfolded, my heartache turned from complete helplessness and disappointment to some stark revelation involving the fundamental nature of this wretched universe. At some point, Shady made eye contact with me as I stood nearby, with a familiar look—a desperate longing—an open-eyed gaze that I had seen so many times before when offering her aid. I could bear neither my helplessness nor her disappointment and had to simply turn away.

Shady survived this ordeal, and, drawing on some endless well of courage, regained the strength to join her mother. Since her mother, Charm, had recently lost both her fawns in their first days, and had already rejoined with last year's surviving fawn, Bangle, it appeared that the three were reunited in some communion of shared sorrow—Bangle with broken jaw, Charm with deep, stratified sadness in her eyes and lame on her right front foot for some reason, and now Shady with only three viable legs and a crushed spirit.

Still, Shady's existence and the existence of her fawn were triumphs—fleeting, but triumphs nevertheless, deserving of recognition and celebration, for they are clearly outside the bounds of ordinary expectations. When assessing the cards that life often deals to those innocent individuals found poorly situated somewhere within the normal range of random variability, that Shady survived and that she had a fawn was, without question, a handful of aces.

The Eyes of Shadow

Recently, a deer wandered into the backyard and lay down in the plum thicket. The plum thicket has always offered an occasional deer some haven or refuge from annoyances such as high wind, blowing snow, burning sun, the hubbub of mule deer society, and possibly even predators. But late spring had arrived. Most mule deer had forged ahead up the mountain to the prospect of more abundant green pastures, and only our native resident population of deer remained in the area. The buck with two inches of velvet showing was obscured by vegetation, and because his winter facial mask was almost completely shed with only tattered remains, I couldn't easily identify him. But with the demands of spring ranching tasks and the return of abundant browse for the deer, I paid little attention to a deer on a warm day in search of a little shade and solitude.

While involved with some menial but demanding ranch task the following day, I marched to the equipment shed in the backyard, and in my blind obsession failed to notice the buck still lying in the plum thicket thirty yards from the side door of the shed. He bolted out of the thicket in fear, which seemed odd, suggesting it was not one of the more familiar deer. However, as he ran, I observed a distinct limp in his front quarter that reminded me of Shadow, but I assumed it must be another injured deer that I had observed in the area for over a month. I would be very surprised if Shadow had behaved in this way, considering our long-term relationship and his relative degree of trust. Again I dismissed the significance of the occasion.

Two weeks before, however, I had found four strands of barbed wire in a section of nearby fence where a deer had become ensnared to such an extent that all the wire was twisted into a single rope-like tangle that I could not untwine with my gloved hands. There, scattered on the ground below, lay a double handful of deer hair, with several shreds of skin with hair attached. The forces that bound this wire together in such a single mass must have been enormous, and it seemed impossible that a deer could have avoided critical injury in such an entanglement. Because barbed wire is a leading cause of mule deer injury and death, I had maintained a constant vigil for such an injured deer, and although deer are perpetually displaying all manner of wire cuts, no deer had appeared with deep lacerations or other severe injuries. The next day I immediately observed that the nervous deer had returned to his bed in the thicket, and I knew something was not right. While not wanting to flush the buck again from his bed, I approached carefully and, with cautious words of assurance, soon found myself within a few meters. As we made contact through the thicket, the great eyes staring back at me were completely familiar. I spoke softly: "Shadow?" Although I had not seen this deer in weeks, he responded with a look that was unmistakable, and I knew without question that Shadow was in trouble.

Shadow remained in the thicket in the exact same location, although his position changed daily, suggesting that he was up and moving on occasion. I placed a heavy rubber tub of water nearby, as well as a container of grain. And spring was well underway, with suitable mule deer browse abundant and within easy reach. On occasion I would observe the troubled deer closely and offer words of encouragement but normally kept a distance that would not make him feel uncomfortable. Curiously, even with close-focus binoculars, I could discern no overt sign of injury, and he still maintained the weight and the overall appearance of the healthy, robust deer I had known all winter and spring. Although surprising that a deer in distress would choose the yard, there was no question that this was in fact the safest place he could possibly find, and he obviously understood this.

Orphaned at an early age, Shadow was one of those individuals cast into social limbo, and although accepted and generally ignored as a peripheral herd member, he was always without any true affiliation, either maternal or fraternal. I was probably the only creature who had ever shown Shadow any true interest or ever suggested that his company was desirable; as a gravely injured young deer, he had always been somehow aware of my investment in his well-being. We were in many ways attached, and here, in his desperation, he had clearly chosen to come to the safety that he knew surrounded this place.

By the fourth day Shadow had become completely sedentary, remaining in the same position with his head lowered to the ground. That morning I entered the house after observing him for several minutes and reported to Leslye that I thought Shadow was dying. At midday, he curled his head back like a cat sleeping and put his head across his flank. At some point in the afternoon I feared he could be dead and approached close enough to see that there was still a gentle rise and fall in his ribcage. Only once the day before had I seen him stand but then immediately lie back down. Later in the day he was lying with his neck outstretched but periodically raised his head in a way that suggested he was in serious pain. It just seemed so unlikely that this fine, robust specimen of a deer, at last in his prime and who had successfully overcome so many adversities, could become deathly ill in such a short time. While never approaching too close, I began a constant vigil from a few meters away as I became increasingly aware that my attachment to this particular deer was profound. After so much history and so many years, Shadow was not just a subject in my mule deer study, but had become an important member of my family—and I was his.

As evening approached, ten mule deer wandered into the backyard briefly milling around, browsing on a few desirable plants peculiar to the yard, and generally ignored both me and Shadow. Eventually, however, several deer wandered by, and, without alarm, they observed with a peculiar disturbed curiosity and concern that distinctly indicated the recognition of a fellow deer in distress. Then, to my surprise, perhaps because he had gone days without mule deer company, Shadow stood up, staggering briefly, as in some desperate attempt to join once again with some familiar herd members. But he could only stand trembling and could only manage a few halting steps that led him from the plum thicket. He stood momentarily on a patch of grassy lawn with his mouth partially open. The look in his eyes was one of helplessness and pain, and the sight of it made me grab the pail of water and walk directly to him. Shadow was standing at death's door. There I dropped down on my knees at his feet and began scooping up water and holding it to his mouth. He barely acknowledged my presence, refused any attempt to actually drink, and only made a feeble effort to moisten his dry mouth and tongue. My heart sank as I stared directly into his pain, his desperation, and something that was clearly akin to an overwhelming disappointment.

Shadow's eyes were tired and bleary, but as I looked into his great black orbs I saw two extraordinary objects suspended on the inside corners of his eyes. There, poised on the edge of each eye, were identical, perfect, liquid, crystal spheres—like small, transparent pearls.

They were tears, for lack of better language—but not the cloudy discharge—the sagging milky exudates that I have seen leaking from the eyes of a hundred sick, injured, or dying mule deer. These were two perfectly limpid orbicular objects of absolute and uncanny clarity. Like unfaceted diamonds, they gathered the evening light in four seemingly geometric balanced source points that as physical phenomena were unlike anything that I have observed in the natural world. For a single moment I was absolutely transfixed—perhaps like the unexpected vision—a momentary glimpse of an unexpected but nearby universe. Shadow then took one last awkward step and collapsed in a heap on the ground by my side as both of these remarkable, tear-like pearls fell from his eyes.

Shadow lay on his right side with legs outstretched and head oriented slightly downhill, as I sat helpless with legs crossed just behind his neck and shoulders. As evening approached and the sun slipped behind the mountain, I watched the rise and fall of Shadow's breath as he slowly inhaled and exhaled in a predictable rhythm that was not shallow and halting but rather slow, relaxed, and steady. There was the occasional light groan—a gentle moaning exhale of air, but then again the slow, steady rise of his breath. Besides his gentle breath, the only other movement was from his left front leg, which he would lift slightly every few minutes, extending the foot forward, as if reaching out. I sat at his side for an hour as darkness approached, not knowing whether this could go on for many hours or even days, but I knew I could never leave him as long as he had breath. Then Shadow moved. He stretched his neck back and lay his head at my crossed feet and, to my astonishment, looked me dead in the eyes. The tired, bleary look had left these remarkable eyes, and they once again appeared translucent, knowing, and black, like large, liquid globes of obsidian. Again I was transfixed—I was captured by his gaze and could not look away. I soon found myself lost in Shadow's eyes. Then, as recognizable as if it were my own brother, his mouth opened slightly, and he called to me in the familiar voice that I had heard so many times throughout our years together. This was the all-too-familiar call that he would make when he wanted my attention, my assistance—my acknowledgment. I felt a helpless agony in that moment, not knowing what this particular voice was expressing. Was it a desperate plea for a help I could not render? Was it a cry for me to somehow relieve his suffering? The sound only served to draw me deeper into the apparent eternity of those eyes. Uncharacteristically, I even prayed at one point for something good and just in the universe to take this innocent being from his suffering—from a life from which there was no more to be gained. Again he called to me, and some deeply interior part of me ran to him, some part of me dove into his eyes, and I was there for him with all that I had. Shadow then briefly began moving his legs. Like an old dog dreaming, it was as if he was running, as all four feet gently moved in a steady but abbreviated motion. Shadow had spent his entire life eluding death every day, but as it approached, was this an attempt to elude this inevitability one last time? Or, had Shadow finally recognized that death was now his only refuge, and, thus, was he in fact at last running to meet death in final desperation? Then, in a moment, he stopped and became motionless—his chest rose weakly one last time, and as a gentle sigh left him, he went silent and still. I watched for minutes for yet another breath, but there was none. Yet Shadow's eyes remained transfixed on my own, and it appeared that the life would not go out of them. I waited for all sign of life and spirit to pass away, but Shadow seemed as if he would not leave me—as if he would not leave my world or his. I reached forward to hold his head, to feel the last warmth that might be preserved—a glow and warmth that I had known and enjoyed for so many years. At last I attempted to close Shadow's eyes and break his gaze with mine, but they would not close—his eyelids simply would not close, and my irresistible attachment to him became disturbing—as if his death would not deliver him from all this meanness and tragedy that had been the stage on which he had played out his life. With bitterness and resentment I wondered if Shadow ever knew even one perfect mule deer day that filled him with satisfaction or even joy—a single day that could have seemed to make a difficult life all worthwhile. At last, half a day and perhaps a light year beyond tears, I forced myself to look away and lay Shadow's head gently on the ground. An hour may have passed, but I was shocked that his ears had already begun to grow cold and that the life could be so thoroughly and quickly gone from him. How could something so great and powerful—so otherwise enduring—pass away in these few moments? As nightfall finally surrounded us, and not wanting his remains to be disturbed in the night, I retrieved a tarp and carefully covered my old friend—the bright light of his eyes now enveloped by the penetrating darkness.

The following day I examined Shadow closely, and there on his shoulder were the telltale bruising and cuts that indicated that it was he who in fact had become ensnared in the fence.

Always lame on his left front hoof, creating difficulties negotiating fences, his right humerus (the large bone of the upper forelimb) had been completely broken in half in the mishap. He must have suffered horribly in those weeks, and recovery would have been a complete impossibility. That he could walk at all was extraordinary.

Something remarkable occurred during these intimate moments sharing in Shadow's life, his final hours, and his death. After some months, I find with a certain detached curiosity that I am somehow not the same, and I will always suspect that Shadow took some part of me with him—or perhaps it was a willing departure, and I was entirely complicit, for I may have found the moment and the company irresistible. But clearly something of me that was vital appears to have either died or went with him. I suspect that perhaps it may have been

⌃ Shadow in better days.

the best part of me, and if this is true I give of it willingly, for I would gladly share an eternity in oblivion with that fine creature and certainly be the better for it. Only now do I fully understand that Shadow was without question a most noble creature, an embodiment and realization of a perfection on this Earth that I will likely never know again.

Peep's Update

In the fall of 2012, many of the does returned from their summer grounds completely emaciated. The summer had been one of severe drought and plagued by grasshoppers. By October, many of these deer and their fawns succumbed in an unprecedented prewinter die-off.

That summer, we had not seen Peep. Although Peep had migrated in her first year, she had not migrated the following year, giving birth to PomPom and Boo in her winter home range in our proximity. The powerful and seemingly inseparable connection of Peep and her two older buck fawns was an interesting phenomenon, but I worried, as she became increasingly gravid with her rapidly developing new fawn, how and when was she to rid herself of this overwhelming attachment. But again this year, she finally disappeared with her older fawns, so I have no idea how she finally resolved this dilemma. Throughout the month of July, I hoped that she would soon reappear with a new fawn or two and spend the summer with us, but she chose to remain far away in some unknown location for the entire summer.

By September, as other familiar deer began to show up from their summer ranges, Peep did not arrive early, and I began to fear for the little deer who had known such a tough life. Early one morning long before first light, I was out in the dark interacting with a few deer, when an odd but somehow familiar shape approached. Although I knew with complete certainty that it was Peep, I also recognized in the inky darkness that something was terribly wrong. She seemed to be almost luminescent—almost as if she was glowing in the dark. Peep had left for her summer migration in absolute perfect condition, but even in darkness I could tell that she was a pale, walking skeleton—nothing but skin and bones and scantly covered in this strange, bleached-out summer coat. As we exchanged greetings, I ran my hand across her back, and my anxiety swelled as I could feel every bone in her body. I had never observed a living deer that was this wasted.

As light began to reveal the extent of Peep's condition, I was shocked to see that not only had she failed to shed her summer coat; there was no trace of her emerging fall and winter pelage. Nights were becoming cold, and now Peep was without any protective undercoat. I could clearly see her bare skin that, although dry, showed no sign of dermatitis or infestation by ticks or lice. There were no signs of ocular or nasal discharge but only some crust deep within her ears, which she seemed happy for me to remove. As I immediately started her on a mixture of nutritious feed and examined her body carefully, it became perfectly clear that although she could be suffering from a high internal parasite load, she was not suffering from some common viral or bacterial infection. This was not an infected "sick" deer, but rather a deer who was obviously starved close to death. I wondered where she could have been—in what mule deer hell had the environmental conditions been so destitute? Despite a summer drought and a severe grasshopper infestation, this seemed like an ecological impossibility. Peep looked more like a concentration camp victim than the spunky, healthy little mother that I remembered from only three months before.

Then, to my complete disbelief, I realized that there were two small, frightened fawns in the yard and that they belonged to Peep. The fawns were unmistakably hers, and their appearance was a glance back in time, recalling Peep's distinctive and adorable appearance, but also appearing emaciated and wearing the dry, brittle hair of that once all-too-familiar starving fawn. I examined Peep's udder and quickly noted that she was completely dry and had not lactated for many weeks. Healthy does are still nursing in September and will often continue lactating into November and occasionally into December. Peep was starved, had stopped lactating early on, and her fawns were now underdeveloped and in terribly poor condition. Of course they were confused and frightened by these strange new circumstances and failed to immediately recognize the food that I was attempting to offer. The fawns seemed perky and alert, but it was difficult to know whether this was because of some meager sense of physical well-being or just the result of fear and adrenaline. It seemed physically impossible that a perfectly healthy deer could slip into such a decline so quickly. Peep and her new fawns were not just in poor condition but clearly on the brink of death.

Of course I could not handle the fawns and closely monitor their condition, but at least their fall coat was in much better shape than their mother's. I began ensuring that the desperate family had access to a variety of nutritious feed at all times, although it was hard to tell how much the fawns were eating. Peep seemed unenthusiastic about the food, as if she had almost lost the will to eat. Within a few days of around-the-clock availability and encouragement, she began to eat with more interest. However, I saw no way that Peep could survive such an overwhelming insult to her body.

In a week, one of Peep's fawns lay down, and in twenty-four hours she was dead. Peep never left her side, and I was certain that this was the blow that would end her life as well. She maintained her intermittent vigil over the dead fawn for several days, with her surviving fawn, Puck, always remaining close by her side. A week later, Puck found a spot below the front meadow, lay down fifty feet from Rosebud's skeleton, and died within hours. Peep was not to be consoled as she hovered around the remains of her last fawn for several more days. For two days I brought feed to her in containers. This was the second pair of fawns Peep had lost in a row. Although I could neither share nor console her apparent anguish, I too slipped into a state of despair and resignation. That this diligent and gentle creature could endure so much agony—both physical and emotional—seemed like a complete impossibility. Now my only concern and objective was to try and save this sad little deer's life one more time.

Peep managed to survive the next few weeks, by some means that I do not fully understand, as she gradually began to eat, and in a month Leslye and I debated that she may have actually gained some weight. A downy winter undercoat of charcoal grey hair began to appear like a shadowy undergarment as it contrasted with the exhausted, pale hair of summer that was falling out in handfuls. The emergence of her winter coat coincided with the first winter plunge into the frigid abyss of subzero temperatures. For a month, Peep was one freezing rain away from certain death.

Now, it is spring, and although I am not certain, I believe that Peep is again pregnant, although I wish she were not. She has seemingly made at least a tentative recovery and is once again reminiscent of the stocky little doe from the previous year. However, this last year has taken a heavy toll on this tough mother mule deer, and as Peep enters her sixth year, she now bears the look of a tired, old, and distinctly disappointed deer. Once again it appears I am her only family, as PomPom and Boo either left their home range or were killed in their first hunting season. I fear that Peep will never have a true family and experience that valuable

⌃ Peep in the bloom of perfection: A healthy young mule deer doe.

⌃ Peep. The price of motherhood in an unhealthy ecology.

opportunity to pass on her many contributions as the wise matriarch of her own maternal clan. Peep might represent the ultimate survivor, and, like most surviving mule deer, she is possessed of some undeniable brilliance. There can be no question that she is very good at what she does, but, surely, if Peep chooses to migrate again, she will die. Now I spend as much time as possible with her, and she seeks my company at least twice a day. Offering her every spare minute, I recognize that she is a rare wonder that is momentarily sure to pass from my life.

Depending on a perspective that changes daily—whether I am looking up the mountain or down the mountain through the eyes of a deer—I have begun to observe my own life with either less—or perhaps more—objectivity. I'm no longer certain.

CHAPTER EIGHTEEN

Provisions of Consciousness

Look in your computer's spell checker for *ethology*. Your spell checker will probably not recognize this particular "ology," and only by consulting a more comprehensive dictionary will you locate the word. The word has become familiar in the academic lexicon only in more recent years as the direct study of true animal behavior has gradually been recognized as a legitimate area of scientific inquiry. In my rather protracted academic experience involving much of the 1960s and early 1970s, biology barely acknowledged that animals actually had a true life experience, as they were viewed more as organic phenomena with little conscious or even behavioral significance. If you wanted to explore the nature of animal minds, their society, or their awareness, you were sent with your tail between your legs to the halls of behavioral psychology to study animal "intelligence," exploring primitive and rudimentary Pavlovian concepts, or those of Skinner, involving stimulus and response and habituation. To suggest that animals could be thoughtful, rational creatures—or, God forbid, to suggest that creatures could be sentient or even conscious—was tantamount to scientific heresy. Ring a bell, flash a light, and feed the dog enough times, and he eventually salivates upon hearing the bell or seeing the light. There was no suggestion that the dog had actually "learned" a preposterously simple corollary—that he could actually have mental images of a warm, moist bowl of kibble! In spite of the fact that every dog owner has clearly observed the phenomenon of dogs having dreams—cohesive, mentally fabricated images—these most simple deductions never seemed to be introduced into the apparent thoughtlessness of the day.

I know all about peer review, and as a scientist, I highly approve of its usefulness and necessity in the academic process. However, the brutality of this process has often prevented the introduction of common sense into the rigorous scientific equation of empiricism and strict objectivity. During those years, there was no suggestion that the dog had simply put two and two together, but had rather become only habituated to the stimulus and exhibited a predictable response. And, of course, there was never a suggestion that the dog's experience was identical to the human experience of driving by the billowing wood smoke of the barbeque restaurant and thinking you might like to have a sandwich—as your mouth starts to salivate profusely at the "thought" of spicy sauce ladled over pulled pork!

This was the sad and all-too-recent dark ages in the study of animal behavior and experience. Institutions such as Keller Brelan were established and dedicated to the exploration of common barnyard animals and primates and their apparently unremarkable intellectual abilities as lights flashed, bells rang, and then perhaps a kernel of corn or a piece of Purina "monkey chow" might automatically tinkle out into a dish as a reinforcing reward to a staggeringly correct response. These were merely the most meager insights into the workings of the animal mind. In spite of making contributions with new techniques for the training of animals without the use of punishment, there was little advancement in understanding the experience or intelligence of other creatures. These were somewhat embarrassing times in human intellectual and scientific development, as academics blindly perpetuated various archaic cultural traditions and concepts by nervously trying to divorce our species from any relationship to the "beasts of the field"—the old "dominion over all things" concept. For, surely, the thinking went, no creature other than human was capable of having actual thoughts or could have an integrated experience of its own life as perpetuated by the conscious abstractions of learning, memory, communication, and society. Thanks to the groundbreaking work of people such as Konrad Lorenz, Dian Fossey, and Jane Goodall, most scientists and thoughtful people now generally uphold that many other creatures share in a fully integrated life experience, satisfying all the criteria for true consciousness.

I am not an authority on consciousness, but I have pursued the subject as an ardent student for many decades. My many explorations into the lives of other creatures have in essence been an exploration into the nature of consciousness and the way in which other creatures envision the world. My objective has always been to simply try to see the world through their eyes. Of course consciousness involves everything that resides in empirical opposition to science.

The nature and definitions of consciousness have at last been explored in earnest by many scholars, and a few ground rules have been established in actually agreeing on a comprehensive set of criteria that can be said to define the basic elements of the conscious experience. Basically, these criteria are relatively easy to satisfy and first involve the simple recognition or awareness of having an actual body, or some sense of "being." Second, a creature may also have the experience of recognizing that its body is operating in a particular space, a location, or at least some rudimentary sense of place. Third, a creature must then typically have some sort of memory that will provide the integrated continuity created by body, space, and time, and consciousness may then be said to occur. Clearly, these elements can be found in most any organism that is relatively well organized biologically, with little necessity for extraordinary or so-called higher brain function that might be found in dolphins, apes, or humans.

At least from the perspective of one of the more self-conscious creatures—a human—it appears that the most fascinating outcome of biological existence is the mysterious phenomenon of self-awareness—of the conscious experience. However strange and abstract, it could be that the most important elements of consciousness are the emotional and experiential revelations that are provided. Even though the tenets of consciousness seem simple and the criteria defining consciousness easy to satisfy, as we all know, the behavioral and experiential elements—these *provisions*—may be varied and complex. Various forms of representational information that facilitate communication between one organism and another—the sharing of consciousness—can further define the experience, and it could be said that human consciousness is characterized by our elaborate, language-based representational system. However, a vast number of creatures, including mule deer, also have highly evolved systems of communication that could be considered differing forms of "language," such as using scent, body language, and senses far more acute than our own. Also, consciousness can have unfortunate consequences in the extreme—the burden of "existential consciousness," the haunting awareness of our own mortality. Some scholars suggest that this particular awareness sets the human experience apart from other creatures. I disagree.

My involvement with mule deer, as well as highly socialized creatures of other species, has given me reason to suspect that humans have no privileged access, either to the conscious experience, or to the familiarity with, and prospect of, certain mortality. There are many creatures that appear to acknowledge the inevitability of death as a provision of their lives. I suspect that now, in contemporary times, it is only through the exposure to combat or extraordinary disaster that a modern human can come to realize that the expectation and dread of death resides in the depths of our most primal and visceral organic experience, and as such is not peculiar to the human conscious experience or any other characteristic peculiar to superior human brain function. Do not be consoled that some other creature with a basic awareness of its own existence clings to its life less desperately or with less passion, or faces death with less fear than you or I would. The creatures with which I live fully understand the implications and are no strangers to the most dreadful reality. It is the daily condition in which they live, and they know full well what is at stake at all times. If you have seen your buddy take a large-caliber bullet to the groin, or watched the animal standing next to you as it is grabbed by some great predator—unlike the usual antiseptic theatrical stereotypes—perhaps you have seen the look of real, deathly fear in a creature's eyes, and found the similarities of the horror and desperation to be unmistakable and indistinguishable.

And now, after observing the mule deer for more than seven years, it is my suspicion that the observation, consideration, and acknowledgment of the mysterious inevitability of death is not an exception among many advanced life forms, but is often characteristic. How often have I observed an animal displaying a desperate attempt to understand and learn from the death surrounding it? Learning the significance of the death among members of its own species can take on the proportions not of an obligation, but of an obsession. Interestingly, many of the predatory species with which I have lived and worked have shown less need for an understanding of the phenomenon of death, perhaps because it is simply the everyday milieu that provides them with sustenance. The so-called "prey species" are logically and of necessity more concerned with the significance of mortality—and its probability.

⌃ The fawn Elvin dying with the entire herd responding and gathering around.

Mule deer visit the sites of recently deceased herd or family members repeatedly—often multiple times per day, and perhaps for weeks. Obviously, the intense, concentrated effort to understand and extract some significance could only be described as laborious and excruciating. Mule deer have made a study of death. After observing these reactions for so long and with such frequency, I am persuaded that their behavior offers strong evidence of a dedicated inquiry that may involve certain fundamental questions: Who is dead? How will the death of this particular individual change my life? What may have caused this death? Can this happen to me? What are the valuable lessons that can be learned from this particular death? In fact, many animals, certainly mule deer among them, do not simply walk away from death and just "go on with their lives." To the contrary, death clearly has profound emotional consequences for these creatures. The exhausting experience of investigating death gradually pervades their lives, and the disappointment that fills their once bright, eager, and optimistic eyes is heartbreaking. They appear to become worn down physically and emotionally. I see the immediate, dramatic, and permanent changes in personality that accompany the death of fawns and other close affiliates and family members. Clearly death has profound emotional consequences for these creatures. Deer grieve. The days when we could conveniently separate our experience from other creatures with the familiar reference to anthropomorphism has come and gone. Another vast underestimation of the experience of many other creatures, the term *anthropomorphic*—like the term *habituation*—has all but lost its usefulness in any informed discussion of animal behavior. Like it or not, we share most if not all of our most important qualitative behavioral characteristics with other creatures and can quibble primarily about quantitative differences. That ship has sailed and has been proven empirically to be a boat lacking integrity that will no longer float. But it is important to remember that when we talk in terms of shared traits and experiences like language and consciousness, any organism may manifest these experiences in ways that are entirely peculiar to that individual species. Although many species may be said to have "language," for example, the experience of so-called language may differ in profound ways. So, in referring to the experiences of grief or mourning, it is not meant to suggest that we necessarily experience the loss of an affiliate in the same way, but without question humans and many other living things share some version—some common approximation—of sorrow with the elephant, the dolphin, and the deer.

I have all too often observed a doe in a condition of exhaustion and despondency after losing a fawn. Days may pass as the apparently grieving mother finally gives up the anguish for a fawn she clearly knows is dead—whose ravaged remains she has examined multiple times each day for a week—whose remains she may have faithfully guarded night after night from the onslaught of scavengers, including coyotes. Eventually, as she lies or stands in solitude, rarely eating, occasionally looking longingly into the distance with pathetic resolution, she voices her "lost fawn" call. And even though the degree of inconsolability can vary greatly from one individual to the next, the stress on these mothers—physical and emotional—can be overwhelming. Recently, I closely observed the familiar doe Rag Tag after losing one of her fawns to a lion at fourteen weeks. In her sixth year but having only recently returned from her summer range badly stressed from poor nutrition, the loss of her fawn sent her into a decline that claimed her life in less than two weeks. Early one morning, in desperation, I literally watched her abandon the remaining fawn, retreating among the willows a half-mile up the gulch, just below the bones of her mother, Raggedy Anne, and there in secrecy she chose to make her deathbed. I observed the closely affiliated doe we named Rodenta lying near Rag Tag in her final hours. Now we are struggling to supply nutritious food and preserve the life of Rag Tag's surviving doe fawn—Rag Doll, who is known as Molly. Every evening for weeks, Molly mewed for her mother's return, and the confusion and sickness in her small spirit was palpable. Only yesterday evening as darkness and danger neared—a full six weeks since her mother's death—she finished her grain, and as we became surrounded by the night, she suddenly remembered and once again longed for the protective comfort of her mother's side. Calling repeatedly, she ran to the edge of the meadow—desperately searching for that familiar face and those penetrating eyes that say to a young deer, "Follow me, and I will keep you safe."

Yes, without question, that conscious provision—sorrow—born of attachment, loss, and regret is an experience we have in common with other living things.

If I could choose the one perfect existence—that personal utopian ideal—an existence that would keep me entertained and satisfy all my ecological, social, and even spiritual

« Rag Tag, at one time a healthy doe.

« Rag Tag, starved from a summer in the
mountains and a hungry fawn.
She will be dead within a week.

« Molly, waiting in vain for her mother's
return.

requirements, and assuming I could somehow be physically sustained, I would surely be content with a permanent life within the rich experience of the mule deer. Ignoring the fact that I may be attacked by some large predator or even mistakenly shot for the company I keep—and in spite of certain physical hardships, enormous frustration and frequent heartache—I have never in these seven years had a moment when I longed to be somewhere else or to be involved in other activities, or ever tried to imagine better company. Without exaggeration, every moment spent with these deer has been the most extraordinary gift. The experience of sharing life with a creature that appears so seamlessly interwoven into its ecology has, by association, immersed me in an unexpected ecology of perfection that I have certainly never found in my own ordinary human existence. With amusement I observe my changing mental landscape and, like a few previous involvements, notice that when leaving the company of the deer, life immediately loses a measure of richness and significance. Now there is some absurd but distinct dread of the prospect of simply being me—the resumption of some necessary and tedious human identity encumbered with paper, electronic devices, mechanical transportation, and the inherent stress bound into the human cultural experience. But this magnificent ecology that has given rise to a most magnificent animal has now changed.

By accepting a distinct but unspoken invitation, I have been *allowed* to become a member of an exotic society, and within this society I have developed relationships that may have numbered in the hundreds. Do not for a moment think of these animals as pets—an inaccurate concept including some implication that would involve dominion, stewardship, husbandry, or control over these animals. Our relationship exists entirely of their choosing. While living on this mountainside in their unimaginably complex world for most of each day—and now, after more than seven years—I find that I become increasingly humbled by the extraordinary company I keep. My admiration and respect for their intelligence, resourcefulness, and physical prowess are unbounded. While sharing their life and their experience in this exquisite but rugged ecology, they are clearly, on every fundamental level, my superiors. I can only be a weak, impotent, and incompetent member of this rich and highly developed society. That my comparative impairments, handicaps, and severe

⌃ Orphaned Molly called for her mother every night for a month.

⌃ Molly survived the winter. Photo by Dawson Dunning.

challenges are so thoroughly indulged by my affiliates is testimony to some unexplainable but distinctly privileged membership that they have afforded me.

Of course, a few of these animals have simply chosen and rejected me outright, but many—perhaps most—have become acquaintances, some have become friends, and some know me as a family member. I cannot say that I have never achieved this level of intimacy with another species, but I have never sustained this level of intense involvement with a creature so complex, intelligent, and capable of sharing so much communication for so many years. Above all, I will always be amazed and mystified that this remarkable animal has contained, somewhere within its fascinating realm of complex behavior, the capacity to allow such an improbable and unexpected membership in its community. It is no testimony to my talents but entirely a result of the deer's mysterious willingness to be accepting.

Again and again it seems impossible, as I am reminded that my life has been thoroughly interwoven with this phenomenal animal for so many years. And after sharing so much history, it is hard to know how this has changed me; it is hard to remember who I once was, and harder still to understand who or what I may have become. My identity has undeniably been reshaped and redefined by this community—this family into which I have in some strange way been assimilated. Increasingly, it appears that my world—my frame of reference—has been irrevocably changed. Perhaps, at last, I am in fact seeing a different perspective—seeing the world through another creature's eyes. Now, when a bullet passes through the body of one of my family members, or a throat is pierced by the teeth of a 180-pound cat, there is no more displacement or refuge from my attachment—that mindless, objective space where previously my emotions would have safely resided. Now there is only the shared pain and agony and the loss of one that I care for deeply. Now with that understanding comes the recognition of the magnitude of all that the deer have lost, the magnitude of their individual disappointment, and the magnitude of the loss it also represents in the order of their community. It is all about shifting perspectives—the deer's, and, now, mine.

I now realize that the objective, safe haven wherein we conveniently assign all unpleasantness in this world—"the natural order of things"—was always a house of cards, merely a childish and inadequate domain lacking a fundamental grasp of a more wondrous and confounding, but stark and undeniably pernicious, reality.

These animals are facing grim new challenges, and I wonder whether their vision of life can continue to include a world that offers them any sense of joy and optimism—for I know this animal, and the potential to experience great joy is a natural and defining part of who and what they are. But now it appears that, for them, there is no refuge, no solace, and no place of safety where they can for some brief moment be restored. They are tired, they are sick, their bellies are not full, their young do not survive, and mule deer populations are under assault at all times and from every direction.

Epilogue

For all its current advances, the mule deer, so different, so uniquely American, so young and promising, is nevertheless a species marked for extinction. That is not inevitable, but very likely, given the circumstances mule deer find themselves in.
—Valerius Geist, *Mule Deer Country* (1999)

As anyone with a knack for the obvious knows, everywhere there is an inexorable tide of humanity washing across the landscape, and the various creatures that seem to loom so large in this ecology are of little consequence in comparison to the forces that are in play—the forces that perpetuate our humanity. I fully recognize that in the grand scheme of our civilization, these creatures, this ecology, and certainly my observations of them bear very little significance. In fact, I have known for many decades that land management and wildlife management are well intended but relatively petty forces on the landscape, and in the long run the fate of all this is primarily directed and driven by the hands of political and economic interest. Any veteran wildlife management employee understands this principle as a given and is simply resigned to do the best he or she can in an ecologically imperfect world. We all know with complete authority, for example, that, without a second thought, these forces would gladly let the seas boil over before they would do anything that would affect the price of gas at the pump or would insult the Dow Jones Industrial Average. Manage your wildlife, but never lose sight of the fundamentals. That is just the way it is—that is just the way it works, and the fundamentals ultimately leave precious little room for negotiation. The welfare of a mule deer is not a force that can effect, much less drive, cultural and economic change. In addition to these stark realities, I now see that I have inadvertently set myself up for an even more complicated fall by the company I have chosen to keep.

I have accidentally stumbled into the lives of these remarkable creatures and made many discoveries that were unforeseen. And, for what it is worth—and regardless of its probable irrelevance—I must say this at least once: the mule deer is without question the most sensitive, affectionate, and imminently lovable creature I have ever been associated with. But I can't simply remain standing on this mountainside watching them disappear into oblivion.

And so, now, with almost overwhelming regret, I must somehow find the means to return to a life that in a perfect world would not be of my choosing. Sadly, I would argue, I have not lost my perspective—my grasp on reality—but, rather, gained it. Emotionally, intellectually, and spiritually, it seems as if the darkness defining the lives of these animals has now overtaken my own. I find that I must retreat for lack of strength and courage and the simple wisdom to know how to proceed.

If I could be their voice, I would say, where are the allies, where is the refuge, where can they find some respite? How can we as ethical humans admiringly gaze up the picturesque mountain so oblivious, and not see the oblivion that quietly resides there, as so many species gasp in our suffocating wake? Can you not see them among the rocks and sage brush and see the wounds, the scars, the shrunken hide stretched across the barren ribs, and the burden of their quiet disposition of insignificance? Their sadness and disappointment has become my own.

⸎

Ironically, ubiquitous in the human ecology, mule deer are the ones who, by their conspicuous presence, become to our eyes invisible. However, the unfortunate reality is that all the deer we see near our roadsides, our agricultural areas, and our urban ecology in winter months are, in essence, *all* the deer. This is the large mammal that can be seen along any roadway, in any hay meadow, lounging around the city park, or wandering through your yard on a winter morning. The mule deer has not chosen our urban and rural habitat because of safety or convenience—we have selected theirs—and, for them, this habitat is neither safe nor convenient. It is the misfortune of the mule deer that humans have a preference for the identical ecology in which this animal is biologically obligated, and that will be their undoing. The illusion of an abundance of mule deer is facilitated by the fact that they are a predictable feature on what has now been redefined principally as the agricultural and urban human landscape. Elk, moose, and even the antelope in many agricultural and urban environments often represent a novel sighting and a rare treat for the human inhabitants. The sight of a herd of elk or the lone moose wandering through most mountain towns in the West, although not extraordinary, is still always cause for a moment of intense interest and perhaps even a photo in the local newspaper. With the exception of that rare surviving mature buck, the mule deer receives no such celebrity and rarely invites even a disinterested glace from a passerby.

The general population of human inhabitants has no concept of how many individual elk exist in their area because elk do not, in general, choose to live in the same habitat as humans. As elk numbers have soared in recent decades, mule deer have been in a steady state of decline. Where we saw one hundred deer ten years ago, now we see fifty. That seems to most casual observers to be plenty of deer, but applying a steady, ten-year logarithm to that simple equation amounts to no deer in the blink of an eye. Mule deer numbers are down all over the West—declines of 50 to 70 percent are not uncommon—and when mule deer have alto-gether vanished from a location, their disturbing statistic vanishes along with them—they are no longer a part of anyone's equation. Bighorn sheep and moose are in similar cata-strophic declines, but as some interest and regard gain a foothold concerning these more exciting and economically significant species, the mule deer seems to languish in relative obscurity. I am constantly shocked as I relay population statistics to otherwise intelligent, well-informed citizens—including sportsmen—who are completely unaware of a dramatic decline in mule deer numbers that has been underway for thirty years. Their decline does not in general appear on the radar of consciousness, either by common citizens or even state governments that ultimately have been charged with the responsibility of monitoring and protecting all wildlife populations.

This is not a resilient species like elk, pronghorn, or white-tailed deer, which have seemed to readily recover from drastic fluctuations in populations in the past caused by habitat destruction, catastrophic weather events, disease, or overhunting.

Wild sheep are typically well defined by the distinct geographical isolation of individual herds. Many of these herds have not simply declined in the last ten to twenty years—they have completely ceased to exist. Those are clear cases of extinction, and red flags should be going up everywhere. A formerly viable herd of hundreds of individuals reduced to complete nonexistence in less than twenty years is not a part of some "natural cycle," especially when these are unrelated herds that are dispersed over wide geographical areas of the Rocky Mountain West. Like bighorn sheep, mule deer across the West are faring poorly in the midst of the "new" Western landscape, and once any wild population slips into a steady and persistent decline, it can be mysteriously difficult to reverse.

Having lived almost every day with this species for many years, I have learned things I could never have imagined. Their memory is impeccable, and their brilliant awareness—their consciousness and keen sensitivity to the workings of their world—is a trait that far surpasses my own tendencies toward awareness and wakefulness. A mule deer is a creature that is wide awake on this planet, and I feel safe in saying that the human organism by comparison is a creature asleep at the wheel. The human brain is developed around a highly complex, language-based representational system, and we are proficient at collecting and organizing large quantities of information, but there appears to be little correlation between the acquisition and accumulation of these vast amounts of information and the achievement and expression of a corresponding wisdom. It must be bound up in the complexity of the human brain, but, ironically, we are creatures who find it exceedingly difficult to simply pay attention.

While struggling with my specific difficulty remaining conscious, I have attempted to pay attention to the mule deer and, at least, have regretfully learned that these deer are not well. The most important single effect of the mule deer's many problems in technical terms is poor recruitment of new fawn-bearing does, and, naturally, the reproductive success of the many surviving does with chronic health problems has also been impaired. The quality and duration of the reproductive life of the mule deer doe has grown shorter. Many does are returning from their lush mountain pastures in frightfully poor condition at a time when they should be in their annual prime. Inspection of these high mountain ecologies reveals that habitat degrada-tion does not correspond and account for the degradation of the animals living there. Rela-tively young does who have survived winter in relatively good condition return from their summer range displaying a decline in their overall health and appearance that can be shocking. Young deer whom I have known every day of their lives come into their winter range after a brief summer and are almost unrecognizable. That these deer could fall into such a state in four brief months on ranges that in summer are still relatively lush and bountiful seems impossible. A catastrophic die-off occurred in the fall of 2012 as starved does and fawns returned from their summer range. By the middle of October and the onset of hunting season, the creeks and drainages on this mountain were already littered with the remains of dead does and fawns. I documented more than twenty individuals within a one-mile radius. An adjoining rancher with his finger on the pulse of his land correctly observed that returning deer were emaciated and that many had not properly shed their summer pelage. He voluntarily closed thousands of acres to hunting as he clearly recognized a crisis that was already underway.

If I were to direct a study in an effort to reveal possible underlying causes, my focus would be not on the multitude of differing maladies that are clearly plaguing this animal, but on exploring those factors that may be contributing primarily to an inability to assimilate plant nutrients and, more fundamentally, to a uniformly compromised immune system within the overall population. But, whatever the causes, the stress of bearing and supporting twin fawns by these gravely impaired does often represents a death sentence for the entire family. Upon returning from summer ranges to the lower rangeland slopes of the mountains, they find that cattle have heavily grazed their winter range, which, along with drought and insect infesta-tion, has left them to starve, unless they rely on the relative abundance of the irrigated ranch lands below. Most ranchers are more than respectful of the right of wildlife to share and exist on land that has been sequestered by human agriculture, but I have heard the few who suggest that mule deer and antelope are worse than a plague of grasshoppers.

In the past seven years, bucks have begun to display an increasing tendency toward poor development in overall body proportions and poor antler development. It is now common for three-, four-, and even five-year-old bucks to have an antler configuration that would be typical of a two-and-a-half-year-old deer, and even the most trained observers would have no reason to suspect they were seeing an older animal. Had I not known many of these individuals since they were spotted fawns, I would have never guessed this myself.

Like much of the state, it is suspected that mule deer populations in this area of the southern Wind River Mountains are down 50 percent in the past ten years, although no one knows the exact figure, as census data on deer in this area have been cursory at best. By direct observation on the ground, I know for certain that this immediate area, including a ten-mile length of mountainside running from north to south along the southern Wind River Range, composed of former ideal mule deer habitat, has declined more than 30 percent in just over six years, and three winter herds have completely ceased to exist in our immediate vicinity in the last four years. This is also the heart of one of the smallest designated "general" hunt area in Wyoming. In 2011, three hundred doe/fawn tags were issued in this area, which surely constitutes a significant percentage of the entire population of does.

Most hunters rely on the wisdom of wildlife managers, presuming that common sense and good science have prevailed, and they infer from doe/fawn permits that mule deer must be overabundant, and they naturally wish to participate in the effort to eradicate the excessive numbers and bring populations into equilibrium with carrying capacity. Furthermore, it is legal for does and fawns to be taken with bow and arrow, as well as by youth under eighteen years of age in bow and rifle season. At this time in history a live mule deer doe should be considered an incredibly valuable commodity.

༄༅

There has been a crisis underway for decades, and it is continuing to develop and worsen. The limiting factors for mule deer are complex in nature and legion in variety. In recent years, ironically, the only outcry that seems to be heard has come from many older, concerned hunters who are aware of an almost complete lack of mule deer in habitat that in recent memory virtually swarmed with them. And, of course, there are the concerned ranchers and landowners who actually spend their days on the land and even on occasion get out of sight of the pickup truck.

These ranchers count the dead deer accumulating around their stack yards in winter, and correctly observe that does returning in fall with fawns are malnourished and that there are indications of disease, heavy parasite load, malnutrition, or a combination of all of the above.

The Mule Deer Foundation, like Ducks Unlimited and the Rocky Mountain Elk Foundation—organizations that have perhaps protected more wild land and aided the recovery of more species than have all other conservation organizations combined—is an organization of caring hunters in partnership with other concerned citizens who share an admiration and love for this phenomenal species.

Now, perhaps, the mule deer may have an ally and an advocate who can carry enough political weight to help tip the balance of responsible management in this troubled deer's favor. For clearly it is only the political weight of many caring individuals that will force the hand of governments and their various wildlife agencies, causing them to yield to the virtue and ethics found in good science and common sense, and not to the selfish politics of big money. Godspeed the Mule Deer Foundation, for they have taken on a heavy load.

The balance has tipped—there is no question about that—and for many reasons the magnificent mule deer is losing its fight for survival. This faltering animal needs to be quickly recognized as one of our precious species that receives our attention and our special concern. I can foresee a day when this familiar deer is a rare sight in its once bountiful and prosperous ecology.

This is not prophecy or conjecture, as this dreadful day has already arrived in much of the West. I've had the advantage of a thirty-five-year observation of the mule deer and a continuous perspective through time in one general geographic area. In November 2011, while traveling from Interstate 90 in southern Montana north along Flathead Lake to Kalispell near the Canadian border, and back south through Swan Valley, I drove on a loop that included the eastern boundary of the entire Bob Marshall Wilderness and crossed vast expanses of Montana ranch lands. This was a transection of hundreds of miles of Montana's most productive wildlife habitat and in a season in which mule deer should be highly visible at lower elevations. I saw many dozens of whitetails, numerous elk, and one lone moose in that long, two-day drive, but, incomprehensively, not one mule deer—not one! Thirty years ago I would have seen hundreds.

If this current decline continues unabated, we may soon see a time when a once-abundant creature has slipped unnoticed from our grasp—all but vanished from our midst. This cataclysm is, at this moment, well underway. We may in fact lose this creature before we have come to understand and know *who* it is and what its special relationship to the landscape might be. For this animal is far more complex and interesting than all of our present understanding.

The mule deer is not unique in its apparent dilemma, as so many creatures large and small within the Rocky Mountain landscapes are also suffering. Iconic creatures such as moose, bighorn sheep, and mule deer are species whose very presence has always defined this ecology and are now all rapidly slipping into obscurity with vanishing populations. As go the mule deer, so goes the entire ecology of the Rocky Mountains. As go the Rocky Mountains, so goes the health of our entire planet. Nothing lives or dies in a vacuum.

It would appear that our collective vision of preservation, which was fostered in the middle of the last century by visionaries such as Aldo Leopold and Olaus Murie, has also largely slipped into obscurity as our *needs* steadily overtake our consciousness and our conscience.

The concepts of "growth" and "development" have become embedded in our contemporary thinking with a strange moral authority and righteousness, ascending to a cultural significance that is patently religious. There has never been a more culturally infantile concept than the suggestion that "growth" can be sustained and perpetuated indefinitely. Without this most basic understanding of our position as fellow organisms on the planet, it seems that the catastrophe for this ecology and the creatures living on it—and, of course, for us—is assured.

Merriam-Webster's Collegiate Dictionary defines *civilize* as follows: "to bring to a technically advanced and *rationally ordered* stage of cultural development" (italics added). It appears that we have achieved the advanced technology but clearly without an accompanying measure of rationality.

Humanity was endowed with the extraordinary gift of reason that has, in part, catapulted us to a unique pinnacle of biological success. Reason allows us to merely imagine wisdom— we can postulate the definitions and describe the possibilities that wisdom might afford a creature, we can even strive to attain wisdom, and, to some extent, we can serve wisdom— but we are seemingly helpless as a species to possess it.

Of all the creatures that have made their appearance upon the stage of life and been catapulted into apparent dominance, our peculiar challenge might be to make some extraordinary leap, not in fundamental intelligence, not in technology, but in simple conscious awareness of our trajectory as a living organism on the planet. Without some fundamental change in the way in which we envision ourselves and our relationship to all that sustains us, we may become the ultimate evolutionary flash in the pan—a truly extraordinary organism that now seems to have become a biological projectile speeding toward the windshield of reality. And we're taking so many other living organisms with us on this collision course.

If there is perfection in nature, it is defined not by rigid universal dogma, but rather by a system based on the pursuit of the ideal through a universal dialectic of trial and error—an exquisite and elegant negotiation of physical and biological possibilities. Indeed, nature has always been defined more by developmental failures than successes. Failure is, in fact, built into the system. However nature does not lament failed experiments; it thrives on them. As in the methodology of all good exploration, all failed experiments are by definition successes. It is equally important to know what works and what does not—what has functional validity and what is inherently dysfunctional. This symmetry is the driving force of all existential agency. Balance can be sustained only by polarity—the dichotomy of opposition. On which side of this negotiation will our humanity ultimately reside?

Having arrived at a pragmatic as well as an ethical and moral crossroads in our peculiar biological existence, we may have a small window—the most fragile possibility of a choice. History may prove that we have chosen poorly, or that perhaps we simply have failed to make choices, or that our choices lacked the flame of common sense and moral integrity. The historical model does not bode well for the inherent ability of our species to make wise decisions. In fact, history clearly testifies that a wise choice by any human civilization is essentially unprecedented in nature.

What will we do this time? The river of life is only so wide and so deep and as we continue to draw down the levels with our ever-increasing thirst for all that it provides. Will we continue to be the agent of death? Or will we ultimately prove ourselves to be worthy to share membership in these perfect waters.

⌃ Blossom and the author, sizing up the world. Photo by Dawson Dunning.